Bon Iver

Bon Iver

MARK BEAUMONT

OMNIBUS PRESS
London / New York / Paris / Sydney / Copenhagen / Berlin / Madrid / Tokyo

Exclusive Distributors
Music Sales Limited,
14/15 Berners Street,
London, W1T 3LJ.

Music Sales Corporation
180 Madison Avenue, 24th Floor,
New York,
NY 10016,
USA.

Macmillan Distribution Services,
56 Parkwest Drive
Derrimut, Vic 3030,
Australia.

Every effort has been made to trace the copyright holders of the photographs in
this book but one or two were unreachable. We would be grateful if the
photographers concerned would contact us.

Printed in the EU

A catalogue record for this book is available from the British Library.

Visit Omnibus Press on the web at www.omnibuspress.com

Contents

Wembley Arena, November 8, 2012

FROM the lighting rig hang antique cloths, brown and tattered as old fishing nets or an acre of sackcloth. The front of the stage is lined with silver rods that resemble a metallic cornfield. After an age, darkness falls on this calm and peaceful scene, until ticking clocks and chiming bells mark the coming of the time.

From the wings stalk nine men, settling into a broad landscape of instruments – dual drum kits, percussion pods, pianos and boudoirs of brass. At their helm, centre-stage, a hulking figure of thinning pate and bushy beard, strapping on a guitar as the horns rise into volcanic turmoil.

Then this rickety shanty shack lights up.

The nets become ice caves, mountain ranges, sunrises and bloodbaths. The stalks glow like inverted icicles or flash like Christmas woodland. And just as the music of Justin Vernon had billowed out from a secluded woodland cabin, reaching far beyond anything he'd ever dreamed possible, the beast he'd blossomed into – Bon Iver – floods the arena with tremulous, tremendous noise.

Clarinets nuzzle sweetly against glitch beats and jittery guitars, saxophones turn maniacal for mid-song jazz interludes, lonesome guitar arias – Justin's fragile falsettos tinged with the soulfulness of Al Green – build into rollicking mass folk chants. 'Holocene' lands as delicate and urgent as a butterfly landing on a steam train's wheel; 'Creature Fear' has grown trombone washes redolent of Elvis Costello's 'Shipbuilding'; 'Towers' twirls away into a vibrant hoedown. There's humour – Justin introduces "a new song, we were going to premiere it on the BBC but decided to save it for you" before playing ten seconds of avant garde freak-out he calls 'Ninja' – and there's scintillating communal empathy – and 'Re: Stacks', stripped down to just Justin and a trio of singers from support band The

1

Staves, finds 10,000 people holding their breath for fear of fracturing the ice-thin frailty of the song, the silence so thick you could choke on it.

Then, come the encore, a bold volte-face. "Everybody fucking flip out," Justin demands, claiming it's "your duty to sing", and the arena becomes a howling choir for 'Wolves (Act I And II)' and a chorus of love-lorn condolence for 'Skinny Love' and 'For Emma'. In a room so vast it usually takes lasers, floodlights and pyrotechnics to quake the back rows, Bon Iver do it with sheer sonic inventiveness and poetic emotional pathos. Wembley has never felt so intimate, so much like a cathartic confessional booth. In a crowd of thousands, every single one believes Vernon is singing his pained paeans of devastation and reconstruction specifically for them.

It's not just Wembley that's been swept away by the tidal wave that is Bon Iver the arena rock band. Across the globe, witnesses claim to have seen fans clutching their faces, dumbfounded in amazement at the trans-formation, this sparrow become a roc. It's staggering how seamlessly Vernon's Bon Iver project has expanded from one man at a microphone in a forest hideaway in 2006 to tiny, seated acoustic shows in the back rooms of bars in 2008 – Justin playing a bass drum with one foot as he taps along to his own acoustic – to blasts of noise from a nine-piece band bulging arenas, topping Albums Of The Year polls, bagging multiple Grammys and exploding the possibilities of bearded, maudlin alt-folk into shards of psychedelia, shadows of post-rock and shots of hip-hop today.

But it's wrong to call Vernon's success 'rocketing', let alone 'overnight'. His has been a slow-burning wildfire talent, fanned from a flicker over the decade before his famed retreat to his father's cabin and the agonising birth of Bon Iver. Virtually from infancy Vernon has steadily perfected his art: honing his lyrics, refining his songwriting and altering his voice through a broad plethora of formative bands, collaborations and solo albums until one fateful heartbreak tipped him towards greatness.

You'd be wrong to think his story is encapsulated in Bon Iver too – in the shattering, regluing and pumping full of life of a hollow shell of a man that one endeavour narrated. No, Justin Vernon's story is one of dedica-tion. To friends, lovers and bandmates old and new. To the wilds that reared him and the Wisconsin ice that cradled him and ultimately pierced his heart. To a pride in, love for and devotion to wherever you call home. And to an inclusive vision of musical communion, the inspiration of friends, the wonders of music shared and revelled in, art springing from the mingling of souls.

Bon Iver may have been born of a crumbling, but Vernon is the foundation stone of vaulting creative towers. And to witness its laying, let's ride the flume, back to a time when Emma was still a femme fatale of the distant future, to the very start of this quite superlative winter . . .

CHAPTER ONE

Forever Ago

SOMETIMES you just can't get far enough away from the world.

When Otter Creek, Eau Claire County – population 531 – gets too much, take a drive northwest, out into the snowy wilds of Wisconsin, the Driftless Zone. Feel the barren aspens shroud and tower over the narrowing roads, the hills and forests suck you into their elemental calmness, nature engulfs you like a homecoming soul. There's a power here, a belonging, a deep repose and a mournful threat. And, for someone attuned to its frequencies of isolation and enormity, there's inspiration.

Ninety minutes out into Dunn County, traversing the icy river valleys and lakeshores sprawled out between Medford and Menomonie, take a turning onto a dirt track, onto The Land. Beneath wintry pines that huddle together like crowds of ancient skeletal pillars, watched by wild wolves and turkeys from the snow-smattered undergrowth, cross The Land's 80 remote, overgrown acres to the very end of the earth: the cabin in the woods. A timber building in an alpine style, it emerges from between the trees like a lost slice of Midwest history, built in 1979 by a local university professor with a hankering for weekends in the wilderness, as a homage to a pioneer-era forest homestead. It's faithfully ramshackle – the dirt floor was only covered over a decade after its construction, a lavatory plumbed in even later – and its eaves are full of the noises of its years.

The crunch of knee on cone. The crackles and squeaks of conception. The buzzing of chainsaws, the crunch of logs dragged through bracken, the pop of hunting rifles and the bubbling of stew pots, the laughter of children. Nails being hammered, trees felled, family ties tightened.

And later, many years later, the killing of an engine, the cracking of a beer-cap, the sound of silence. Then a gentle guitar, strummed like an only friend, and a voice, a rich falsetto drenched in soul; a voice, becoming a choir, lifting out through the tiles and chimney stack, drifting beneath the doorframes, seeping out into the woods, up through the bare, clutching branches into the cloudless night sky, a voice full of redemption and despair, a million miles from anywhere, singing only to the pines and the turkeys and the wolves and the snow.

A voice from nowhere, that would soon reverberate right to the tender heart of the world.

★   ★   ★

The bar door swung closed; the glass hovered at Justine's lips. A little entranced, from her stool at the end of the bar she watched the new guy in the collegiate suit and trench coat cross the floor, take a seat at the counter, order his pitcher – a cheap house speciality – and bury a glass into his moustache. He seemed refined for a patron of The Joynt, Eau Claire's rowdiest old-American bar and jazz club*, more studious than the usual denim-hoiking beer-swillers that frequented the town's cheaper drinking holes. Eau Claire† was, as its most famous resident would one day explain, "a town of normal, beer-drinking people . . . five bucks gets you hammered in this town."[1]

Set amidst the rural backwoods of lakes and valleys in Wisconsin's Driftless Zone, Eau Claire was the eighth biggest city in the state, built just north of Highway 10 on the back of the logging and paper trade. With a population of just over 66,000 it was big enough to warrant an airport and a university but small enough to maintain a sense of communal isolation, particularly through the long winters when the snow descended like an annual choke chain. Though regulars at The Joynt still spoke in hushed awe of the year the mercury hit minus 45, every winter tested the resilience of Eau Claire, snowed in tight from December 'til the great April thaws, rarely above freezing for months at a time, the town's 300 salt and snow removal trucks working virtually around the clock for a third of the year. Locals were proud of their hardiness through the hibernation period, for surviving the snow-ins and the March madness. "You start to

* The Joynt was once a major stop for blues, jazz and rock tours between Chicago and Minneapolis in the Sixties and Seventies, hence today its walls are lined with autographed pictures of some of the artists who played there.
† Named after the French for 'clear water'.

go a little crazy around March," the town's famous son would say, "but in the main people from the Midwest are proud of two things: beer and the weather."[2]

Eau Claire was the sort of town where newcomers got noticed, especially if they exuded a sense of style and worldliness. What's more, it was a rare night out for Justine, always tough to get a sitter for her young daughter Kim and venture out to The Joynt for a pitcher or two. She wasn't wasting any chances.

She lowered her drink, caught the barman's sleeve. "Who is that guy?" she asked over the hum of classic jazz. Before the night was out she'd wangled an introduction – his name was Gil Vernon and he was new to town, just landed a position as professor at the Eau Claire campus of the University Of Wisconsin. Although, it just so happened, he already owned some land up near Medford, 80 acres on which he was building a cabin.

Justine was a teacher too; the pair instantly clicked. As 1979 tumbled recklessly into the neon decade, Gil and Justine's romance tumbled with it. Within weeks of their meeting, Gil drove Justine out to the cabin and proposed; they were married within four months of their eyes locking beneath the council of jazz and blues greats peering down from The Joynt's walls. A few months later they were basking in the happy news that they were expecting their first child. A child they believe may have been conceived one rainy summer night in a house up on Gil's plot, north of Menomonie. A son of The Land.

Justin DeYarmond Edison Vernon, his middle names chosen in honour of his grandmothers' maiden names, arrived in Wisconsin on April 30, 1981. Though his family settled in the tiny town of Otter Creek, five miles south-east of Eau Claire, many of his childhood memories grew out of the cabin in the woods. It was here that his father, now working as an arbitrator settling disputes over labour issues in the professional sports and airline industries, would take Justin and his younger brother, Nate, to bond as a family over the earthy activities of young manhood – processing maple syrup in a specialised shack or wood-cutting and carving in the sawmill Gil built on the property, intending to hand-build separate 'contemplation cabins' for each of the children.

"It's not a getaway, there's no lake or recreation," Justin said in 2008. "We put in a toilet only last year. We'd go as kids, my dad would pretend

7

it was fun, but we'd basically be there to use a chainsaw all day and haul trees to the sawmill. It's his bizarre hobby. He spends more time there than he does at work . . . I'd like to see myself in him, in knowing how to be alone. He treats life sacredly without saying much about it."[3]

His time out on The Land gave the young Justin Vernon a fondness for the beauty of the wilderness, an appreciation of nature's primeval pull. "The cabin's like a little alpine-style, timber-frame cabin, [it] used to have a dirt floor," he explained. "There's that ancient vibe, because you're so far away from everything . . . When it's winter out there, there are no leaves on the trees and the pines are really tall, and there's lanes of light inside them, and bare hills, and so much space."[4]

Over venison stew and beans cooked in a pot, while the wolves and wild turkeys prowled the undergrowth outside, Gil would pass on wisdom to his sons. "There are three rules you should live by," he'd say. "One, be a good person. Two, if you can't get something for nothing, you haven't got anything. And three, throw a good party."

It was back at the house in Otter Creek that Justin received a more valuable education though, in music. His parents were fans of zydeco, jazz and the classic blues of acts like James Booker[*], but also the legendary songs of Bob Dylan, Neil Young, Jackson Browne and John Prine. The toddling Justin soaked it all in, sparking a lifelong love of artful Americana, folk music with deep and ancient roots. It was a sense of classicism and respect reinforced every Easter, when Gil would take the family to sing to their ancestors.

Another drive out of Eau Claire, this time 40 minutes due south into Trempealeau County, brings you to a valley of cornfields and farmland, ringed by forested hills. Down in this calm, windswept plain, close to a public hunting ground and precious little else, sits a church, the East Bennett Valley Norwegian Lutheran Church. Justine regularly took her children to church and encouraged them to talk about their questions and beliefs about religion with her, but this building has long since stopped holding services. The Vernons would make the trip because in its graveyard rest Justin's grandparents Gordy and Lucille, as well as several other members of his family – cousins and uncles that include his great uncle

---

[*] Justin's love of Booker is evident in the fact that he often plays his track 'Feel So Bad' to visitors.

Kermit, the man who first taught his mother, Justine, to play piano, launching the family's musical lineage.

Gil had a unique way of paying his respects to lost family each Easter. Pulling up at the church, he'd check for witnesses then take out a credit card and slide it into the jamb of a sturdy wooden door. The lock was nowhere near as sturdy as the door; a click and they were inside. Skipping up the deserted aisle, the Vernons would take to the church piano, Justine spilling out old hymns while Gil and the children sang along. It was always a wonder that, year after year, the old instrument remained firmly in tune. To Justin it made music seem timeless.

The piano at the Vernons' house wasn't quite so harmonious. Keen to encourage her kids musically, Justine guided them all towards the house piano, but Justin, hitting puberty, was the only one of the three who didn't take to it. "Music was always around the house, we made all the kids take piano lessons," Justine says. "With Justin, he didn't really like the piano all that much, especially when I was teaching him for a while. That did not work out, but he asked if he could quit piano if he went to guitar. From that point on it was him and his guitar always."[5]

Eventually Justine and Gil agreed to swap his piano training for guitar lessons and the sound of Justin strumming John Prine tunes became a constant hum around the Vernon household. "He had a passion and obsession for it,"[6] Justine says, adding, "He has wanted to be a musician, for sure, by ten."[7] "Justin practised in the garage, practised in the basement and you know that's where dreams start,"[8] says his father, Gil.

One of the first kids with whom Justin practised around the house was Joe Westerlund, who had the locker next to his in sixth grade at South Middle School. They found common ground in music, since Joe had started playing drums around the same time Justin had picked up the guitar. Together with a few other friends, they started piecing together Neil Young covers in the Vernons' laundry room, enthusiastically filming their early attempts.

"It's bizarre to watch," says Justin, "because we're both very, very prepubescent. We played in a whole bunch of different bands with the same people, different names. You know, classic middle-school stuff."[9]

Amongst that flurry of shape-shifting middle-school combos were early incarnations Skillet and Big Ed's Gas Farm, bands for which Justin would pen his first songs, play gigs in the middle-school gym and record his first demo tapes. "Justin was one of the first people that I got really excited to play music with and to start bands with," says Drew Christopherson, an Eau Claire schoolfriend whose band Wondermutt played alongside Skillet at those early shows and who would go on to found Wisconsin label Totally Gross National Product. "I think we felt it together. We would make a tape one night, and then the next day go to RadioShack and buy like 30 cassettes and hand-package them and sell them at school for a dollar apiece. It was a fun thing to do when you're 12."[10]

And heaven knows, sitting in their front room straining to hear the TV over the racket, what Justine and Gil thought the day, soon after Justin started high school, that Pleeb arrived in the Vernons' cellar.

"He loves all the early, unacceptable things," claims Ryan Olson, a schoolmate a few years above Justin at Memorial High School, who was also fascinated by the possibilities of music and starting his own bands. "His band Pleeb, which was James Buckley* and him and this guy Mark Thompson playing crazy future prog, fucking music up in our practice space in Eau Claire . . . it was insane. They were like 14-year-olds playing the shreddingest, most amazing shit ever.

"I was a freshman and [James] was a junior," says Justin, "and he sort of recruited me to be in this really strange band where we wore like Antarctic winter masks and koala hats and stuff. And that was when we started showing up at, like, confirmation classes and playing these really weird, really weird shows."[11]

Justin was equally enthused by Olson's band at the time, Sled Napkin, even going so far as to send them his first ever piece of fan mail to describe how excited he'd been watching them at the school's various Battle Of The Bands contests. "It was just like the energy up there, and the fact that they were just kids from the Third Ward in Eau Claire, it was just kinda like my mind exploded."[12]

And Justin's enthusiasm for music went hand-in-hand with his love of words. "Lyrics are important to him," says his mother, "but when he puts them to music, he's looking more for a feeling."[13]

The young Justin's lyrics were as much decoration as they were

---

* An upright and electric jazz bassist who would eventually form The James Buckley Trio, The Vandals and Mystery Palace and become a member of Gayngs alongside Justin and Ryan.

declaration. The first songs he wrote, aged around 12, were, according to Gil, "not trite songs"[14] but they were obsessed with living in Wisconsin and Eau Claire. They were paeans of pride and dedication to a place he was already worried he loved too much. "Even as a teenager," he says, "I was already worried that I wanted to live there my whole life. Like: 'dude, you should probably not love it so much here'. But the idea that I could live in Eau Claire and I could not know every nook and cranny or that I could not know every nook and cranny in my own home, or my own land . . . I think it's pretty telling how widely travelled people are and yet they never maybe examine where they are as much as they could. I really like locality, I like permanence. I like people being in one place and knowing it."[15]

So intrinsically connected were Justin's words with his home that he took the concept to its most literal extreme. One afternoon Justine would open the door of a downstairs closet in the house to find that Justin had permanently etched his favourite lines into the walls, surrounded by doodles of the main players of the songs or illustrative props like newspapers. The words were punctuated with huge cartoon exclamation marks and a starburst hemming the word SKILLET.

"Frivolous, nowhere to go, his relatives rejected him," went a lyric called 'Lyro', while later lines told the fragmented tale of characters called Jack, Barney and Thor-H, all involved in an outbreak of civil unrest: "So Jack spread the news around the town, everybody believed it but with a frown, the township started a civil war, hail to the Silk man, the Silk man will die!" Whoever the Silk man was, he won the day. "In the end the conclusion is run, the two good guys lost and the bad guys won." By the end of the song, Jack and Barney, our presumed heroes, were killed. Even so young, Justin was at one with the idea of unhappy endings.

One day, he'd similarly scratch the shape of his home county across his heart. But for now, his music was about to become embedded in it.

★ ★ ★

Peering down from the tower 20 feet above the water, you shuffled your toes to the edge of the wooden platform. Heaving in a breath, you spotted your friends perched on the huge inflatable cushion below, waiting expectantly for your jump, grinned to yourself, closed your eyes and launched yourself into the air. As you hit the blob – as the water pillow was called –

you sank deep into the inflatable folds, throwing any kid already lounging on it high into the air to splosh into the water beyond.

The blob tower was one of Justin Vernon's favourite attractions at the Eau Claire YMCA Camp Manitou*, the summer camp he attended in New Auburn as a boy. A mixture of regimentation and adventuring, children and young teenagers would rise early to ceremonially hoist an American flag before breakfast and a day of canoeing, water-skiing, climbing and games. But the development of social skills was a key element to the weeks kids spent at Manitou too – they'd be allocated a cabin of other kids to stay with, becoming a seven-day family, eating together and having 'individual nights' of getting to know the people in their cabin. The idea is to form firm friendships, sealed on the last night of their stay at a 'friendship fire', and scrawled forever on the cabin walls. In one cabin was written the legend "as close to heaven as the living can ever get"; even if Justin didn't share the sentiment, he would have appreciated the act of writing it there.

For such a dedicated child of the winter, Justin threw himself into the Chippewa Valley camp scene, eventually becoming a camp counsellor in his own right in his later teens. And soon his summers would be made all the more colourful by his immersion in jazz camp, an eventual result of the night, aged 14, that music truly claimed him.

It was 1995, and Justine and Kim were major fans of a folk duo called The Indigo Girls, then touring their fifth album, *Swamp Ophelia*. Justin liked the music and allowed himself to be convinced to go to see them playing with Michelle Malone and Joan Baez. "I was like 'Ah, whatever, I'll go see the show'," he later told Pitchfork, "and it honestly . . . it just changed my life."[16] He'd later describe the gig as "the first major moment when I remember music having such a profound, overwhelming effect on me . . . they were doing 'Wild Horses' by the Stones. I felt like I had grown up in about five seconds. I totally had a moment where I flash-forwarded my whole life, and I knew I could never give up on music. Completely devoid of any religious or iconic context, I felt like music was handed down to me, this is what I was going to do."[17]

His father, Gil, recalls the moment. "We were sitting at a concert venue outside of town and he always said that at that moment I'm going to do what they're doing."[18] He recognised the raw spark of purpose in his son.

---

* So much so, he would later name his personal Twitter account after it.

"You don't prepare the path for the child, you prepare the child for the path and that's what we try to do and he had to choose the path."[19]

Justin instantly became obsessed with The Indigo Girls, particularly *Swamp Ophelia*'s opening track, 'Fugitive'. "It's absolutely without question my favourite song of all time," he'd claim in 2008. "I've realised over the years what kind of rep the Indigo Girls get, and I guess I'm not going to get in the business of trying to change that for people. But this specific record is super brilliant and the guitar solo is unreal and the drumming . . . and it's some of my most favourite lyrics. I've actually got some of the lyrics tattooed on my body, that's how important the song is to me. I've got so much nostalgia attached to it, but when I throw it in and listen to it, it's still got so much shit in it."[20]

Passionate, beautiful and brooding, the simple intensity and acoustic power of the song set the bar for Justin's own musical endeavours, and its lyrics about running away and hiding as a way to truly expose yourself to your loved ones spoke to him deeply. There was a romance to retreat, a heroism in vulnerability. It sounded like his father's shack, singing.

To be so moved by traditional fem-folk might have led many a young man down the dark roads to hemp trousers, sandals and hand-whittled perching sticks. He could have lost himself in the fixed tones of antique folk, become Lady Antebellum before their time. But Justin's tastes, thanks to the diversity of his parents' record collection, were far too explorative and interesting. He was drawn to post-punk hardcore and alt.pop too, embracing the febrile vigour of Fugazi and the quirks and kooks of Primus. He became fascinated by the free-form progressive rock of Phish while also adoring the rootsiness of gospel music. He got into both crazed prog rock and the mainstream AOR of The Dave Matthews Band.

"Justin always teetered on the edge," Drew Christopherson recalls. "He got way into grunge and everything back then with us, but he simultaneously dove into Dave Matthews Band and stuff like that. I never saw eye to eye on the DMB shit."[21]

Justin also found himself drawn to the intricacies and possibilities of jazz. So as he hit high school he joined both the marching band and the jazz band, a major ambition of almost every kid in Eau Claire, since the jazz band was held in such high esteem locally. Steve Wells, Justin's high school jazz band director, remembers Vernon's intense enthusiasm for music, even then.

13

"Homecoming was crazy," he says. "Justin was in football [and] band and after all that hoopla going to Friday night's game, the next day we had a parade and it was hot and it was downtown. I could remember driving down to Wilson Park and getting out and the first person I saw in full uniform sweating profusely was Justin and he's ready to go. He wanted to be there, it was important to him."[22]

"The music program at Memorial High School was just life changing," Vernon would say. "Bruce Hering and Steve Wells were very tightly knit with Bob Baca, Ron Keezer and the university, so basically we were getting a college-level education as high school kids. And I think, at a certain point, I'd reached a level of understanding of music that I just wanted to hang out there for a while. I felt like emotionally I understood enough about what I wanted to do with music, and I wanted to branch out a little."[23]

Through the band he met several like-minded wannabe musicians, and he quickly began to gather the strongest team around him. In his sophomore year at high school the school badly needed new instruments, so Wells came up with a cunning fundraising ruse; he'd put together small groups of players and charge local community events a fee to hire them, all money going towards the instrument fund. One such collective was formed of Justin, Joe, a brass and djembe player, Keil Jansen, and a saxophonist and singer who particularly caught Justin's eye: Sara Jensen, middle name Emma.

As section leaders on their respective instruments, they were a strong quartet, and Wells soon had them pulling in bucks by the bucket-load at Christmas parties. The foursome found a firm connection so, even when the fundraising efforts came to an end, they kept playing together.

Justin also began attending Wisconsin jazz camp every summer and it was during one such vacation* that he first met a kid called Brad Cook from Chippewa Falls. They bonded quickly and spent several summers at camp along the shores of the North Wisconsin lakes. Through a shared love of music and sports, Brad and Justin became close friends, an inseparable pair.

Brad was a curly-haired, outgoing, direct-speaking sort of kid who suffered from extreme Attention Deficit Disorder, which made him a

* Either at Manitou or jazz camp

14

troublesome joker at school, only tamed by painting and drawing exercises such as stippling, an art form his parents introduced him to in order to maintain his focus. The process consisted of condensing thousands of dots on a page to form a picture, a practice that he would ultimately rediscover in music. "I had no patience in my life, but I could sit down for hours and do this," he'd later explain. "With minimalism, that same technique of art applies. I had enough curiosity in my *lack* of an attention span that I would want to wait and see what would happen."[24]

Brad's ADD may have contributed to the fact that, for his entire childhood, he hadn't gotten on too well with his brother Phil. Though they'd shared a house all their lives they had conflicting personalities; Phil was the easy-going one, Brad the tense, confrontational one. But shortly after Brad started high school, the rift was miraculously healed. By jazz.

In his high school freshman year, Brad's ambitions towards joining the baseball team were stymied by a skiing accident which broke his collarbone that winter. To cheer him up, Phil, 18 months older and studying jazz and bebop, invited him to replace an errant bassist in their school's jazz band. Having never played bass and unable to read sheet music, Brad turned him down. But Phil persevered. He and the band director eventually talked Brad into it, and the pair bonded over Brad's bass training. From the moment he picked up the instrument and turned on the amp for the first time on the last day of the school year, Phil taught him to tune the guitar and pick out the notes. "Every day we would come home, and I'd memorise all the parts note for note," Brad says. "Phil would sit there for three hours and play one bar at a time until I had it memorised, and then he'd play the next bar. He really taught me how to play day by day."[25]

Before long Brad introduced Justin to Phil* and the three started jamming together in various combinations of bands. Over the summers of 1995 and 1996 the first swirls of a long-distant Eau Claire scene began to congeal. At jazz camp the year after Brad started playing bass, a 15-year-old Joe Westerlund ran into Phil Cook; the following year at camp Joe met Brad too.

"That was a major turning point in our lives," says Phil, "to be at a camp and be immersed in music and also to be meeting each other and be influenced by a lot of other music, not just jazz. From where we grew up,

---

* And their cousin Brian Joseph.

small winterised towns, it is really quite a welcome relief to meet other people from your own area that can scat every note of Miles Davis' trumpet solo on 'So What'. The release that that gives you, like 'I'm not alone in this world and I'm 15' was unreal for all of us. It was so cool to meet other kids that were that into jazz. Obviously we formed a very specific and fast friendship."[26]

Brad, Phil and Joe had Justin in common, the link that bound them all. Though they'd soon be challenging each other in Battle Of The Band contests in high school – the Cooks in one band, Justin and Joe in another – there was something about the four of them that felt like a unified force.

Justin had way too much experimenting to do to be tied down to any one line-up yet, though. By his mid-teens, he'd become a bubbling maelstrom of influences in need of vent. His dad was gonna have to get a bigger basement . . .

CHAPTER TWO

Mount Vernon, Ascending

"It's a pretty lukewarm cultural experience, to be clear about it. But there's also just so much talent and I think that the schools there and where I grew up . . . I was lucky. I think that the public school system and their general societal ways of doing stuff really treated me well. I know that it didn't treat everyone well, but for some reason it worked for me . . . Every year that I live there there's something new that I can discover about it that I like about it, whether it's sort of a weird underbelly thing about the town that I don't know, or whether it's a new band, some high school band or something . . . There were a lot of cool musicians that were my age and a little older, and then there were all these different eras of people playing at the bars and the clubs. Some people knew each other, some people didn't, but you could definitely tell that it was a music town with a knowledge of itself, and that kind of connected it . . . I've heard people say that they were born in the wrong place, and I just feel like I was born in the right place."

– Justin Vernon on growing up in Eau Claire[1]

I N Midwest America in 1997 it was tough to be a musical rebel. Grunge's alternative edge had been dulled – Nirvana were gone, leaving bands like Pearl Jam, Soundgarden and The Foo Fighters to shift their sound firmly into the US rock mainstream and become seriously huge business. The hardcore and post-hardcore scenes were thriving in the shape of Fugazi, At The Drive-In, Unwound and others while Shellac and Slint had originated a complex and intricate hardcore hybrid known as math rock, but other offshoots of the punk scene were also racing towards populist acceptance – the emo pop of Green Day, Weezer and Jimmy Eat World was charting big and Blink-182 were just a few years from adding a chart-smashing puerility to the mix. Metal, too, was about to get seriously scatological; Limp Bizkit's debut album hit the stores that July, garnering little in the way of sales but auguring the arrival of the abominable cultural apocalypse that would be nu metal.

17

The more traditional genres showed greater promise. Inventive new blends of country, pop and psychedelia were being touted by Mercury Rev and The Flaming Lips, both soon to reach their critical and creative peak, and the first sparks of a folk reinvention were catching hold. Conor Oberst, in his new guise as Bright Eyes, was about to launch a career that would bring fresh vitality and energy to trad folk styles and, in Denver, the Elephant Six collective – Apples In Stereo, The Olivia Tremor Control and most notably Jeff Mangum's Neutral Milk Hotel – were concocting free-form psychedelic folk albums liberally doused in fuzz and distortion. The future of folk would soon emerge from this sizzling lo-fi soup.

In the summer of 1997, though, the coming of age of these anti-folk sounds* was still 12 months away and, to the dedicated Midwest musical adventurer, the future of traditional music seemed rooted in experimental jazz rock.

Of which a H.O.R.D.E. was coming to town.

The Horizons Of Rock Developing Everywhere tour – H.O.R.D.E. for short – was the jazz-rock Lollapalooza. The touring festival, hitting amphitheatres across the US, was instigated by the rootsy rock band Blues Traveler in 1992 as they were tired of playing the East Coast club scene all summer while bigger acts packed out the outdoor arenas. So pooling their draw with their friends bands – Spin Doctors, The Samples, Widespread Panic, The Aquarium Rescue Unit and Phish – they built a big enough show to make the communal leap to the amphitheatres.

And communal was the key word. A central tenet of the H.O.R.D.E. philosophy was the revival of the jam band. The bands would mix and merge onstage, improvising and jamming live, and would invite local bands to play at every stop on the tour, to leave a trail of collaboration and unity in their wake.

Out in the crowd when H.O.R.D.E. hit Wisconsin, Justin Vernon took the tour's collaborative ideals deeply to heart. Having sprung to a skinny six feet and boasting a shock of thin hair he was a natural focal figure, not just among the musicians he'd met at high school marching band and jazz band but in the shifting Eau Claire band scene and even in the sports arena – he was captain of the Memorial High School football

* With Neutral Milk Hotel's *In An Aeroplane Over The Sea* and the first albums from Bright Eyes.

team and a star of its basketball team.* He'd gathered players around him in various formations throughout his high school years, now he was about to become the focus of his first full-on music collective.

It was at the 1997 H.O.R.D.E. festival date that the group of musicians who would come to form Mount Vernon finally cohered. To the core unit of Justin, Sara, Joe and Keil were gradually added Brad on bass, Phil on piano, a trumpeter called Trever Hagen and several other interested players. Becoming a close-knit group over subsequent jazz camps, the revolving crew of up to 10 players that made up Mount Vernon held their first rehearsals in Justin's basement, necessitating Gil making a few home improvements.

"We actually partitioned a room in the basement right below us with soundproof in the wall," he says, "so we could actually sit in the room . . . and watch TV and have a full conversation in spite of the fact that we had nine kids down there with trombones, trumpet, two saxophones, three guitars and a keyboard all plugged in."[2]

"We always thought that he had talent," adds Justine, "but we're his parents, you have to take that with a grain of salt."[3]

Over 1997 and 1998, Mount Vernon grew into a solid fixture on the Eau Claire scene. A preppy-looking outfit, their unofficial uniform consisted of blue turned-up denim jeans, white promotional T-shirts, plaid shirts, the odd Hendrix-style hippy shaman smock and a smattering of caps – a blue baseball cap for Justin, a looser checked affair worn backwards for Sara. But their faintly dorky image as they trod onto school hall stages belied the communal sense of enthusiasm they exuded, infecting everyone who was caught in their sphere. Such was Vernon's ethos of all-welcome inclusiveness, of building a widespread community of musicians and friends around Mount Vernon, that even their sound guy would eventually join the band.

"Even in high school, his band had a lot of team spirit to it," claims Christopherson. "It's very easy for him to get people to feel connected. He played our graduation party in high school, and our whole gymnasium filled with the graduating class was practically up in arms watching him play these songs. Everyone was kind of tearing up."[4]

---

* One of his high school reports was on the basketball history of North Carolina, where he'd eventually move to seek his musical fortune.

Their sound, at first, was heavily jazz influenced, emulating the funky swing and improvisational interludes of classic jazz and ska shows as Justin's guitar, Phil Cook's electric piano, Joe's drums and the brass section's array of saxophones, trumpets and flutes took turns occupying the eye of their six-minute Stax storms. They were the epitome of the accomplished high school jazz camp band, but one thing really made them shine – the vocals. In one corner, Sara Jensen's luscious soul warble oozed a clean-cut classicism with hints of Dusty Springfield, Joni Mitchell and Carly Simon. Centre stage, Justin's deep, husking rock growl was far more indebted to Eddie Vedder and Dave Matthews than any you'd find most trad jazz nights, although he'd later equate his voice to more credible reference points "like Waits or Springsteen. Over the years my fave singers have been more gospel singers, but every time I've tried to sing like that before I always ended up sounding like a complete asshole."[5]

When the two voices combined, backed by the full-throated choir of their Mount Vernon counterparts, they created a powerful, glacial choral shiver that predated the lush harmonies of Fleet Foxes by almost a decade. Together, Justin and Sara made a raw kind of magic.

After a year of playing together, Mount Vernon did what came naturally to Justin. Obsessed with keeping a record of the sound of this ever-shifting band, in 1998 they travelled to Minneapolis and, over the course of a single weekend, recorded their debut album. Adorned with a mauve-tinged cover picture of three shadow figures on a lakeside waving to their two friends in the water – an image that reflected the themes of wilderness, community and chill that would come to define Justin's later work – *We Can Look Up* was an hour-long collection of Mount Vernon's 10 biggest showstoppers, few of them galloping in under the six-minute mark.

Those that made the wise investment of buying one of the limited run of vinyl and CD copies of *We Can Look Up* at one of Mount Vernon's shows, or received one of the copies hand-mailed to local newspapers and fanzines in the hope of drumming up a review[*], may have been bemused by its ramshackle recording, its musical fumbles, its incongruous improvisational solo segments and its meandering mash of traditional jazz, folk,

[*] The copy sent to the Eau Claire *Leader-Telegram* was unearthed in a forgotten cupboard 14 years later and formed the basis of a news article describing it as 'Vernonabilia' in April 2012

ska, prog, grunge and even hardcore punk. But within its eclectic grooves they'd have found formative glimpses of inspired new ideas and the origins of a stylistic approach that Justin would develop into a formula that would make the globe shiver.

Justin Vernon's first 'official' album release opened with one of its starkest pointers to the sounds that would ultimately secure his success. A lustrous choral harmony laced with falsetto, twice singing an aching three-note refrain. It struck a note of alt.folk credibility belied by the upbeat lounge-style track that followed. 'Sprinkler', the first song on *We Can Look Up*, swung into action bedecked with a cheery jazz-pop hook on flute and horn and a lilting springtime soul bounce that smacked of a Seventies New York sitcom theme. It was only when Justin's gnarled voice enters two minutes in, singing of a summery weekend amongst the sprinklers, that the tune took on a grittier edge, even though his lyrical imagery was saccharine in the extreme. "I look to the sky and I see a rainbow swallowing my eye," he sang, picturing children playing in the water sprays, idyllic as a *Sesame Street* segue. Though it ultimately dropped into a darker middle-eight of strummed guitar, bulbous bass and strident piano building to a crescendo, it climaxed with Justin bellowing "I can hear you smiling!" over the sort of flute flurry that Sufjan Stevens would soon make his own. For an artist whose currency would one day be in winsome melancholia, 'Sprinkler' was a surprisingly joyful and jubilant introduction.

The second track, 'High Five', relaxed us into the upbeat mood. A twinkling flute, high-neck guitar and floaty piano convened over a spritely melody before the loping funk beat and prowling jazz brass introduced another sunny Vernon lyric. It found him wandering the streets with a gang of friends "looking back on a year that's weathered like a pair of shoes". The song's opening verse gave Justin's first hint of wintry reflection as "a cold Sunday evening hits me like the evening news", but there was little lingering dislocation since, he continued, "a phone call means so much, I've got the dudes on the line . . . we'll get together anytime". 'High Five' developed this sense of community into one of communal living; the second verse found Justin "waking up in a cold room" in a large shared house on a hill in Chippewa Falls "looking out on Wisconsin's land" as a jovial pancake breakfast was being prepared by his laughing band of friends, throwing his stuff into an "evening knapsack" and going about his day, whatever day it might be, the roving troubadour.

Here was the core of Mount Vernon's atmosphere of inclusiveness and 'team spirit' – "We are one, we are having fun, we are out in the sun," Justin bawled, declaring that everyone was "welcome to our house". It was another idyllic boho scene – the band of jazz rock brothers living under one "groove", a girl so "funked out of her mind" that she's passed out on the couch – and one that was close to his heart. One day, a decade away, he'd set out to recreate this environment in the form of a communal collective of musicians based in a shared studio complex.

'High Five' closed with Mount Vernon indulging in a spate of trad jazz jams before coalescing into a sweet soul choir, and even featured Justin launching into a lengthy free-form scat of a brand you could never imagine coming from the inventive folk hero of 2013. But it also pointed to Vernon's ability to build and then break a swelling wave of noise, as well as his growing tendency to ink himself. "I've got a koala tattooed on my neck," he sang, precluding the appearance of Indigo Girls lyrics across his chest and the outline of Wisconsin over his heart, with places of key significance to him individually marked.

The structurally focused but loosely recorded 'Today Is Just A Day' brought in the album's catchiest hook yet, the backing choir lacing the song's slinky ragga groove with an addictive but fairly surreal chorus line, reflective of the random wordplay Justin would adopt on his most famous albums: "It's like kettles and pots, it's like shoes and knots in my shoe-laces." Justin's verses, despite a further bout of speed scat, were more direct, reflecting on an average summer day, possibly at summer camp ("all those sunny days . . . all of those days by the water"), spent "with the girl in the sunlight". Justin is entranced by this unnamed woman, right down to the way she holds her phone – "I'm wondering why she shines so bright . . . I'm wondering why she's so mysterious . . . I wanna know what makes her move, I wanna know what makes her groove." Conjecture may point at the girl in question being Sara Jensen since, during Mount Vernon's four years together, the band's two singers became a couple.

'Thompson', the longest track on the record at over seven minutes, opened in a darker, rock-heavy mood. After an interlude of in-studio voices too quiet to be comprehensible, Justin's guitar struck in with a glowering desert rock strum akin to early Pixies, albeit with a ska upswing. Joined by trumpet and drums, this furious opening proved a red herring;

after one minute 'Thompson' switched to an urgent ska rock pulse, the vehicle for the album's most extended solo interludes, Joe beating out a two-minute drum battery before handing the spotlight to Phil's piano for the closing few minutes as Justin wailed Vedderishly in the background. But far more fascinating were Justin's two anguished verses, the first sign of the broiling waters beneath his sunny jazz persona. Racked with stress and isolation, he roared about the loneliness and defiance of the performer: "Mellow lit room with four exit signs, four pathways home/When you're in a room that's full of people and you're speechless, then boy you're all alone/I found my way through the mikes and I am here and I'm not letting go/This is my stomping ground, I walk through the door, this is home". His second verse broadens the theme to include a more general isolation, based on the fear that his warmth and friendliness tends to frighten people away. "Should I have acted a little less kinder?" he asked himself. "Should I have taken a step back, did I scare them away? . . . Now I've got an empty dinner table."

The mood suitably darkened, Justin passed the mike to Sara for the album's central ballad 'Alexander'. Her rich soul voice illuminated a Sade-style lounge song full of stuttering piano, sultry saxophone and poetic imagery of a dangerous and unpredictable lover: "Purple light painted on the eyes from a dim lamp, a street tramp in a faltering light/He breathes the smoke to ease his dancing mind . . . I have to wonder what can I mean, what can this be to a man whose soul is tamed to cloak his brain, insane, a spinning barrel part of the game?"

Gradually, the strains of holding the relationship together despite Alexander's distance and introversion got too much: "As the years unwind, a dying tear that I'd hoped I forgot how to cry . . . What I'd give to see his face unfold, to know his truths, to have and to hold/I've climbed inside his grand, built-up wall, I can tell by his trembling lip he's ready to fall". And this title character who "finds strength in strangers' lives and from his own tries to hide", could this, in turn, be a cypher for Justin, who's already admitted on the album that his deep interest in others can drive them away?

Unlikely given the timescale, and the next lyrical sidestep. This tense and downbeat segment of 'We Can Look Up' gave way to a stirring reveille of marching piano chords, delicate guitar and a drowsy duet of trumpet and saxophone akin to the brass swoons that would eventually become Beirut's trademark, before 'So Red' took a sudden shift of tempo and picked up the pace again to a joyful ska skank. Vernon's lyrics, though, remained downcast, bemoaning that he'd "never had to buy a wedding ring or any other sort of thing/Been a couple of years . . . since anyone's looked in my direction". By verse two the desperation reached critical: "sometimes my lungs cave in, sometimes my heart gets thin, sometimes I need to be with her". It was as if, having brushed aside the album's initial positivity and opened his emotional floodgates, Justin could no longer hold his murky waters back.

These anguished revelations were by no means the only signpost to Vernon's future as a craftsman of sublime, melancholic mood pieces. Four minutes in, 'So Red' dropped down to a near silent guitar refrain full of restrained tension, a bleak hopelessness and words unsaid. A rattle of snare drum and plaintive trumpets strike up, rousing an air of nobility to the struggle and, as more brass rallies to stir a sense of heroism in the face of emotional adversity, 'So Red' builds to a euphoric crescendo of a hue that saw far beyond the remit of traditional jazz and would eventually become the foundation stone of alt-folk. Though they were some years yet from emerging as a recognisable force or movement, Vernon was already thinking along the same lines as Band Of Horses, Fleet Foxes, Beirut, Iron & Wine and Bright Eyes: traditional instruments building grand swells of intoxicating noise.

The album's title track was the first recorded duet between Justin and the girl who'd give her name to his breakthrough masterpiece. Returning to a stoutly upbeat groove with an Afrobeat rhythm resembling Paul Simon's 'Graceland' and the kind of frivolous Soweto guitar work that would come to characterise Vampire Weekend's Afropop, the song found the pair ironically cooing to each other about a doomed affair: "Sweetly done wrong, singing lovers' songs, we tried so hard, we tried to be strong." Picturing bittersweet romantic images of "glossy beaches reflecting an orange and blue sky", their affection has now cracked, sending the couple spiralling into a bleak wintry despondency – "Weeks fly by in timeless time, we're just measuring seasons by the mind, leaves still die on Jefferson Street and winter's a dark, dark time." As the track progressed through a cheerful Afrobeat party section of bongos and breezy horns more suited to the Glastonbury World Stage than the icy Midwest – and entirely at odds with its lyrical fragilities – the duet became ever more spiteful and desperate, the pair barking "prove you're more comfortable now with these people and with these friends" at one another, and "spill your guts out on the sidewalk, we can slip, slip around". Their dissolving relationship clashed with their need for security with opposing reactions for both; as the song reaches its finale Justin is yowling "I don't wanna stop talking to you" while Sara responds with a firm "I'm running away". Though presumably not a song about their own relationship – after all, they were singing it together – 'We Can Look Up' arguably exposed a propensity for conflict and discord between the two. If not a public airing of laundry, then, certainly a premonition.

After several tracks of heart-wringing and bawling out its troubles, Mount Vernon's debut album needed a lift. 'Happy Song' was precisely that. "Life, it's been good to me!" the choir chimed in a jubilant gospel swing that erupted in occasional bursts of handclaps and whistles, while Justin sang of nostalgia for his childhood toys and his idealistic dreams of racial integration ("I got brown hair, you got brown skin, we can spread the love together"), yodelling a heady chorus of "when we shine tonight, we will be so bright-lit". A simple, throwaway three minutes of naivety, optimism and celebration, it stopped 'We Can Look Up' descending too far into darker emotional leagues.

Any jazz/ska band worth its salt needs no excuse to wander off into free-form experimental interludes, and 'Superstatic' was Mount Vernon's chance to meander through a variety of styles and genres in honour of keeping prog alive. A Ween-esque six-minute slab of very wonky jazz rock that shifted its perspective roughly every minute, it opened as a slinky jazz club saunter topped with serrated metal guitar chops and drowsy horns, became a spritely Twenties skat Charleston number for a few bars, then a sleazy striptease. From there it went medieval on your ass, slipping into a lyric-free madrigal choir version of 'God Rest Ye Merry Gentlemen' complete with sleighbells, then a burst of double-speed Tudor Christmas minstrel song: "this is Christmas time and we travel far and near".

By now you had the tune pegged as a quasi-comedy caper of six or seven attempts at random genres strung together, and it didn't disappoint from there on in. At the three-minute mark it turned into a nu metal chunder of spiked power chords and Justin grunting, goblin-like, over the top as if he'd just turned his baseball cap backwards and transformed into a proto Fred Durst. And from the ridiculous to the sublime; this gnarly chunk of rap rock gave way to a slice of rattling choral folk that was the closest the album came to envisioning the suave country of Bon Iver, with its lush harmonies and home-made tin-can percussion. Unfortunately it lasted mere seconds before the nu metal made an unwelcome return.

After such a sprawling, schizophrenic splurge of styles, 'We Can Look Up' closed as it began, deep in NYC sitcom territory. A languid, autumnal folk pop ditty laced with flutes, piano and hushed-yet-passionate bar-room emoting, 'Black Pirates' was by far the most mature, natural and accomplished moment on a record that often felt like an amateurish first stab at making an album. There'd been bum notes, trad cheese, cornball playfulness, lengthy solos both fumbled and unnecessary and awkward teenage poetry by the gallon, but having succeeded in actually making a debut album speckled with flashes of true inspiration it felt that, come 'Black Pirates', Vernon was relaxed and confident enough to begin making the sort of music he heard in his head. 'Black Pirates' was a Lilith Fair-friendly brand of flute folk reminiscent of Suzanne Vega, sure, but it didn't sound like a high school jazz band playing at being professional musicians, it sounded like, well, professional musicians. At times, it even sounded like his future.

There was a maturity to the lyrics here too as if, after gushing out his growing pains and teenage party songs throughout the album, Vernon had reached a fresh plane of wisdom. The story, swapped between Justin and Sara, smacked of fantasy – a character known as Black Pirate "rides his black horse out of the moonlight", watches a tornado brewing in the distance, considers "the monsters he has slain and the ones left to be done" and then races into the very heart of the chaos, "into the core of the horror, right into the eye of the storm". But come the chorus the artifice dropped and Justin, accompanied by Sara and another male voice, seemed to sing from the heart: "Alone is not a word, it's just a reconciling herd that seems to run us down when we're sleeping". It was an abstract concept that seemed to say that loneliness is an unconscious human impulse, suggesting Black Pirate was a metaphor for our innate compul-sion to race towards emotional catastrophe. But crucially, it was open to multiple readings, a first tentative hint of the intangible sound-built imagery to come.

Today, 'We Can Look Up' sounds like what it was, an album-length demo tape showcasing the raw talent of a songwriter still deeply in thrall to the standard practices of jazz, ska, world music and other traditional formats. But throughout you can hear Vernon learning how a song should work and beginning to find his musical footing, explore his own voice and ingenuity. You sense him trying to weave into these fixed sounds and structures elements of his post-grunge rock tastes, classic US folk songwriting and explorative lyricism. Firm – but brief – flickers of his future direction sporadically rise out of the melee, in the choirs of 'Sprinkler', the crescendos of 'So Red' and the folk lope of 'Black Pirates', as if daring him to snatch at them and run.

As they completed mixing on the album though, Mount Vernon could hear nothing but its flaws. They already hated their old sound and knew they could be fresher, more inspired. Still, they set about sending CD copies of *We Can Look Up* to the local press and, since actual albums from semi-professional local bands were few and far between, they made a small splash. In 1998 the Eau Claire *Leader-Telegram* sent a rookie journalist called Ken Szymanski to conduct Mount Vernon's first ever interview, all nine members and Ken crammed into Gil and Justine's living room. The newspaper filed a photo of the band* posed on a wooden balcony over-looking frozen fields on the outskirts of town, all flyaway hair and geeky grins. They looked like the archetypal backwoods hobby band overjoyed at feeling their first hot flush of flashbulb.

Little did the photographer know he was snapping history; the roots of a future Eau Claire scene, and a burgeoning love affair that would beguile a generation.

* In the shot they numbered nine, but their live line-up rotated to include up to 10 members at some shows.

CHAPTER THREE

A Towering Love, A Thundering Wave

ON the widening banks of the Chippewa River, separated from the water by the red brick edifices of Governor's Hall and Horan Hall and the green expanse of Putnam Park, the Towers dominated the skyline. Two imposing grey slabs, more sprawling residential estate blocks than vaulting spires, that sat at the hub of the University of Wisconsin's Eau Claire campus, home to almost 1,300 students and the beating, rutting, puking heart of UW-Eau Claire.

"They're pretty iconic if you go to college here," says Justin. "Everyone barfs at Towers. Everyone studies at Towers. Everyone has to see those, if you go to college here for four years."[1] Many students also lose their virginities at the Towers including, by his own admission, Justin.

"It's made up of these two towers – North and South," he later explained when describing the meaning behind the song he'd come to name after the buildings. "My girlfriend lived in one and I lived in the other. ['Towers' is] about falling in love, but also about what happens when you've long fallen out of love and those reminders are still there. You drive by them, these two buildings, and you look, and you realise that we really built that up. That we really built that love into these things, and for a long time afterward looking at them really made me feel sad; to see these empty buildings that I don't go in to any more. But then, as time goes on, they start to become kind of joyous in their own way: you can look at them and think 'that love was great and these buildings still stand tall'. But there's also an element of the fact that they're just buildings – they're gonna fall down one day, and they're not that important because there's new love in your life and you've got to break things down that get built up."[2]

All that heartbreak was still to come the day in the fall of 1999 that

Justin, then sporting Vanilla Ice dreadlocks, and other members of Mount Vernon arrived wide-eyed at UW-Eau Claire to launch their college careers. The band had built up such a following around town, graduating out of school hall shows into local venues such as The Metro even though none of the members were yet old enough to get in for anybody's gigs besides their own. Their rambunctious, open-hearted sets had helped them become one of the most popular bands in the city, and no-one wanted to split after graduating high school. The University was famed for its impressive jazz programme[*] and played host to the Eau Claire Jazz Festival every year, drawing such greats as Gary Burton, Rufus Reid, Charlie Byrd and Ira Sullivan to town, so it seemed a natural home for Mount Vernon, sat right there on their doorstep.

Justin had signed up for four years majoring in Religious Studies and minoring in Women's Studies. It was an unusual combination for such a musical soul and he did try his hand at studying musical theory but, he claimed, "I didn't want to be proficient . . . It seemed like other people were valuing things that were more about technical ability and not, like, feel."[3]

"Even now I'm not completely done with the idea of going back to school to study music, or even film," he told his university newspaper, "but when it came time to decide . . . you know, I wasn't a great reader, and I wasn't a great practiser, and I didn't have great theory, and the music programme at UW-Eau Claire is very difficult."[4]

It was perhaps Justin's familial make-up, or maybe his Indigo Girls obsession, that prompted him to minor in a course studying the philosophy of feminism – he certainly claimed not to have chosen the course in order to meet girls. "It sounds like the stereotype of the one guy sitting in a class full of women," he says, "and sometimes I was, but I really didn't do it to try to pick up girls or anything. It was just after I took that first class, it was like alarm bells started going off in my head. It just seemed so obvious that our society, at its really deep core, is so patriarchal, and it seemed so important for me, and everyone, to understand that something is really wrong with that."[5]

---

[*] UW-Eau Claire's Jazz Ensemble I has received two Grammy nominations and been voted Best College Big Band by *Down Beat* magazine six times.

His parents certainly had an influence on his decision to study religion, however. "He talked a few times about the influence of his parents on his decision to study religion and philosophy in college," his tutor Charlene Burns says. "They apparently told him they didn't care what he majored in, as long as he was passionate about it and got a degree . . . Justin was a real delight in the classroom, very smart, great sense of humor and personal humility, engaged in getting the most out of his educational experience and always looking to be challenged. He cares deeply about the meaning of life and struggled with the genuinely difficult questions, like how to make sense of the reality of evil and suffering. I recall his becoming intrigued by things like the powerful expressions of suffering and hope in African-American spirituals and the implications of the Dead Sea Scrolls for understanding Christianity."[6]

"The world of religion resonated for him," she said. "He's a really deep thinker and very caring. He's very compassionate."[7]

"I was always kind of a spiritual kid," Justin adds, describing Burns as his "guiding light" through university. "I was always real interested in people and why things like love and memory or any of those things are important. I wasn't an A-plus student at all, but that was one of the reasons why I appreciated Charlene so much. She knew that I wasn't an academic; she knew that I wasn't going on to graduate school. And even though she never let up on me, pushing me to do the right things academically, she allowed me to study what I wanted to take away for my life, and the whole experience was just very good for me."[8]

He'd be more dismissive about the subject itself. "All it taught me was that [religion is] a pile of garbage. People need to think more and pray less,"[9] he'd tell *The Times*, and by the time he came to compile his senior thesis he would see his studies shift back towards music, basing a paper on 'The Problem Of Evil' around the question of why artists suffer while bad people thrive.

But this question had a deeper drive. By the end of his course Justin was an artist who had done his fair share of suffering. He'd lost his formative band, split with the love of his life and fled the country to lick his wounds. He was beginning to question not just who he was, but where was 'home' . . .

★ ★ ★

In Justin's sophomore year of 2000, reduced to a solid seven-piece*, Mount Vernon set about recording the follow-up to *We Can Look Up*. Ascribed to Move Music and assigned the catalogue number movemusic1† to give the recording more credibility despite its very home-made feel – the sleeve was another nature painting, this time of a tree leaning in the breeze across a summer field – the six-track mini-album *All Of Us Free* was a leaner, brighter and far more accomplished undertaking than its predecessor.

Opening with a brazen double barrel of Joe Jackson/Ben Folds bar-room piano and saucy E Street horns, it took only a few seconds of 'Sandlot' for the listener to realise that this was a far more confident band than that which made *We Can Look Up*, and one far more in control of its talents. Brad's five-string bass filled the space, Justin's guitars sounded full and alt.folk rich; engineer Scott Sugden had done a fine job in velvet-cladding their sound. Here was Mount Vernon reaching a peak.

Just like the first, the second Mount Vernon started full of the flush and thrill of life. His voice maturing into its husky timbre, Justin sang again of idyllic summers "bumming around", spinning images of the same sort of laid-back boho living that had characterised the likes of 'High Five' on 'We Can Look Up'. "Morning time, dry sun, waking up next to a good friend, start out with bowls of cereal, then video games," he sang, with only the merest hint of any conflict to come – "I never began to see the end." Again, there was a strong sense of contentment in his surroundings, a feeling of belonging as he wailed "Slammed on my baseball cap, shut the door and head out into the world, the neighbourhood is bumping with the sound of summer . . . To this love, this world, I am forever bound/These dusty afternoons tucker me out but I feel found". For all the ice and dislocation of Eau Claire, as 'Sandlot' built to a double-tempo crescendo of hazy trumpet solos, funky bass, chiming piano chords and rampant cowbell abuse, Vernon again made his hometown sound like a dream community of perpetual summer.

The smoky summer vibe continued into the second track, 'Morning',

---

* The line-up that recorded *All Of Us Free* was Brad on bass, Phil on piano, Justin on guitars, Joe on drums and percussion, Sara on saxophone, Trever on trumpets and Keil on trombone and djembe.
† Since no official record deal was signed for *All Of Us Free*, it's likely this was a label invented by the band in order to release this album.

the closest yet to the soulful folk sounds that would make Justin famous. At least, it was for the opening two minutes. A solo Vernon strummed and slapped his acoustic guitar with a funk flourish, recalling the likes of Joan Armatrading or Jackson Browne and revisiting his recurring theme of romantic and easy-going starts to immaculate days. "I wake up in the morning time with the sun breaking in my bedroom," he sang, "let joy rush in when I open the scene and that's when I know all the angels are here with me". He sang of "bright new tune"s and rural peacefulness: "The sun's coming up, the wind is blowing through the trees, my country road is quiet now, as quiet as it can be". Had he added a falsetto and some surrealist lyrics oozing heartache, he might have found his ultimate calling seven years early.

He didn't quite have the courage to venture into a full song alone though. One hundred seconds in Mount Vernon struck up some drowsy horns and a breezy harmonica and Justin embarked on what can only be described as a pastoral rap. In the vein of Red Hot Chili Peppers, Justin rhymed about the liberating effects of nature, dreaming of leaving behind all of his worldly possessions and losing himself in the countryside. "I'm bleeding because I miss the country wind," he rapped, enthusing about the "sacred bees" and how "the folks out there are so kind, where time isn't money, time's a place". He painted nature as a place of spiritual purity and freedom from mental constraints – "we all got to shake down the baggage and bend those bars of those mental cages/And then one day everyone knows everything's alright and everything's okay/And if our fear becomes our courages then that day I hear all of the beautiful people say/It's alright, it's okay, nothing wrong with today/And I don't need to find out what I'm afraid of".

It sounded a glorious utopia indeed, and Justin found philosophical nourishment there too, an unlocking of life's mysteries and a – rather hippified – emancipation from materialism. "Out the window I can see all the key to human simplicity," he claimed, "I said 'burn all your money and you can finally feel free, compassion heals thee'." There was a real idealism at work, but despite its affecting gospel chorus refrain and sweet whistling interludes, this was one track that Justin would later look back on with a certain embarrassment. "Out of all the songs, ever, I think I might have been a little off my rocker because it's like a rap song, or what-ever," he'd say. "That'd be one I'd wanna re-think a whole lot."[10]

Re-think it he would, only the following year, but more immediately the mid-paced blues of the next track 'Feel The Light' rethought Justin's attitude to nature. This time it was destructive rather than regenerative; the leaves were burning in autumn, the wind blowing the smoke away, the fire sucking the heat into the ground against the chill of the nights descending into icy stasis. Yet here too Justin found contentment. "The moon is almost warming us and there is an absence of sound," he sang, "peace on earth tonight, let the stars shine bright/Let our souls feel high, come on feel the light". By verse two he was transmogrified into the city of Eau Claire itself ("I know that this valley that I live in will hold me safely in its keep, rivers run right through me") and while he felt the presence of people "making the best of their day" he was constantly aware of the land the city was built on, thrumming with energy beneath the foundations.

So the themes of *All Of Us Free* were set; finding yourself and eradicating your fears through the psychological freedoms inspired by nature and community. It was a philosophy carried right through to the end of the mini-album and arguably Mount Vernon's melodic high-point, 'Breathe'.★ Built around an effervescent folk twangle, dense bass, warm piano and horns that may have been nudged a little towards a tone of strident disharmony by the cult success of Neutral Milk Hotel's *In The Aeroplane Over The Sea* album in 1998, it was once again imbued with the atmosphere of antique coffee-house comedy shows as Justin and Sara swapped verses of escaping the weight of city life into the golden fields and windswept country roads. "You pass through my heart like a ton of steel," sang Justin, finding solace in some lonesome retreat, possibly the cabin on The Land, "here I'll never feel alone because here is a place called home, I've made this drive up to heaven so many times . . . where the soul feels no cold".

Crucially, the lyric, if taken at face value, suggests the possibility of a disruption in the pair's relationship, a realisation that their personalities were beginning to clash. Sara's verse speaks of two different kinds of people, those to whom "a face of a planet breathes . . . more sorrow" and those who "laugh free". She casts Justin as the former and herself as the latter,

★ The two intervening songs, 'Here I Go' and 'Back Down', are the closest Justin Vernon has to 'lost tracks': unavailable to anyone who doesn't already own *All Of Us Free*, currently changing hands on auction sites for upwards of £110, and unrecorded for later albums.

singing "with a darkened light . . . I asked you to come in and balance me". Yet, by the end of the song they're unbalanced and dislocated, singing entirely different lyrics at the same time, both singing of the sun's harmony with the earth but from different rhythms, cadences and perspectives. It sounded, in retrospect, like a sour break-up set to sweet, sweet music.

An interpretation tempered by later events perhaps, but one thing is certain. Before many copies of *All Of Us Free* could be sold or much promotional live activity undertaken, Mount Vernon had been scattered across the globe, like seeds in the wind.

★ ★ ★

"There is an Emma," Vernon admits, but he is reticent about offering up anything but the sketchiest biographical details about her and their time together. He alludes to their being together for years, going their separate ways and leaving the country to get away from each other, resisting the urge to start the cycle over again no matter how tempting, and regret over that decision that lingers in his heart to this day. "It's obvious there's this long-lost love of mine," he says. "Doesn't everybody have them? But the majority of the record isn't about this person, it's about what happened to me afterwards and the long years that followed."[11]

★ ★ ★

Winter, 2000. His relationship in tatters and his band hanging in the balance, for the first time Justin Vernon retreated to the wild unknown. And this time he fled halfway across the world.

Aged 19, in the second semester of his sophomore year, the rural backwater he chose was on an entirely different continent altogether. With his university career put on hold for a year and a limited working visa in his pocket he arrived in Galway in the windswept west of Ireland, looking for a small chunk of a new life to help him forget his broken old one.

"I always wanted to go to Ireland," he later told Irish newspaper the *Sunday World*, "so, at the age of 19, I came over to check it out and stayed until my work visa ran out."[12]

In Galway, Justin took a temporary job selling mobile phones at an Eircom shop in the picturesque open expanse of greenery that was Eyre Square, and supplemented his income by busking around town and entering local open mic nights. "I was pretty much a nobody down there at the time," he said, "but I did win an open mic night in The Cellar pub. My prize was a €30 gift voucher for a local music store; one of the albums I bought with it was The Pogues' *If I Should Fall From Grace With God*. I'm a big fan of Shane MacGowan."[13]

Drowning his sorrows in Murty Rabbitt's bar by night and licking his wounds between securing 24-month contracts by day, Justin's months in Galway were a means of physically separating himself from facing up to his split with Sara after several years together. It was just the start of a long recovery process. It would be some years of mourning, soul-searching and exorcising his loss on record before he'd finally come to terms with it – enough, at least, to dedicate his most famous record to Sara Emma Jensen in the wake of another break-up, as if finally laying his memories of his relationship with Sara to rest.

The clearest insight we have into the workings of Justin's heart during his time in Ireland came with a song he wrote about the period called 'West Coast Of Ireland', released on a self-burned CD of one takes of tracks he began playing solo around Eau Claire on his return.* Accompanied by a plaintive acoustic guitar and singing with a damaged depth of feeling unheard in his Mount Vernon recordings, Justin's cracked soul husked through tear-strewn lines, the spaces between the words taut with devastation: "sitting on the west coast of Ireland looking out onto the ocean, knowing you're looking straight on back, feeling that same wave of emotion".

Yet the song doesn't wallow. Though Justin here found that his emotional turmoil made it "hard being spiritual", he was saved by the three core stalwarts of his life – home, nature and music. He sang of kissing the sand, tasting the salt water of the Atlantic, of the sun shining "right on through to the core of my bones"; he dreamt of the day he'd land back at Minneapolis International to be met by his entire family and his plan to immediately "lay right down in the cool April sun, gonna lay in the grass until I start itching and I'll find I'll probably mow the lawn a few times". Having reconnected with his homeland earth, he'd reconnect with the city he loves, "watch another Wisconsin sun go down, have dinner with

---

* The seemingly home-made CD was titled with the hand-written legend *In The Room – Live – 2002*.

my parents, then head on in to my small, small enough town" and if that wasn't enough, he could tour the country to lose himself in its music – "I can get out to California, I have San Francisco on my mind, I can get down to New Orleans and have that music knock me to the ground."

By the end of this lament of heartache and hope, he was grinning into the face of death and declaring "I wanna be able to feel the air and be where the river meets the sea, where the sky meets the ocean and where space meets the sky, I'll be singing 'all of us free'." For all the reputation he may one day earn as a clinger to old, lost loves, here was an artist determined not to let his misfortunes drag him down.

When he did return to Eau Claire in April of 2001*, it was to tidy up business. Mount Vernon, the band decided, was no longer viable; besides the issue of Justin and Sara's fractured relationship, the band felt they'd begun to stagnate. From working in the University of Eau Claire's Media Development Center Justin had learnt much about electronics and had started to gain an interest in the electro works of Steve Reich, David Tudor and Brian Eno, fresh influences he wanted to put into practice. What's more, just as Justin had run off to Ireland, the other various members were scattering too. Keil, having never been that interested in studying at UW-Eau Claire in the first place and only signing up because the rest of Mount Vernon had enrolled, headed to England, giving up his studies in Eau Claire for good. While Phil remained in Eau Claire, Brad left for Minneapolis, where he spent four months living with a married couple who turned him on to Brian Eno and "totally blew my mind"[14]. Trever, after completing his course in sociology at UW-Eau Claire, also moved to England to study music sociology at the University of Exeter, eventually earning a PhD and going on to teach in Prague and Japan. Justin has never spoken about what became of Sara†.

Joe, meanwhile, had skipped town to Vermont, where he was busy

---

* If 'West Coast Of Ireland' was accurate, Justin spent around three months in Galway at the very start of 2001, returning in April; although some sources claim he stayed in Ireland for a full year, returning in 2002, this is unlikely since he released the solo album *Feels Like Home* in 2001, featuring his Eau Claire resident brother Nate as well as other Eau Claire musicians.

† A Facebook scour does uncover one Sara Jensen living in Eau Claire with her young family and, whether the 'Emma' in question or not, not inclined to reply to requests for interviews from members of the press.

studying jazz at an arts school called Bennington College, taught by the legendary free jazz drum pioneer Milford Graves. Graves, having played with the likes of John Coltrane and John Zorn, had some unusual and out-landish techniques for improvisations that he'd developed around the practices of martial arts and cookery. "Milford opened my eyes to a different set of values in music altogether," Joe said. "He's an artifact, and it got me excited about jazz again, having contact with someone who had looked up to Elvin Jones not because everyone said he was good but because he was the guy to go to in New York at the time . . . It felt like I was taking something from a pure source."[15]

It suited Justin at that point in his life that, musically speaking, he was largely alone. After years of open-armed collaboration, he now felt most comfortable expressing himself via an acoustic guitar and his own voice, it felt like his time to get introspective. Yet he was invigorated by his trip to Ireland, warmed to be home and keen to get creating again. He struck upon an idea of artistic consolidation, of marking his progress in music up to that point at the same time as edging into the future. He decided to select the best songs he'd recorded with Mount Vernon and re-record them solo alongside other tunes he'd come up with in high school and the best of the songs he'd written since leaving for Ireland. By doing so not only would he compile his best material to that point in his life and stamp his individuality and spirit on his songs – explore them within the free-doms of a new, more personal solo identity – he'd uncover fresh emotion and meaning by separating them from the context of the full band. It was as if the adult Vernon, in the midst of the hardest period in his life so far, wanted to devour, dramatise and demolish the naïve pleasures of his teenage self.

One third old material and two thirds new, *Feels Like Home* opened with its six-minute title track, and immediately we were thrust into the sparse and intimate folk world that would eventually make Vernon the darling of the alt.folk universe. You could practically hear Justin hunched over the belly of his guitar, plucking and strumming at his pains with a new-found virtuosity. "It's a little overt at times for me to listen to now," Justin said, perhaps acknowledging that the track reverted to his well-worn lexicon of idyllic pastoral imagery – country skies, passing seasons, breaking mornings, homebound roads, fields, leaves and trees, "but it is everything this record is about."[16] It was a paean to security, safety and the comfort of familiarity in a lost and lonely world, marking the point where Justin shed much of his youthful jazz obsession and embraced the homely sounds of mournful folk music. The timbres of Justin's debut solo album – marked once again with the Move Music label and released under the moniker JD Vernon – echoed space, depth and intensity, its stark and impassioned guitar solo reverberating as if through the shell of a broken man. Bruised and yearning for home, Justin Vernon had come of age.

To prove it, he next tackled 'Feel The Light' from *All Of Us Free*, reimagining it as an upbeat folk-country swing imbued with a timeless sepia hue that smacked of alt.country maturity, all harmonicas, slide guitar flourishes and wooden porch clap-alongs in swing chairs. Here, a third verse about a long plane journey seemed particularly fitting after his jaunt to Ireland, the wonders of nature gleaming through even when stuck in a metal tube for 13 hours – "the morning when you're flying is night, the dawn and sunrise all at the same time/The orange blanket that is the white clouds below, the blue and black horizon that bruises and glows/And in the middle a single star overhead is where resides my fear". Even 35,000 feet of empty space couldn't separate this earth child from the comfort of the elements.

And there, in the final verse of 'Feel The Light', a familiar female vocal. It's uncertain if Justin's duet partner singing "peace on Earth tonight/ Come on, feel the light" is Sara, but this would certainly be in keeping with his tendency to stay loyal and close to those that have meant something to him. Perhaps as a result of coming from such a close-knit community, Vernon would never shut anybody out; he'd remain friends and often perform with the various members of Mount Vernon over the coming years, and he and Sara stayed friends too. As late as 2008, in the wake of the success of the album that bore her middle name, Justin told the *Observer Music Monthly*, "She's fine with it. Now she just makes me pay for breakfast."[17] *

The same stripped-down folk treatment was afforded to a more delicate and defiant 'Breathe', which grew a lo-fi beat like a battered bucket, double-tracked vocals, a shrill harmonica and a whispered coda without

---

* It's also possible that Justin and Sara were still entangled in reconsidering the status of their relationship at this point, that it wasn't an affair that ended with a clean break-off. In the quote from *Mojo* above he's credited as "resisting the urge to start the cycle over again".

losing any of its irrepressible joie de vivre, and 'We Can Look Up', which here ran to a full seven minutes full of impassioned howling, multi-part harmonies, Celtic arpeggios and the sort of artful, skilled flamenco and C&W guitar work worthy of the world music concert hall. His years with Mount Vernon had clearly refined Justin's guitar playing to impressive lengths and his time in Ireland had tenderised his spirit.

For further insight into his frame of mind, though, you turned to the new tracks. Slotted between these re-recordings was a swampland Mississippi blues called 'Leave It Alone', again featuring a female vocalist plus a brittle New Orleans jazz trumpet alongside brushed orange-crate drums and trembling harmonica. It marked Justin's first song about politics, referencing Kenneth Starr, the lawyer behind the investigation into Bill Clinton's affair with Monica Lewinsky culminating in the impeachment of the President and arguably tilting the US against his re-election. Critics of the Starr Report into the affair argued that Starr had overstepped a line from his original remit to investigate the suicide of deputy White House counsel Vince Foster, becoming a 'political hitman', and Justin was clearly amongst these liberal objectors. "Kenneth Starr, you go around snooping on your other people's chief of staff," he crooned. "I tell you one thing about Mr Clinton, he's a good man/You just make me laugh, why don't you leave it alone?"

The rest of the song may have been an attack on Starr too, but sounded more like an assault on the integrity and self-serving nature of politicians in general, including Clinton: "Where are you Mr Powerful?/I can hear your high chair creaking from way across the room/I know I might be insane but I aint never seen someone as weak as you . . . hey Mr Politician, where have you gone to?/When we all know that your money, your money bought your name/Why don't you leave it alone?/You can't seem to keep your hands off of other people's things/When you say you're going to go out, go out and save everything". Maybe as a result of his trip across the world, for the first time Justin's lyrical vista expanded beyond Eau Claire and its surrounds, beyond his social group, his personal relationships and the world he can see around him, to take in global and national concerns. He was realising that songwriting was a platform with clout and the best practitioners used it to explore other topics than their introspective angst, the laid-back serenity of their hometown and the friendliness of their friends. By the end of 2001, in the wake of 9/11, a song chastising Ken Starr would seem like a trite political slash from a naïve era, but 'Leave It Alone' was a pivotal step in Vernon developing a wider, socially conscious perspective in the vein of his protest folk heroes.

And in the vein of his Deep South blues heroes, the next track 'Trainyard Blues (Live)' was exactly that, a playful duet of slide guitar and harmonica like a hobo's mail-train blues in which Justin tipped his cap to the delta blues legends Robert Johnson and Willie Brown while simultaneously impersonating them. As a reconstructed tribute to the blues it felt throwaway but sincere, but Justin had fresher fish to fry.

'Jefferson St.' was a contemporary folk number that syphoned some of Bright Eyes' tremulous emotion into a tender, spacious recording of Justin spinning funk riffs out of his acoustic guitar, so sparse you can hear the creaks and echo of the room.* Besides his guitar, a sultry bongo and a backing choir of double-tracked Justins, his solo voice, quivering and on edge, wove a wintry scene on Jefferson Street over Thanksgiving and Christmas, a backdrop to his musings on a life gone awry. "Something terrifies me," he sang as if grit-toothed in the face of his trials, "the world ain't so simple, you see/The riddles are the same but the answers change/Why does it cut me down to size?/Why do the leaves inside me die?" He seemed resigned and philosophical about it all but the tsunami of emotion soon overcame his mask of restraint. The climax line "I am a lonely boy with my cover soaked with rain" began breathless, the tension of losing his grip, and ended with an almighty, anguished wail that felt like tear-strewn catharsis, Justin warbling "why are you crying? Why aren't you flying?". It was the first real sign that Justin was using the *Feels Like Home* album as a sort of self-therapy.

And just as when the floodgates opened midway through 'We Can Look Up', there was more to come. Bedecked with mournful guitar strums and pining violin, the nine minute epic 'When It Rains Down Here' was Justin's attempt to paint Chippewa Valley in the same mythical folk colours with which Springsteen painted Nebraska two decades before, in the hope that by being the man that seals Eau Claire's place in eternal Americana folk legend he'd somehow heal himself: "before my arches are rebuilt it must have a song". Realising that to do so meant

* An effect Justin would develop over the years to create a famously intimate effect that would contribute greatly to his breakthrough.

imbuing his imagery with a sense of the history and hardships of the people who inhabited his homeland, he switched his scene from dreamy summers to "the grey background" of the desolate rainy season, "floating in an atmosphere of truth and hidden lies". He trained his eye, characteristically, on the soft-focus beauty of the scene, on the "silver mountains and blue streams . . . those moss-green pines, heavy raindrops clinging to electrical lines", yet his words were weighty, sodden with unspoken tragedy both personal and political. The rain held two metaphors: of Eau Claire's political isolation ("the rain is so quiet it's sad and the liberty rings so loud we can't hear/It's so hard to see outside when it rains down here") and of Justin's downpour of personal miseries stifling his life ("I can't proceed until the rain is gone").

Ultimately, the rain metaphor couldn't contain Justin's pain. Listening to Louis Armstrong "play his horn on the short wave radio", Vernon's overwhelmed by the sadness in the music – "his sound breaks my heart with a stone in my throat, like a sword through a heart, leaking tears onto the ground". "Alone is where I've been needing to be," he admitted, and as a crashing piano stirred the mood grander he took the watery imagery a step further, imagining himself as a ship's captain on an ocean of troubles, besieged by beating waves of woe but fighting through: "the wind can blow me wherever it needs to take me/The skipper taunts the sky/A thundering wave crashing into the side/It will never break him, it will never save him". It was the testament to staying unbroken by it all that was the key. Justin was a survivor, not a sinker.

His steady march to maturity continued with 'May 27th, 1999 (5.23 a.m.)', a contemplative travelling folk tune that saw Justin start to recognise the transience of youth and friendship. It was set at the point where high school ends, social groups dissipate, adulthood stretches ahead like "a long highway with nothing ahead but the red sun" and you realise that "everything good must have an end". His "endless childhood nights" blown away, Justin found himself aged "eighteen, wondering where all the days have gone" while a friend called Kate was packing up her things and moving away, tears running down her nose, leaving her old friends with a final message, "'laugh while you can, you're never gonna see them again/Hold their hand as tight as you can/I say to you, if you can never look down you're never gonna land'".

Having watched his band ricochet off around the country and the world, Justin had seen that family is the only true, dependable rock in life and expressed here a sense of regret that he hadn't appreciated them enough: "mother's love and father's hand can always pull you out of the quicksand/But you get up and you just dust yourself off, when you're walking away all they can do is cry/And hope maybe that they'll catch your eye". It was an idea that flew in the face of Mount Vernon's songs waxing lyrical about a communal unity that would never end, and something that Justin would endeavour to fight against within the Eau Claire musical community, striving to keep everyone playing together in one form or another. But he couldn't ignore the shifts and fractures of human nature and, as the song reached a noble roar of defiance, he saw a fatalistic heroism in the death of his childhood. "Forget all drugs and leave all rock'n'roll aside, you aint helping us get through," he bellowed in the face of age and decay, "it's love that gets us through, it's time that makes us doomed, we're all leaving soon/Who needs a grave? Who needs a tomb?/But for now I am gonna miss you, let's all lock arms and shout to the sun, hey look at what we have done/We've finally come together just in time to come undone/Even if victory isn't written in our stars, boy, we've still won". In the end he'd come to terms with his fading youth, seeing childhood as all part of life's schoolyard game, a barrier to bounce off on your way to somewhere altogether more exciting – "we're gonna touch the wall of our childhood and then we're gonna run".

Justin's lyrics were developing a poetic adult complexity, but it was his stylistic dexterity that he showcased over the next two tracks. 'Lullabye Of The 3 Dancers' was a virtuoso, Iberian-tinged flamenco flourish on the solo acoustic guitar, interrupted only by a silent interlude of Justin lilting "little baby sleeping", and then came the album's big folly, a reworking of 'Morning' from *All Of Us Free*. This time, over seven minutes and now called 'Morning (AM)', Justin wholeheartedly embraced the soul and hip-hop vibe of the original, free-forming brand new lyrics alongside an appearance from his brother, Nate, rapping in the guise of his hip-hop alter ego I.D.E.A.

Over the crackle of vinyl, the trickle of a waterfall, synthesised bass, beats and xylophone and a jazzy Seventies early-Jay-Z sort of organ groove, Justin riffed around the images of the original track, clearly having fun messing with the rap genre. After an earnest Seventies soul introduction from Justin, it sounded like two brothers making a home-made Soul II

Soul spoof and one that flew in the face of the aggression and violence that inhabited most Nineties hip-hop. Alternating lines, like the small-town nature boys they were they rapped about their warm-hearted friends ("we don't need to fight, the message seems clear/When you steer away from fear/We ain't got nothing but lovers up in here/Beautiful people equals good cheer"), their love for Eau Claire ("we have a home that we'll forget never, may the love flow and keep us together . . . Home is what I praise when I raise to the sunlight/I comes into my place, I embrace the good life") and their childhood family memories ("we've got John Prine blasting through the house, making us feel we can't live life without"). On the rare occasion they tried to assimilate some of rap's confrontational imagery ("you'd better detach, reattach and blow up like a bomb"), they couldn't help ruining it with a rhyme lifted straight from a Sunday School jamboree ("you can help straighten out the world by being a good mom"). When they cast a shout out to inspirational rap troupe Jurassic 5, it was virtually in the same breath as a reference to San Francisco bluegrass combo The Bay City Ramblers.

Justin and Nate were too awkward and way too nice to convince as rappers, but 'Morning (AM)' was notable for its brief acknowledgements of teenage years fading ("green grass, basketball, long summer days/But now I'm getting packed up for the next phase"), a philosophy of selflessness that was largely unheard of in hip-hop ("strive to think about yourself a little less, give back to the world") and, crucially, the way Justin constructed his words. For the first time, when scrambling for rhymes that seemed ungrammatical or nonsensical in lines like "I keep absent of things applicable to my mind/I try to form a clean river free of pesticides", he was forming his lyrics around the sounds of the words rather than their meanings. And that was a technique that would one day bear him solid gold fruit.

Rounding off with a tinkle of Bontempi jazz piano, 'Morning (AM)' was the album's novelty burst of light relief, a sign that Justin's bright soul hadn't been entirely shrouded. The final track, 'Home Is . . .', bridged and unified the two opposing frames of mind of the record. An experimental mood piece with no words or melody, it juxtaposed dislocated, melancholic piano notes and the sounds of torrential rainfall against the giggles and chatter of friends huddled against the elements claiming "we just laughed for two hours straight" and watching TV news reports. The atmosphere was one of oppression and sadness, but filled with a real warmth; 'Home Is . . .' was the sound of love and friendship getting Justin through a storm.

He acknowledged as much in his self-written liner notes for the album. "I feel I need to sketch, emotionalise, thank and play to the people and places that have shaped me," he wrote. Eau Claire didn't return the love in equal measure though. Despite playing solo shows around town he sold few of the 100 copies he printed up and to this day owns an unsold box of the CDs. Hence it's understandable if, from that point on, Vernon saw his self-recorded solo albums as recordings he was making largely for himself, therapeutic exorcisms that he expected no-one else to hear.

No, it would be a far more upbeat country rock noise that his Eau Claire public would come to love him for. And to make it, he'd recruit some familiar faces, carved forever into the side of Mount Vernon.

CHAPTER FOUR

Sparks Of Edison

JUSTIN Vernon wasn't the only Eau Claire musician messing with hip-hop in 2002.

After eight months living in Minneapolis, Brad Cook arrived back in Eau Claire with his head full of beats. It wasn't just Brian Eno he'd been turned on to in the big city, he'd also learnt about an experimental rap collective releasing music under the banner of Anticon[*] in California. Described as "the hip-hop equivalent of post-rock", Anticon developed into an alternative rap label for avant garde hip-hop artists such as Alias, Doseone and Jel, acts bringing drone and electronica elements to the rap form. It was something Brad was itching to explore himself, so he hooked up with Joe to form a left-field rap group called Mel Gibson & The Pants, working around Joe's course at Bennington. Brad was fascinated by Joe's course, often ringing him in Vermont to find out what Graves had been teaching him, while Joe would send him back interesting oddities he'd unearthed in the college audio library.

"Playing in Mel Gibson was weird without Phil," Brad says, "but, without him, I definitely developed my own confidence apart from him and my own musical voice."[1] And Mel Gibson & The Pants wasn't Brad's only foray into off-kilter sonics. He'd met a guy in Chicago called Thomas Wincek who was making a name for himself as an experimental electronica pioneer, having created a glove made out of needles from record players for his senior thesis at Chicago's Art Institute. After college Wincek moved to Eau Claire to live with his wife, and Brad would come over to immerse himself in Wincek's music collection – John Cage, Alvin Lucier and Jim O'Rourke – and create esoteric soundscapes of their own.

Brad hadn't abandoned the simpler rock thrills though. Hooking up

[*] Sometimes styled anticon.

with Justin again, he found Vernon boasting a raft of 50 new songs and unhappy playing them solo. So Brad and Phil rejoined Vernon alongside Joe's younger brother Danny on drums. The four-piece once more took on Justin's name, this time his two middle ones – DeYarmond Edison formed with the intention of playing rock music with what Justin called "a certain kind of tenderness".[2]

"It felt so right, the three of us," Justin said. "And Danny was the closest we could get to Joe. We had this really intense emotional connection from high school. But in Mount Vernon, we were still reacting to this post-Phish kind of thing, complex music. It felt really good to get back to being OK with being really rootsy."[3]

Concentrating on the best 25 of Justin's new tunes, DeYarmond Edison's debut show saw them augment Justin's songs with two covers, one of New Orleans funk rockers The Meters and one Grateful Dead number they'd heard Bruce Hornsby playing. At first DeYarmond Edison was little more than an excuse for the three friends to play together, but a healthy burst of friendly competition soon spurred them on.

Dinner With Greg were an alternative C&W band that had filled Mount Vernon's vacant slot as the biggest group in Eau Claire. Watching them, Justin, Brad and Phil were stunned at their professionalism, amazed that their town had produced a band that, to them, sounded like world beaters. Brad considered them the best band he'd ever witnessed; Justin was inspired by their shows to seek out the works behind their sound, classics by Neil Young and Paul Westerberg. And, most importantly, it made him realise that, in songwriting terms, he had to up his game.

The gang of four set about honing their set in earnest, Justin determined to focus himself as a professional tunesmith. Investing in instruments and equipment, they tried out an array of new techniques, Brad's new electronic drone tendencies underpinning the solid Midwest rock howlers that Justin was writing to create an intriguing stew that critics would come to align with the likes of alt.country legends Richard Buckner and Sun Volt.

For two years, DeYarmond Edison ploughed the Eau Claire clubs and bars, building an awestruck fanbase of their own. Before long they'd reached the same level of local success as Dinner With Greg[*], and had

---

.[*] When Dinner With Greg eventually split, several members joined with some of DeYarmond Edsion to form a new electro-rock side project called Amateur Love.

gained a slide guitar player in the shape of UW-Eau Claire graduate Chris Porterfield.

"I was playing in a different band at the time," Chris says, "and then those guys had already been together playing music for several years. And then I joined them and played pedal steel guitar for a few years. Eau Claire was sort of . . . the scene was really close-knit, and there ended up being a lot of collaborating and sharing of players and different projects and stuff, and that's how I got to know the guys in DeYarmond Edison."[4]

Chris recalls the writing process in the band. "It was mostly just sort of a fleshing out of the ideas. Justin Vernon was the primary songwriter in that band. Occasionally we worked on lyrics together, but primarily he would bring song ideas to the table, and then everybody else would flesh them out."[5]

Chris wasn't the only new musician Justin was playing with at the time. He was earning spare cash giving guitar lessons at a local music store and for four years one of his students was a school kid named Mikey Noyce. Over their first two years of lessons Justin's tutoring of Noyce would turn from intense guitar study to sessions of merely listening to music together and picking out the parts on guitar. Eventually Noyce began writing his own songs and playing them to Vernon and, by the end of their four years, the 'lessons' would simply entail Mikey turning up at Justin's house and talking all day; they'd become close friends. And it was a friendship that would one day produce powerful music.

By 2004, DeYarmond Edison were playing packed shows to enthused crowds around Eau Claire, and sounding like real local hopes. Their gigs were a flurry of intriguing instruments – blues harp, vibraphone, banjo, pedal steel, organ and an old Thirties drum set, their photo shoots ranged from candid dressing room lounges to shots of them in suits and ties on the steps of grand derelict buildings. Simultaneously, MySpace was just building steam as a platform for bands to promote their music to a potentially global audience. Now all the band needed was some music to invade the internet with . . .

★ ★ ★

"This was like a re-beginning of something for us. It was our first glance at Eau Claire from an adult sort of standpoint. It was sort of one foot in the past and one trying to figure out what the present was . . . and not having any clue what the future was." – Justin Vernon on *DeYarmond Edison*, 2008.[6]

★ ★ ★

Brooding piano notes. A faint lilt of what sounds like a violin played back-wards. Then chiming chords, the heavy beat of drums, stadium guitar strikes and a Springsteen highway charge. This was 'Leave Me Wishing More', the opening track on DeYarmond Edison's self-titled debut album and, on its self-release in 2004[*], the first recorded introduction to the band's sound. Fans of Mount Vernon would have been stunned by Vernon's dramatic transformation. Gone were the jazz and world influ-ences; in their place a sturdy American rock adorned with freewheeling guitar solos and thundering piano, redolent of sweeping canyons and wide, windy plains. The three years since Justin's last release had also seen him find a more settled emotional footing; here he sang of a secure, serious and comforting relationship and difficulties overcome – "the boat I'm in/It's capsized, it's good again" he sang, "the target's a bended knee".

'As Long As I Can Go' was a more familiar sort of tune, a mid-paced acoustic country folk number akin to John Prine or Jackson Browne that built to a stirring climax, with Justin basking in the glory of an Eau Claire sunset and spinning another paean to his home town. "In my future I hope there's no other place," he crooned, wishing for little more than a dog to share it all with. It was a vein the album would continue in, with 'Dusty Road (So Kind)' coming on as a low country rattle, the distant drums beating out a soft railroad beat, Phil's piano drifting as if through a rich fog and Justin, to warm arpeggiated guitar, turning his emotive husk to a story of a summer's day spent driving with his partner, the two of them brim-ming with love and assurance. "I know I never ever had the blues," Justin sang, lifting his hushed tone to a joyous bellow, "But the man says that a whole lot of rain is gonna fall/But down my country road/No rain, no rain's gonna fall at all".

From this opening triptych, with Justin sounding like the polar opposite of the devastated 20-year-old that had recorded *Feels Like Home* three years earlier, you might assume that his life had taken a major swing for the

---

[*] Its sleeve once more smacked of a warmth for nature, featuring a tree brushing up to a whitewashed building, shot in sepia.

positive. 'There Is Something' was the first hint that some anguish still lingered. A slow, funereal ballad with a mild jazz bent, it found Justin wrenching his way through lyrics about a relationship cracked at the centre. "I leave, you enter . . . I awake, you go to sleep . . . I begin, you end," he whispered, a fractured affair that left him "falling down to a shattering, deafening sound".

One of their most popular tunes at the time, the next track 'The Lake' was a moment of raw intimacy, the brushed drums, a marimba melody and sparse guitar adding weight to Justin's musings on death and the afterlife. Yet despite its grim theme 'The Lake' had a surprisingly upbeat mood, Justin's "grieving" was "not sad, it's more of a longing that comes for the season that I'm in" and his dream of his soul staying put in Eau Claire and living in the memories of the city's inhabitants rather than ascending to any sort of Heaven was warm-hearted and full of hope. Restrained and artful, the song was a fan favourite, but a source of frustration for Justin. "Even though I like what that one's about," he said, "we could hardly ever play that song because we couldn't re-create that moment. The moment was tied down to this recording."[7]

At over seven minutes, 'Conquistadors' was the album's centrepiece and its most intriguing lyrical work. A glowering ballad of piano and ethereal background warps, it appeared to concern the historical connection between religion and imperialism, referencing not just the Spanish and Portuguese colonists of the title but also mentioning Pope Pius XII in the same breath as Hitler – the head of the Catholic Church during WWII has long been criticised for remaining silent about the Holocaust as it was happening. It was almost as if the song was narrated by a Jew who had died in the Auschwitz atrocities ("I was killed by my own kind in a Holocaust . . . My blood has been spilled/Henceforth, the Catholic guilt") and this, along with 'The Lake', marked the first signs of Justin's study of religion creeping into his songwriting. Where 'The Lake' explored the sense of security and belonging that can spring from believing one's soul or memory will live on, 'Conquistadors' tackled the reality of organised institutional religion, its inhumanity and failings, with chilling condemnation. At last Vernon was starting to prove that, when necessary, he could hit hard.

DeYarmond Edison was transforming into a dark and haunting beast, and the swirling textures of the instrumental 'Jackson And David', building from a ghostly hush of guitars plucked and treated to sound as though they

49

were playing backwards to a chug of wordless elation, was a fitting atmosphere piece, bridging to the album's final third. It gave way to the subtle,
downbeat 'The Unseen', a quiet ode of self-assurance with all the trade-
marks of *Feels Like Home* – the essence of Springsteen's *Nebraska* and
Bright Eyes, the background shuffles and creaks of chairs, floorboards and
instruments – but none of its desolation. Flooded with the sort of surrealist
imagery that would ultimately serve Vernon so well ("the landscapes
unravel/And I'm on that train they call time/And I take the words that
come to me/And fire them from the tops of trees"), the sense was of a man
who was shored up and fulfilled by the simple knowledge of romantic fate.
"I've never watched your face," Justin mumbled, "and I've never felt your
embrace/And maybe I never will/But at least I've had them with me to
keep me filled". It was an ode to a future love that, for the moment, was
intangible – he felt it in the gold hue of the autumn leaves, heard it in the
whoosh of passing cars – but somehow he knew it'd eventually find him.
It made for a deeply touching tune, tapping into the fundamental hope
and belief in us all that we couldn't be alone forever, that fate would find
us The One.

As heartfelt and honest as 'The Unseen' was, it wasn't the song that
Justin felt the most personal connection to on the album. That was 'My
Whole Life Long'. "I'm still in that song," he'd say of the seven-minute
ballad some years later, "that was a rare moment I think where a song
peeked through in this sort of overt writing style."[8] You can see why;
more than any track in his canon thus far, it consolidated his core concerns
into a cohesive, affecting whole. The first verse alone linked images of the
natural world (a lush lawn "under a mist", the rain "pounded the ground")
to the apprehensive uncertainty of young love ("now I'm old enough for a
kiss/So I'm headed for your tongue/It's gonna burn"). Subsequent verses
brought in his religious learnings, from images of a hanging Rabbi in a
tree, "blood running to his feet", to the resurrection myth hinted at in the
line "Mary roll away the stone". Lushly crooned, it was a song bathed in
peacefulness, a summation of Vernon's life as a universal free spirit: "in a
starry map I swim" he sang amidst references to breezes, blood, time,
bones, rocks, ravines, the elemental building blocks of life. His meaning
was amorphous and far-reaching – love, religion, history, nature and
music all merged into a mesh of imagery that seemed to suggest a need to
find comfort and satisfaction from the simple act of living. But he'd never

sounded so poetic or at one with himself as when he sang "You got your whole life long/To live your whole life long/And when your whole life is gone/Your whole life's just a song".

DeYarmond Edison, like *Feels Like Home*, closed with an experiment. '(For Bill)' opened with a minute-long free-form collage of sounds; cymbal, guitar and offbeats. Gradually the jazz clatter found its feet and drifted into a cool and casual post-rock organ groove redolent of Band Of Horses and in keeping with the album's deep and dolorous latter half. What had started as a bold rock roar had developed into something far richer and more resonant. A debut that suggested a sonic sumptuousness and space, a band not merely embracing modern folk and country rock sounds, but out to expand them.

The limits of a four-piece restrained Vernon, though. He'd start to work with Thomas Wincek, writing loose pieces as part of an amorphous project that wouldn't come to fruition for some years to come. But it was only when he struck out alone that he could fully explore his musical dark sides.

And his darkest side took him back out into the wilds, the gun steel cold in his hand.

★ ★ ★

There was something about pulling the trigger. The creature in his sights, his knee trembling against the damp earth. The silence before the crack. The animal stunned, falling.

It made him feel so close to death.

"The first time I ever did it, it was kind of beautiful," Vernon said of his first hunting trips in 2004. "I was like, 'wow, I feel more mortal. I feel less important'."[9]

At other times Justin wasn't so enamoured with the memory. "It didn't feel good," he told Laura Barton of *The Guardian*. "You want to hit it [in the side], you want to kill it really quickly."[10]

But up on The Land that year, Justin learnt the art of survival. To hunt down and kill a deer, ironically, was a lesson in the clinical brutality of nature's cycle, and he appreciated being able to create, with nothing but a gun, a knife and the wilderness hoard, one of his favourite meals. "Venison tenderloin medallions. Fresh. The real fresh way. It's the only way to reward yourself after a long day of hunting. If you just toss those in some butter over the cook stove you will never eat anything ever again that tastes that amazing. That's it. I actually eat a lot of grits with venison strips tossed in."[11]

The isolation suited him, inspired him. A reflection of the solo work he'd continued to create and play around Eau Claire throughout his time with DeYarmond Edison. In 2005 Vernon released a second solo album, this time under his own unadorned name. *Self Record* ran to a sprawling 80 minutes and 17 tracks and included Justin's most adventurous creations yet. Encased in a sleeve bearing an unfocussed self-photo of a quarter of Justin's face, it was an equally enigmatic listen, combining the heart-on-sleeve acoustic musings of *Feels Like Home* with a whole new level of sonic and stylistic experimentation.

Blips, fuzz and crackles, like malfunctioning electronics backed with waves of static, set the tone, fading in and out of the background of 'The Whippgrass', all stark metallic slashes of electric guitar recorded as if in a dank basement in the style of Tom Waits or a backwoods Jack White. For a song sounding so subterranean, its concerns were pretty celestial. Justin wailed warmly about sitting with someone he'd known since they were a child and contemplating spirituality and higher planes of the universe: "Just sittin' on the whippgrass/I'm so full and this is so vast/I know we'll all be together, babe/Someday, somehow". The higher place Justin envisioned wasn't any traditional religious idea of Heaven but something "within me somehow", a sense of universal "truth" that provided him just as much comfort.

The theme of abstract self-knowledge continued into the chilling piano snow-tread of 'Pier 39', Justin telling his subject "you will somehow make me learn/What it is inside of me that burns/A carnival inside this mind/Just a divert road sign/Directing you along the way". This was one of the earliest examples of Justin's fledgling ability to swathe the relation-ships within his songs in poetic obscurity that allows the listener to decipher their own secret meanings in the words. The lyric seemed to outline a time spent with a lover in a bayside scene, but the relationship itself was picked out in details rather than painted in broad strokes. There was talk of "old card games" they'd play, notes they'd write to each other, conversations about "affinity" and "habitat", all the small things that bond a couple, that allow Justin to muse "I tie you up with me". It was the dif-ferences between them that caused the most allure and understanding though – "I'm baffled by your symmetry . . . I'm . . . bold, gentle, stubborn/ You're rolling waves," Justin sang, concluding, in an aching refrain, "don't be like me 'cause you love me". Deeply romantic, 'Pier 39' was a road sign directing Justin along his rightful way.

He'd take many a diversion before he arrived, mind. After a plaintive, plucked minute-long mood piece called 'O're The Hills, 'kneath The Grape' we stumbled upon him playing a solo acoustic country ballad in an Eau Claire bar, recording his one and only cover version to date. First he poured out his heart to a crowd of rowdy drinkers, spilling tears like storm water on 'Drinking This Rain' over a lost girl. A portrait of desolation, it saw Justin drinking his sorrows away, "the oak on the bar . . . like the oak in my heart", and poring over the emptiness he felt. "It's coming to me like a baseball to a bat," he husked, "it's like when you're thirsty and there's none in the well/It's like bringing darkness when darkness already fell/It's like breaking dreams of a broken man". Even as he was weeping himself to sleep in verse six, though, there was a hint of security and familiarity in being this drowned, hitting him like a venomous drug ("it slides into my veins and it takes away my head/I don't have to feel the same") and at the end of Justin's lyric it segues smoothly into a 90-second snippet of the subdued ardour of Bruce Springsteen's 'I'm On Fire', a song derived from the same sense of ache and yearning but with much more confidence and a far greater hope of getting the girl.

A confidence that was snuffed within the opening seconds of the cracked country twang of 'Return To You', wherein Justin turned up on the doorstep of an old flame having "busted something/I'm broken inside", hoping to fall back into an old affair. He was certainly determined ("alligators and armadillos couldn't stop me from getting in through your door") and persuasive ("I'm like copper, you're like shoeshine/The best is yet to come, we've got a lot of time"), but there was real futility to the song since Justin openly admitted "I've just been through something/ That's left me in pain/In truth cut me even deeper than you". History or fiction, the sentiment was strangely admirable; Vernon was someone who'd often look to old friends and lovers for support, a tendency that would eventually create an entire artistic community around him.

The distorted impressionist imagery of the more upbeat folk swing 'Above The Code' brought with it a happier scene. Poolside, radio tuned to a Motown station, hot sun flashing in shades. Moments and snapshots caught within illogical phrasings that flit between a summer pool scene and a sweaty seduction just as the lines flit between Justin's brash forefront vocals describing the scene and a whispered background voice inserting philosophical asides between the lines – "you're a baby, I guess that's why they say these things" or "these are times that keep our body coming way too cool". The impression was of a hot, lazy afternoon turning into a lusty night, but the chorus seemed to refer to the molecular science behind love: "the symmetry of genes and feelings is the imagery of love and meaning/It's above the code". Here the album took a turn from the personal to more spiritual matters; Justin was positing science against the traditional spiritual concepts of love, and went on to further question religious spirituality in the final verse. Writing about the idea of a heaven-bound God that had been instilled in him from birth, "hidden by a different kind of mind", he opined instead that love might emanate from a more real, natural and human-based source – "The way that God was painted to me/Up in Heaven, in the sky where I could not be/What is wrong with Earth?" The theme of a paradise we're already living in rather than an amorphous, mythological Heaven we have to wait until the afterlife for reflected the philosophy of 'The Lake', a heartfelt humanist ideal.

Strange, then, that in the very next song he'd use the personas of Jesus and Mary Magdalene around the time of the resurrection as metaphors for a thoroughly modern sort of affair. "Sweet, Sweet Magdalene," he sang in the chorus of a song with that very name, his delivery tender, spacious and folky, "build your time machine/I'm sturdy like the Soo Line*/But I'm one dead Nazarene", using the image of Magdalene tending to Jesus' post-passion wounds in his "cell" of a cave to represent a lover trying to heal his emotional scars. "The smallest part of me is an echoing cavern/Ready to be filled with the light of your lantern," he crooned, bringing an ancient classicism to a Prine-esque story dotted with cameras and recording devices, as a new lover patches Justin up from his own painful tortures and betrayals. Despite questioning the beliefs he was brought up on in the previous song, Vernon clearly still had a fondness for the Biblical characters, relating to and modernising the more human sides of their stories. It was as if he was trying to strip religion of its supernatural aspects and uncover slivers of Biblical truth that people could really believe in.

* The Soo Line was a train that ran through Eau Claire.

The largely instrumental folk chug of 'How Many?', its looping acoustic flurries and electric guitar squalls interrupted only by Vernon's distorted voice murmuring indistinct, half-heard questions – another early example of the sound of words being more important than the words themselves – introduced the most experimental segment of the album. 'Right Down There In Your Tributary' was two minutes of dusky electronic throbs and bubbles bedecked with lustrous splashes of electric guitar and reverb tones, its background ambient noise seemingly created from Justin's voice looped backwards. 'April Four' appeared to use the same technique but instead added improvised free-form jazz piano that was eventually joined by a skittering backbeat.

Oddest of all, though, was the flurry of electronically treated voices that served as brief introduction to 'The Orient And The Gatsby's Slew Of Choices'. The atonal, haunting sound of spectres in the machine, they re-emerged as the song struck up, built on a monotone space drone, layers of synthesized strings and clattering DIY beats akin to Radiohead's more sumptuous recent moments. Vernon's melody had more in common with a Coldplay epic such as 'Fix You' though, louche and expansive in tone. The song concerned a troubled relationship of mutual need – a pair of friends, perhaps, who turn to each other for comfort in their darker hours ("She called me on the phone/It was just a little friendly cry/My middle aches, can you make me fly?"). But its imagery and metaphor was dense and rich; Vernon had "no Gatsby in me I'm running from", referencing the faux-millionaire of F Scott Fitzgerald's masterpiece *The Great Gatsby*, who invents a fake life of money and power to try to woo back an old flame, suggesting that the relationship in the song was purely platonic. But rewarding too, as the line "I'm the sea and you're Japan" brings to mind Japan's Seto Inland Sea, almost entirely enclosed by the country and thereby kept relatively serene.

The moving acoustic paean 'Sides' was far more direct, plainly telling the story of a suicidal religious-leaning gay man who seeks help, advice and support from the church after becoming the victim of a street assault because of his sexuality. Delivered with a clear and unflinching eye, it was Vernon's most blatant condemnation of the faith he was brought up with to date: after initially being welcomed at the church, the man is shunned by the priest once his sexuality is revealed ("I was unfolded, I believed there was something He could do/But you just hung your head and told me it was the door I needed to be going to/Son, there's just principals, I cannot be the one who helps you"). So he denies Christianity ("Father, your cold heart's a smoking gun/Your cross ain't nowhere I want to hang my hope from") and kills himself, believing God will accept him for who he is even if the church wouldn't. His point was that only the church took sides in the debate about homosexuality and was exposed as hypocritical in its intolerance of it – the "unconditional kingdom that stands up high" that the congregation tell him of is apparently far more conditional than we're told, only open to those who are 'on side'. 'Sides' was his most clear argument yet that faith and spirituality was all very well (indeed, he portrayed it as an often positive force), but it shouldn't be left in the hands of organised religious bigots going by the book.

The bold, brazen 'Ring Out', all chiming electric guitar and tremulous bawling, tackled Vernon's stance on religion head on. "This is tougher than I thought," he yowled, "JC's up for another bout and I am ringing him out". Having heard "the sermon on the mount" being recited in church, Justin had noticed that he didn't fit with the congregation hearing it with him. He was considering the actual truth and meaning behind the passages, while the rest of the church-goers were "just listening/Worried, sinned and lacking sight". "I am getting in the way," he decided, and from then on saw himself as an outcast and outsider, positing his alternate, non-Biblical views on spirituality as heard in 'The Lake', 'Above The Code' and 'Sides' while "withering alone . . . this is tougher than I thought". Shunned by the very people he's trying to enlighten to their blinkered view of the universe, Vernon instead finds fulfilment in a girl he meets in a bar, her beauty filling the gap left inside him by the shallowness of religion; all of the meaning and emotional nourishment that the church had failed to provide to him, he finds in her: "holding you, the grace I've caught/'Cause you're made of everything I want/And I am wringing you out". By the end of the song he was using Biblical imagery to describe his adoration of her – "like the kitchen rags of God, I am wringing you out . . . I am water on your feet". As with previous songs, Vernon was arguing that the joy so many look to some dislocated kingdom in the sky to give them is often far more easily found on Earth, in the beauty and lusts of life. It sounds more animalistic than spiritual, more base than holy, but it sure rang truer than any drenching in "Saviour spit".

From the theological torments of religion, Vernon next switched his perspective to the horrors of territorialism. 'Redemption 1: (An Army Man And His Self-Discovery)' turned a noble guitar and piano ache to the ends of honouring war dead, and those that survived. It pictured a veteran standing at a memorial wall, studying the names of the dead and caught in an emotional struggle. One part of him found reassurance in the memorial, "a spark of hope in the dark/No matter what the cost/To know that nothing ever will be completely lost", but another part resented the clinical peace of the monument hiding away the brutality and violence that caused it to be built at all, "keeping us from the rust of what's hurting us all", as though the act of honouring the dead justified the inhuman savagery of war itself: "mistakes we've made, broken families/No, these aren't just little games". As he watched families searching for the names of their loved ones, though, the soldier decided "the warmth of searching for the blood just might be enough", and this thought set off the self-discovery of the title. In double time, Vernon spewed out the revelations as they came to the soldier ("I am open, it is pouring in"), realising that he was confused, angry and lost amidst all of this human suffering ("it is storming out here"), but also one of the lucky ones – "I am loved but not gone". And ultimately, he came to see that his involvement in the battle had made him part of a universal family, both brother, sister, mother and father to these lost comrades and their grief-stricken families. To have been fighting at all made him complicit in the death and devastation and, while it was too late to change the past, he could at least be there for those left behind.

The album ended with two lengthy tunes that brought resolution to its main themes. First, the seven-minute 'Nothing Better Than A Journey To You', recorded faintly and full of tape hiss as if a basic early demo had made it onto the final album, returned to the personal relationship element that had dominated the early part of the record. Mirroring DeYarmond Edison's 'Dusty Road (So Kind)', it hissed and whispered about the happiness and hope to be found driving to an old lover's house, leaving the album with a sense of emotional completion. Despite admitting to uncertainties in the relationship, of having "mysteries at the top of my mind, I've never reached an answer" and feeling "nervously brave" to be heading there, he decided "I've got you on my mind and nothing to lose" and spent the journey wondering "what love is" and poring over his darker moments when "in the thick of the night my stomach is sore/I think I'm unable to carry on". But hope wins through; he knew that "I want to grow old with you, no matter how long it takes", that this woman is "a candle burning at the back of my eyes" and that their love will have grown from the distance between them: "to see the smallest tree and the amount that it grew/At the end of a journey, there's you".* As he approaches the end of his journey, he sums up the very art of lyric-writing itself, singing "It's amazing trying to put into words the message coming truly in song", but rather than artful language or by "quoting some book", he once more lets nature encapsulate his feelings, in the image of the growing tree. Even with the huge leaps in poetic significance that Vernon showed over the course of *Self Record*, words failed him when compared to the sheer miracle of nature at work.

His rounding up of the more theological themes of the latter part of the album was even more simply spelt out. For just over 12 minutes at the end of the album a slide guitar and doleful trumpet slowly waltz over a buzzing background tone. As a final comment on his ideas of an earthly, humanist spirituality, Vernon titled this elegant piece simply 'We Will Never Die'.

In all, *Self Record* was a huge artistic leap for Vernon, both in his sonic explorations in search of a new sound that gelled with his immersive folk and country roots to create something uniquely his, and in his artful tackling of grand themes and the development of cryptic images, open to the listener's interpretation but always underpinned with a firm philosophical reasoning. It was the sound of a talent blooming, and one soon to outgrow the very town that had so inspired it.

★　★　★

In Eau Claire, there's only so damn big you can get. Like Dinner With Greg before them, DeYarmond Edison had reached the town's limits, and there wasn't any stretching them. Off the local buzz around their debut album they were regularly ramming the clubs in town, but they'd never garner enough local support to make the leap to the 3,500 capacity Zorn Arena on campus, and no major label A&Rs were trawling the clubs of

* Some commentators even claim that Justin references Roman poet Catullus in the line "and every time you sneeze, as a wise man once said, I believe in love", suggesting the quotation from Catullus 45 which reads "Love sneezed approval on the left as before on the right".

Eau Claire looking for the next world-beating rock band. They'd out-grown Eau Claire, yet no-one beyond its city limits knew who the hell they were.

Come the March thaw of 2005, as they looked out on another enthused, packed and sweaty local crowd full of the same faces that already owned their record, DeYarmond Edison felt utterly empty. They were going nowhere*, reaching no new people, stuck in their small-town rut and several of their closest friends from college were leaving town, chasing their own dreams around the country. What's more, Vernon was becoming frustrated at the limits of his own songwriting. Over the past two years he, like many of Eau Claire's music buffs, had grown more and more obsessed with *It's All Aquatic*, the 2003 debut album from Amateur Love, the ex-Dinner With Greg band with whom DeYarmond Edison had shared houses and bandmates for several years. Listening to it spurred on, thrilled and niggled Justin.

"They were really my favourite band," he told 89.3 The Current. "Which was distracting when I was trying to write songs with the other guys in the band, because Josh, the songwriter in Amateur Love, was better than me."[12]

One weekend, in a break from recording their second album, they split town – Phil and his girlfriend of eight months, Heather Williams, headed to Nashville for a 48-hour visit to catch three gigs by Americana bluegrass string band Old Crow Medicine Show at a venue called Exit/In. Brad and Justin, meanwhile, struck out for Minneapolis, where they ended up hanging backstage with Wilco. Both pairs saw the same light at the same time. There was a huge country out there, a widescreen world, and it wasn't going to come to them. They'd need to go out and shake it by the shoulders until it knew their name.

Most bands would hire a van, load up on beers and hit the road, playing tiny clubs across the country over and over again until their local fanbase was replicated nationwide. DeYarmond Edison, reconvening after their eye-opening weekends away, decided on a different approach. They'd conquered Eau Claire by focusing intently on one town, why not just do the same in a bigger city?

---

* Although, by the end of DeYarmond Edison, Vernon had landed a publishing deal with Nashville's Bug Music, the band were still self-releasing their own albums.

They considered their options. Chicago? Too close, too intimidating, too passé. California? Too far away. New York? Too full-on. Minneapolis? Too chilly, even for a bunch of Eau Claire kids. Nashville? Austin? Too scene-centric, the sort of places a new band arriving in town would just get buried in the drifts and pile-ups of hopeful young bands clogging the club circuit.

They focussed in on either Colorado or North or South Carolina. Colorado was known for its snow which, although smacking of home, was something they fancied a change from. But North Carolina piqued Justin's interest. The area had been called home by some of his greatest jazz heroes, including Nina Simone, John Coltrane and Thelonious Monk. Justin had written a high school report on the basketball history of the area and was intrigued by the Appalachian musical heritage of the mountains of North Carolina too, the bluegrass and folk that had taken on a particularly localised twang. They began to focus their search for a new base around the Research Triangle area, the corners of which were in Chapel Hill, Durham and Raleigh. The area appeared to be developing a vibrant new scene, with labels springing up and a strong musical community thriving and, most importantly of all, the cities and their climates were 1,100 miles away and complete new worlds to the entire DeYarmond crew.

"We basically picked it because we wanted to have an adventure and move someplace that was different," says Phil. "In our mind, the difference was moving to somewhere that was warm and with mountains and ocean, which we didn't grow up with."[13]

"We thought they were kind of stuck not getting anywhere when they were here," says Justine.[14]

"We just wanted an adventure," Justin adds. "We had been in Eau Claire, what we called 'incubating' for too long. We were like chicks under the light for years and years."[15]

That March, in the decrepit van that Keil's dad had purchased in order to ferry around a high school golf team, a five-strong scouting team of Justin, Brad, Phil, Heather and Keil hit the road to the Triangle. The dusty road wasn't so kind to them; by the time they'd reached the one room they were all sharing in the Garner Holiday Inn Heather had fallen out with both Justin and Brad, in turn, for practically the length of Interstate 94, leaving Phil somewhat stunned, and the van's brakes had damn near given way. They finally went the very next day, causing the group to embark on a dangerous, brakeless drive 15 miles to Cary, where they could rent a Crown Victoria to replace it.

"The only thing that worked was the emergency brake," said Keil, "and it was one of those foot ones. So if you started it, you had to kick it really hard to get it back out."[16]

Having finally found working wheels, they set about a five-day exploration of their potential new hometowns. They quickly ruled out Durham as a possible HQ, the rundown shop fronts and caved-in windows of the downtown area giving the impression of a town drifting towards dereliction. At the other end of the scale, upmarket Chapel Hill was just too pleasant and edge-free, reminding them of the Eau Claire they were there to escape. But when they hit Raleigh, something about the place – the fact that it was a hub of roaming musical outcasts from Iowa, Philadelphia, Michigan and Wisconsin – felt like home.

"Everything seemed really even about Raleigh," Phil said, "and it wasn't like a flash-in-the-pan thing. There was a lot under the surface. Raleigh seemed like it would unfold itself very gradually and steadily to us."[17]

Immediately, the crew began house-hunting. Since eight of them were due to move down – the four band members plus Keil and several girlfriends – they needed somewhere large, at least four bedrooms, and the trip itself yielded no success, all of their enquiries coming to nothing. But back in Eau Claire they found the perfect place on Craig's List, a massive four-bedroom 1,800-square-foot white house at 2209 Everett Avenue, directly opposite Raleigh's first ever mall, Cameron Village. Lease signed, the move was set for July, shortly after the release of the second album they were currently recording.

The move would inevitably cause ructions within the line-up. Chris Porterfield decided to stay put in Eau Claire, for love.* "I was just about ready to graduate," he says, "and I was dating a girl that I eventually married, and actually she was a Milwaukee girl, and that's how I ended up [there]. So I had stuff going on that I wasn't ready to uproot, and they were looking for a change of scenery . . . The actual decision of it wasn't difficult. Like I never really considered for a second going down there. Bands, especially at that age like in college, band relationships really are

* Chris would eventually go on to launch his own music career in Field Report.

like dating a bunch of people at the same time. So there's a lot of emotions and all that stuff tied up, and there was definitely some weird feelings for a while as that particular chapter sort of got wrapped up."[18]

And if the all-new DeYarmond Edison were really going to feel like a gang starting their career afresh, they needed their old drummer back.

Standing outside a yoga studio in Manhattan waiting for his girlfriend, Carson Efird, to finish her class, Joe's cellphone rang. It was Brad. "I knew when they proposed the idea of me moving to Raleigh and me joining them, it was something I couldn't pass up," he remembers. "It was exactly something I wanted to be doing because I trusted these guys to be dedicated and really work hard at it and not just get caught up in a scene thing."[19] Within weeks, Joe was back in Eau Claire adding drums to four tracks on the new album and DeYarmond Edison felt like a band on the verge of a bold new beginning. And with a bold new album to match.

★ ★ ★

A lull of meditative prayer in a Tibetan mountain temple. A ceremony of smoke and bells beneath a Mayan ruin. The gathering of tribesmen on an Antipodean plain. Whichever ancient soundscape it brought to mind, there was something primal and elemental to the drone and tinkles of the instrumental intro piece 'Lift', opening DeYarmond Edison's second album, *Silent Signs*, with a sound drawn from Tibetan singing bowls and resonators. And there was something antique and classical too about the warm harmonic buzz of acoustic guitar, the blare of the fuzz-treated harmonica and banjo, the serrated shivers of the slide guitar that made up the album's taut and downbeat title track that followed.

Just as Brad and Justin's interest in esoteric electronics, world music and drones had expanded DeYarmond's sonic palate to rival the emerging alt.country of Iron & Wine and Band Of Horses, and Joe's free-form training was adding fascinating new percussive edges such as the 20 seconds of delicate cymbal and percussion work that ended the title track, the song saw Justin's lyrics reach a fresh realm of sophistication. Surrealist and impressionist images began to take over his work; he sang of a girl's "star-studded birthday suit" and how "the rivets in my past continue moving me", using abstract objects and images to illuminate the lyric's mood and meaning. Here the hints of nudity and sensuality – the "cold November hands" warmed "under your thighs" and the suggestiveness of the line "that's me you hear roaring in your river/Like how you hold me deep inside when currents quiver" – have led commenters to suggest the song is about sex and its deep emotional connection, or a sweet memory of it. Vernon's intimate delivery fits the reading, although it's not without a sense of lost romance and the "rivets" of relationships faded "like the bellows in bag pipes still blowing melody". His grasp on grammar and syntax was simultaneously slipping, no doubt purposely, as he began to prefer the flow and cadence of words in a line like "the pain is just a comfort gone from missing" to making a plainer sense with his lyrics. His words were now often more about the impressions they left, the echoes they made, the rhythms they inhabited than their strict definitions. "Lyrically, I think 'Silent Signs' was more advanced than anything DeYarmond ever did," he'd later claim.[20]

When the subject matter required it, however, Vernon was still prepared to tackle a topic head on. The adorable country shuffle of 'Heroin(e)' was Vernon's first reference to hard drugs in song, likening the rush of heroin to the rush of adoration and esteem but decrying the fact that he provided such a rush to no-one. Vernon has never spoken about taking drugs himself*, but the protagonist of the song certainly felt a need for and addiction to chemical fulfilment – "won't you jam that needle, holder of my fears . . . won't you put something in me, or else I might be sick" – although Vernon was singing as much of emotional sustenance as he was of narcotics. If Justin was venting his need to give anything up in the song, it was most likely Eau Claire, hinting at the band's move to Raleigh in the line "we all have habitats to kick". And if the song – a country rock standard – pointed his future direction in any way, it was in one of the first appearances of Justin's falsetto vocals in the chorus, a result of his bandmates pushing him to change his singing style. "I was being encouraged by the guys (in the band) to challenge that voice," Justin remembers, "because . . . in a way I was cradled so much by this Eau Claire scene and by the supporters that I just wanted to keep singing that to them and singing what they wanted to hear. But I wasn't really there."[21]

In an interview with internet music site The A.V. Club, Vernon expanded on his thoughts on his vocal technique. "For the most part, I've been influenced by black singers and singers I couldn't sound like," he

---

* Indeed, the female slant to the title suggested his protagonist here was a woman.

said. "Whenever I tried to do a dark note or a bent note, I would just sound like Hootie And The Blowfish. I was really insecure about it, so I just ended up writing rock'n'roll songs where I didn't have to do that. But I feel so much more comfortable being able to access painful melodies. I feel freer singing the high stuff."[22]

His sense of resigned desolation returned for 'Love Long Gone', a suicidal tread of melancholy banjo and close harmonies from the entire band that had Justin repeating verses of lines that sounded plucked straight from a final note to a family: "tell my love that I'm gone . . . sorrow waiting a gun . . . tell my father I'm proud . . . I hope to leave half as much". The tone was one of an alt.country Nirvana, the lowest Vernon had yet gone, unusually bereft of the hope that had even lit up the darkest corners of 'Feels Like Home'. The sublime, loping country languor of 'First Impression' restored a certain normality, with Justin finding security "in the arms of kin" and a "new friend" of whom he claims "I've been feeling your hold for a week or so . . . there's a train in my heart/That doesn't seem to start/Unless you're lying next to me". Lovers and friends were carrying him through again, the deep despondency was gradually lifting. And 'First Impression', arguably Vernon's most accomplished recording to that point, was awash with glimmering guitar mists, baritone croaks and unbridled nobility.

Suffering with honour; it was fast becoming Vernon's trademark lyrical standpoint as he worked his post-college issues towards the fifth phase – acceptance – and it provided the marrow of *Silent Signs*' sixth track, 'Bones', too, an elegy to his still having a long way to go to get there. Over a folkish chug reminiscent of R.E.M.'s more stirring numbers or mid-tempo Springsteen the impressionist imagery returned, a long-dead relationship represented by a collection of bones Vernon couldn't throw away but kept "in a trunk at the foot of my bed . . . always open to show me that they're still dead". If 'First Impressions' spoke of the solace of a fresh romance, 'Bones' concerned the lasting ache of an abandoned one, as though time's natural healing was failing him: "every day it's harder still/I'm flooded and unfilled . . . how I long to be alone/How long will I carry these bones". Describing the lengthy gestation of his sorrow in terms of a sunken ship finally rising from the depths and as a "bruise . . . coming to the surface . . . it's been hidden so long" and frankly exposing it with the exclamation "this world without you is fucked", Vernon brought his anguish to a rousing climax with the chanted harmonies of the band crooning "I'm so far from not caring". A record of a pivotal stage of Justin's emotional development towards coming to terms with the romantic setbacks in his early life, 'Bones' was a bittersweet venting of heartaches he still kept suppressed, but would ease all the easier for such open acknowledgements.

The sullen mood continued into 'Heart For Hire', a maudlin banjo ballad that cast Justin as a hardened emotional shell of a man warning a potential new partner about his damaged heart. "You should know that it's cracked like thirsty ground," he croaked, "you should know that I've hung it all around". Leaving her before she can leave him, he hinted again at suicidal tendencies ("the way I held that kitchen knife/And the way I was fallin' to the ground/You found out when you heard that ugly sound") and closed with the eternal dilemma of the perpetually forlorn, "Have I loved enough?/Have I loved too much?" 'Silent Signs' was fast turning into a portrait of Justin as a young man resigned to a life of weary, relentless melancholia.

Thankfully, 'Dead Anchor' raised the pace and lifted the mood. "I'm on the rebound . . . youth is refreshing . . . I've learnt my lessons . . . never again will I be corrupted," Justin declared as DeYarmond Edison let loose a summery spring-step sort of tune full of breezy organ and sunny xylo-phone. At first it was a sunburst of recovery and rediscovery yet, as the lyric progressed, there were signs that Vernon's upbeat new attitude might be skin-deep. "Spray on a coating/Then I watch it age/It crumbles relent-less," he sang before admitting to being "attacked" by a girl who was "on his back" and talking of feeling "paralysed and fake". Still, the pivotal line was a note of positivity, "I'm getting free, see", a rare and much needed glint of sunlight through 'Silent Signs'' deepening gloom. Justin, however, would come to think poorly of the number. "I would definitely take "Dead Anchor" off of this because I don't think it's a very good song,"[23] he said later, and also said of it, "Man, have you heard 'Dead Anchor'? I hate that song! No, I don't hate any of those songs, but there isn't a lineage that I feel connected to there."[24]

With its lightly tripping, lo-fi pastoral folk rhythm, understated banjo, synth chimes and muttered, indistinct vocals, 'Ragstock' was the most modernist of all of the tracks on *Silent Signs*, predating the snow-flurry spectre-songs of Fleet Foxes by three years. 'Ragstock' was more cabin fireplace than icy waste, but held the same haunting quality, largely down to Justin's whispered, half-heard lyrics of violence, demons being canon-ised and tongue-tied tapeworms, evading meaning and sung with a warmth belying their sinister nature. It may well be a drug song, since the only truly audible lines are the opening ones – "suddenly I'm worried/ Times have passed to care/Alone and high/Mind gone bare", after which the song descends into intentional incoherence. But if 'Ragstock' emerged from the haze of a high, it was a blissed-out trip, and one that Justin remembered fondly. "'Ragstock', to me, is the biggest bridge into Bon Iver-land because of the way it was recorded – sort of direct and quiet."[25]

Wilderness, antiquity and family were the touchstones of the earnest country rock of 'We' with its references to cedars burnt, wood split and water carried by "mighty hands". Justin appeared to be imagining himself as a family elder, close to death and communing with his family and history out in the woods, weighing his worth by the labour he has put into working the earth. The lyricism was too vague here to cohere into any distinct theme though and it would stand as one of Vernon's least success-ful DeYarmond lyrics.

'Dash' was far more affecting and direct, adorning a lustrous sweep of keening trumpets and lamenting guitar with the sort of religious question-ing that Vernon had explored at length on *Self Record*. Aligning himself with Carl Jung's take on Christianity[*] in the line "Carl Jung and I are out on the ocean", i.e. the ocean of alternative theological thought, he asked his listeners if the "vague thesis" of a Jesus "up in the sky" was a realistic or viable idea, pointed out that religion is a result of the fact that "all of us ache for answers to questions" but that asking "Gabriel, when will you speak to me?" often gets no reply. Offering a different sort of vision of St Paul's enlightenment on the road to Damascus, one in which Paul's appar-ent visitation from the crucified Jesus led us all into "the lion's den"[†], Vernon wielded his pen against the church's structures once more: "we

[*] Jung's interpretation of Western theology was based on the idea that Christian symbol-ism and words were actually references to the workings of the inner psyche and repre-sented our need to understand and connect to our own unconscious, saying "Our age wants to experience the psyche for itself . . . *knowledge*, instead of *faith*", as noted in "The Spiritual Problem Of Modern Man", *Civilization In Transition*. Vol 10, *The Collected Works Of Carl G. Jung*, tr. R.F.C. Hull. Bollingen Series XX. Princeton University Press.
[†] Some doctors have claimed another alternative interpretation of the story, pointing out that the blinding light, loss of bodily control, aural hallucinations and temporary blindness experienced by St Paul have much in common with the symptoms of sunstroke.

think it's all held together by services and sacrament/And faith is a permanence, clay bowls and firmament/Oh honey, I am the honest one". The concluding lines offer the concept of a lost and terrified humanity floating on an ocean of ignorance when it comes to the true meaning of life, and moving in whatever direction anyone cares to push it, "moving along with the slightest swells". As summations of the ludicrousness of Biblical fairy stories, half-truths, exaggerations and superstitions affecting generations go, there's none more succinct than 'Dash'.

The album ended with the most silent sign of them all. The quiet, minimalist 'Time To Know', a song so delicate it was barely there, just the faintest twinkles of piano and Justin's gruff voice barely a hiss, spinning a picture of a couple floating in a rope-tied rowboat, watching the stars. Conjuring an atmosphere of serene isolation, Vernon drifted off into verses of memories of that same relationship as it slowly broke apart. "The struggle came," begins the second verse as the pair found that their differences "broke our back", leaving Vernon shattered, his life an endless torment: "now the seasons have trouble passing/Through the creases in my hurt". Home design magazines in grocery aisles plagued him with images of happy home lives as he realised "it was time to know that it was time to go", and the album wafted to a close on waves of dream-like, hallucinatory images, "every sidewalk sale, every finishing nail, every dress that's worn, every baby born", amorphous lines drenched with regret. A favourite of Justin's ("I really like that still" he'd tell *Volume One* magazine[26]), it was a fittingly bleak end to an album criss-crossed with Vernon's lingering emotional scars and bubbling with suppressed damage, but laid out with a poet's touch.

DeYarmond Edison played one show in Eau Claire to promote *Silent Signs*, the album launch party in July 2005, Joe's first gig back with the band. Again, the local buzz was deafening, but it failed to infect Vernon, and he'd eventually see the fact that the album would fail to get them signed and stayed a cult classic as a blessing in disguise. "If this record had picked up," he said, "I'd be a very confused person right now because we'd still be playing and we'd still be in a band . . . and I'd be lost in this stuff right now. And I'm lucky . . . because it's a good record and it got the attention of a few people, but I'm glad it didn't snowball. I needed that time alone to disassociate myself with myself and attach myself to what I wanted to do. Joey, Brad and Phil were my inspiration to play because I just looked up to them so much as brothers and friends. That, ironically, became the thing that rendered me unable to write for myself – and that's what they wanted me to do."[27]

Justin would be just as dismissive about all of the albums from this pre-Raleigh period, claiming in 2008, "I've made three or four records in the past, and we've sent a billion out to different people. And they just don't land. I'm really glad none of my shit from the past has gotten out there, because I'm embarrassed by it now."[28]

At the time, though, DeYarmond Edison wanted to shed their roots and take their new album out into the world, to show it what they'd got. Within days the gradual evacuation of DeYarmond Edison and their entourage from Eau Claire, bound for Raleigh, had begun. On the morning of July 30, Phil, Brad and Keil hopped in a Ryder truck full of DeYarmond's gear, waved to Brad's girlfriend, Kate Johnson, who'd join them a month later*, and headed south, back along Interstate 94, with Keil's iPod, on random shuffle, delivering some sort of divine countenance in the form of a Tom Petty song called 'Time To Move On': "It's time to move on, time to get going/What lies ahead I have no way of knowing/But under my feet, baby, grass is growing . . ."

These words of hope drifting from the open windows, they believed they were headed for a new frontier where they would make their name.

Instead, the move would tear the band apart.

---

* As would Joe; Justin and Heather would be only a week behind the first truck to Raleigh.

CHAPTER FIVE

Eau Claire, Au Revoir

"The advantage and disadvantage are kind of the same. You're brutally disadvantaged because there is the 'whole world' out there, and you are advantaged by the fact that your whole world can be right here. For me, as an example, I believed so hard in this place that I stopped believing in myself and had to move to North Carolina for a fresh start. So there is a balance. You have to be a strong entity as one person – to help make stronger fabric of a larger community."

– Justin Vernon on growing up in the Chippewa Valley[1]

THE huge white house on Everett Avenue was a model of communal democracy. Cross the porch where the inhabitants – Keil, Justin, Heather, Katie, Brad and Phil* – sat for dinner together on warmer evenings and you'd enter the hallway where a huge whiteboard was erected to display any debts owed between housemates in the form of an elaborate spreadsheet divided into boxes linking each pairing – a scrawled dollar amount in the Phil/Justin column, for example, indicated that was what Phil owed Justin. Elsewhere you'd find a daily chore rota (Justin was a devil for forgetting to do the dishes), lacking the unspoken shared responsibility that everyone took to look after the household pet, Peking duck Crackers, which Keil had purchased for the grand sum of $1 from a student at the Morrisville elementary school where he'd taken a teaching job.

Each housemate had their social role too. Phil and Heather were like the parents of the house, Brad and Katie the playful kids. Justin was the creative powerhouse and Keil was the technical geek. Spotting the vast array of differing musical interests within his housemates, be it roots folk,

---

* Joe and his girlfriend took an apartment about a mile from the house.

gospel soul or avant garde electronica, he used his electronic know-how to put together a network of servers on Linux whereby anyone could individually access one of the 7,000 albums the collective jointly owned, or have it play throughout every room.*

For most of the guys though, this was among their first experiences of supporting themselves, much to the mild chagrin of their girlfriends. "They all have wonderfully supportive and loving, but also enabling, mothers, who have taken care of everything their entire life," said Heather. "It can be kind of hard for them to realise that they do have to do things like buy toilet paper for themselves." "Mom's not going to stop in and buy you toilet paper and change your sheets,"[2] added Katie.

In general, however, there were very few rows between the Everett Avenue housemates, and their system worked a charm. By day the members of DeYarmond Edison's posse worked at record stores, schools, autistic wards and restaurants. By night they drank in the Village Draft House or socialised into the early hours with their nearby neighbours, spreading their community spirit as wide as possible. At weekends DeYarmond Edison would retire to a rehearsal room on Capital Boulevard to practise and write, making sure to put down everything they played on an enormous computer recording system that dominated one wall. After all, they didn't want to miss out on their musical epiphany.

Grayson Currin, a local Raleigh music writer who was among the first to interview DeYarmond Edison on their arrival in town, noted that "with the move, everyone's guards went down and their vulnerabilities as bandmates were exposed"[3], but with this personal openness also came a musical one. The musical community in Raleigh was open-minded and inclusive and inspired DeYarmond to evolve and expand their roots-rock template much further than they had before.

"We moved down there and then instantly . . . were wedged in with this great social circle," Justin recalls. "Chapel Hill, Durham is kind of this big conglomeration . . . the people are holding it together."[4]

"The whole Raleigh thing is just awesome," he'd elaborate. "It's kind of this town where it's not necessarily where everyone wants to be, but everyone stays, because everyone is there."[5]

"When I got to North Carolina our minds were sort of exploded with a

* The system also included hundreds of films and a wide range of video games.

new community, new people, with new perspectives on music," he said. "We got this residency at an art gallery and started doing really experimental music and things like that. And so in that regard, it completely smashed open the windows of music in my life."[6]

The residency at Bickett Gallery – a show a month at the start of 2006 – was pivotal in the development and the demise of DeYarmond Edison. Having made an immediate splash in the Raleigh scene with their initial run of shows and gathered a solid local fanbase within months of hitting North Carolina, they were riding the rush of their instant cult fame and the vindication that they could reproduce their Eau Claire success on a bigger scale in whichever town they happened to stick their pin in. They felt as though anything was suddenly possible, and wanted to take on board the experimental influences they were hearing from their new scene-mates all around them. The plan for the gallery residency was one of total indulgence and experimentation – each member would be allowed to call the shots for one show, leading the band down whichever weird and wonderful path they fancied.

After what they described as a "palate cleanser"[7] show at the multimedia gallery*, playing stripped-down versions of their previous DeYarmond Edison material on acoustic guitar and upright bass, they discarded their familiar canon for entirely new musical journeys. Each member was tasked with delving as deeply as possible into a genre, style or musical concept of their choice then, four times a week for two hours at a time, the band would convene at the Capitol Boulevard practice space and whoever was curating the exhibition piece that month would guide the rest of the band, at great length and exhaustive depth, into their new specific musical niche, working towards developing a suite of music to perform at the gallery.

Joe opted for the relatively safe ground of free-form improvisation, hoping the group would learn from his sessions to play with a sense of freedom and really express themselves through their notes. To emphasise the power of restraint and patience, Brad helped them concoct lengthy ambient phase works called things like 'Four Keyboard Phase In A' that were in debt to Brian Eno, Steve Reich and outré 20th century classical composers such as Philip Glass. To strengthen their knowledge of and abilities in the area of classic Americana, Phil scoured hundreds of antique

* Varying reports put this gig as late in 2005 or in January 2006.

roots records of blues and string band artists to put together a set of traditional songs to be played on the original instruments. When it came to Justin's turn, he decided to focus on the shift he hoped to make in his vocal style, experimenting with what the band could do with just their voices. He made them bawl out spirituals at the tops of their lungs and scream 15-second blasts of demented vocal acrobatics. It was also where Justin sang his first song entirely in his haunting falsetto, tackling Mahalia Jackson's 'A Satisfied Mind'.

"There are these moments when you're not sure, and you're on the cuff of feeling insecure about what you are about to do," Justin said. "Then you do it, and it works."[8]

The intention of the exercise was to develop additional techniques and exotic styles that would add texture, colour and inventiveness to DeYarmond Edison's creative process, but their stylistic advances caused ructions from the very start. On February 3, 2006 the band played their second ever show at Raleigh's Kings Barcade venue, opening a two-night benefit event called Double Barrel Benefit, organised by North Carolina State's radio station WKNC 88.1. With a one hour set to fill, the band used the first half hour to play only two pieces, both lengthy ambient drone experiments built from the atmospheric sounds emitted from Justin's guitar and Phil's Hammond organ, dotted with extreme bursts of ear-splitting volume. The room was enthralled, but even the closing half hour of songs from their two albums occasionally reached such serene and silent interludes that the bartender thought their set was over and turned on a CD of between-band funk music. Joe exploded. "It's OK, you can play music in the next room while we're playing in here,"[9] he fumed as the barman fiddled with the buttons to make the noise stop, then launched furiously into a raging soul song called 'Set Me Free' to drown out the muzak. By the end of the song he'd beaten through the skins and Justin, joining in his destructive fury, was shredding feedback from his amp. Kings was blown away; DeYarmond were partially blown.

Joe's intensity and forcefulness in pushing the band to grow and develop had already been rubbing up against Justin. As the band member most dedicated to the art of a well-crafted melody, he was frustrated at Joe's need to let numbers roam free, as he was trained to do at Bennington. Justin's emerging talent at pinpointing moments and emotions through stark impressionistic images and poetry was clashing with Joe's desire to reach a similar sort of understanding through the vagueness of improv. Justin was gazing into clear skies; Joe was finding truth in the density of clouds.

"Watching those two is fascinating because there is such tension, but it's always been super-productive," said Brad at the time. "Joey is such a thinker, and Justin is such a reactor. They've always done this amazing job of challenging one another. I've never seen two people push themselves closer to the edge of letting go and quitting because of each other – and then grabbing on and completely letting go toward each other."[10]

Anyone attending all four nights of the DeYarmond residency would've been forgiven for thinking they'd seen four entirely different bands. When DeYarmond self-released a 90-minute 2CD album compiling 16 tracks performed at their Bickett Gallery shows called *The Bickett Residency*, it revealed a band truly pushing their limits and boundaries to breaking point. CD1 opened with six tracks from Phil's night including the entire band hollering out the raucous, intoxicated blues of 'I Been Drinking', and throwing themselves into antique travelling folk ballads like 'Going To Germany', Appalachian murder stories such as 'The Banks Of The Ohio' and 'The Longest Train' (about the slaughter of a girl on a train, whose "head was found at the driver's wheel and her body I never did find") and the Forties blues classic 'Step It Up And Go' all performed on harmonicas, washboards, banjos and other such mountain music paraphernalia, often boasting authentic multi-part harmonies, whoops and yodels. In among all the thigh-slapping references to rosy-cheeked girls, foaming beers, dark drownings in Ohio rivers, lonesome émigrés and southbound trains, some of DeYarmond Edison's regular themes reared their heads: for all that 'I Been Drinking' was about being fleeced by no-good cocaine-dealing women, it was in essence about being stripped of all dignity and identity after a ruined relationship, while the idealistic visions of the Promised Land described in 'No Depression In Heaven'* were, considering Vernon's previous lyrics on the subject, being beautifully crooned with every tongue in every cheek.

The four tracks from Joe's night, making up the rest of CD1, consisted of structure-free explorations of cymbal clatter, drumskin wave-rolls and extended silences that invoked a midnight sea swell ('Sea Legs'), irregular

* A song about killing yourself to escape financial ruin in the Great Depression.

73

bursts of formless folk noise, looping arpeggios and ramshackle grandiosity that repeatedly fell apart and reformed in search of a final coherent melody ('Abel + Cain'), four-minute jazz meanderings ('Visual Performance Str.') and tribal psychedelic mania ('Afro Blue'). CD2 was dominated by Brad's 14-minute avant garde synth piece 'Four Keyboard Phase In A', played on four separate keyboards, before Justin's segment dedicated to often a capella spirituals including a faithful rendition of Ada R Habershon's 'Will The Circle Be Unbroken' and a take on 'Bones'. The crowning moment though, was Justin's chilling version of the blues standard 'A Satisfied Mind' accompanied only by subdued electric guitar. Amid a release considered "too jam band" by some commentators and thrillingly challenging by others, the song stood out as a bold and shiver-inducing twist on DeYarmond's rootsy alt.folk formula, and in the annals of modern alternative history it will go down in legend as the first recording of Vernon in falsetto.

The *Bickett Residency* album, on the other hand, would go down in infamy as the sound of DeYarmond being crushed beneath the weight of their own imaginations. If DeYarmond's Raleigh experience to this point had been characterised by Justin and Joe 'letting go towards each other', the Bickett Gallery residency would send the band ricocheting away from one another. "The Bickett residency, ironically, was the most I've ever learned about music and simultaneously the reason we started to break apart," Justin told Currin some years later. "We realised there were so many things we'd never explored as musicians. I had this intense friendship with all these guys, and it was like we had gotten divorced. We made all these life commitments to each other. I couldn't imagine going through something deeper."[11]

"The biggest change [in my musical education] was in North Carolina when my band DeYarmond Edison did a residency at this art gallery," Vernon would later tell *Uncut* magazine. "We did four months. Each month was curated by a different member. We each tried different things – we had 20 minute keyboard phase pieces à la Eno, or we had nights where we played only Appalachian songs. Sometimes we did gospel stuff, sometimes freak-out punk. My residency was the human voice, so we did old slave spirituals. It was a weird concept for us to attempt, but you learn a lot about aches and pains and what pushing a voice can do. It was then that our band realised we needed to dissipate, but also during that time I started to sing in falsetto, doing Mahalia Jackson songs. That was when I started making demos."[12]

The demos he began to make in early 2006 would become the last solo album he'd record under his own name*, and would lead him into his scintillating heart of darkness . . .

* * *

"I was deep heavy into about a five-year process of going in the tank. I wasn't that happy. I was in Eau Claire, my home, and then I was in Raleigh. I was hoping the move to Raleigh would move things in my internal life around, but it stayed the same, and I stayed in the tank."
— Justin Vernon, Laundro-Matinee website, October 16, 2008

Justin Vernon never settled well into Raleigh. When the lease on the Everett Avenue house was up in May 2006 the rest of the band were happy to move into various apartments around town and continue exploring and enjoying their new North Carolina home, but unlike his bandmates Justin had become deeply homesick and ached for the wilderness.

"It was a tough transition for me, and it wasn't for them," he said. "I can look back now and see that for the first time [DeYarmond Edison] were growing apart. But we'd known such happiness together, I was frozen by a fear of never having that again."[13]

Justin just wasn't made for the big city. "I couldn't escape and be in the woods in 10 minutes if I needed to. I like that in Eau Claire, I can walk to a bar or a coffee shop and there's city-ish things, but I can also drive and in eight minutes be at my parents' land outside of town."[14]

Plus, he hated his job working the grill at a local restaurant called The Rockford. "I was working in a kitchen. It really truly did suck the soul out of me . . . I was a grill person and it angered me. Every moment I was in there I felt I was defacing my destiny or something. Like I was disrupting the time-space continuum by being in that kitchen because I was so out of place. I wasn't doing anything with my hands that I wanted to be doing. I would have anxiety so bad about it."[15] Justin despised the job so much he gradually filtered it out of his life — by the end of the year his initial

* At least, at time of going to press.

40 hours of work a week had dwindled to just eight, an income on which he struggled to survive.

Back home in Eau Claire his mother had little inkling of Justin's feelings. "We're a close-knit family so I was sad but I was also happy for him [to be moving away]," Justine said. "And in all honesty, I was not aware of all the difficulties. I knew things weren't going exactly how he wanted things to go. It's not like he called me crying every night to mom."[16]

Indeed, from the outside Justin's life in Raleigh appeared to be heading in the right direction. He had found a girlfriend there in the shape of Christy Smith, singer and songwriter with local Raleigh band Nola and, when the time came to leave the Everett Avenue house in May, he moved into her duplex apartment in a wooded lot on Fairall Drive, just off Wade Avenue. They shared an untidy back bedroom with a broken window, but it was home, and there was an uneasy sort of love there.

And he had a new solo album to show off too, the first results of his latest demo sessions.* He called it *Hazeltons*, adorned it with a stark sleeve picture of himself, hooded, at night, and once again printed up 100 CD-Rs to sell at shows, knowing all the while that it was another record he'd made primarily for himself.

Those that did splash out on *Hazeltons*† discovered a huge leap forward in Justin's artistry. Largely gone was his rootsy country baritone that aligned him with Dave Matthews, Bruce Springsteen and Hootie & The Blowfish. Instead, over avant folk jaunts brimming with far more vitality, inventiveness and life than had inhabited his previous solo albums and DeYarmond recordings, he favoured either his new-found falsetto or a mid-range choral effect of his own multi-tracked voice, as though he was finding support for his new singing style from a gaggle of clones.

The album – at seven tracks and half an hour little more than an EP – launched itself brightly. *Hazeltons* was Justin's evolution into the fresh new folk sounds emerging in the mid-00s, a lustrous, rich acoustic lilt

---

* Some sources claim *Hazeltons* was recorded in Eau Claire before the move to Raleigh, and thus before the new sets of demos he'd begun recording in the wake of the Bickett residency. This is unlikely since the album contains songs sung in falsetto, and Justin has claimed he first sang entirely in falsetto during the gallery residency.

† Though Justin is said by several Raleigh scene regulars to have been a member of a band called The Hazeltons, it's likely that he played shows featuring tracks from the album under that name.

redolent of Sufjan Stevens whose *Seven Swans* and *Michigan* albums had been pioneering a new pastoral folk sound throughout the decade and whose fifth album, *Come On Feel The Illinoise*, featuring Steve Reich and show-tune influences, home-made orchestras and marching band styles, was lauded by critics as having crystallised the alt.folk genre. Indeed, Stevens' dedication to Americana was such that he originally planned to write an entire album each about all 50 US states. In the spirit of Justin's Bickett Gallery night when the entire band were encouraged to sing as powerfully as they could, the multi-tracked choir of Justins on 'Hazelton' belted out this nebulous tale of a woman being emotionally savaged by a man ("you came, you saw, you sawed her brain/Cut out all the parts that held your stain"), before drifting into a closing section of lullaby falsetto harmonies mingling with soft opposing melody lines that, in terms of sheer sonic wonder, surpassed anything he'd achieved on record before. The lighter tone also gave the tune a more objective slant; he was beginning to step outside of emotional situations and view other people's relationships from a distance in the same way that he had commented on the clash of religion and homosexuality in 'Sides'. It was a minor but crucial shift – Justin's songs were no longer so deeply personal, his lyrical world had widened.

'Frail Sail' saw him taking on some of Joe's improvisational experiments, beginning the song with electronic hiss and blips, as if the file of the song was corrupted, and ending it with wild crashes and rolls of free-form drums and wiry, discordant guitar plucks, as if played on the strings between the headstock and the tuning keys. In between nestled a bright, delectable tune flooded with warm acoustic guitar and carried by Justin's first example of a full song in falsetto on a 'studio' record. "It felt more internal, more realised,"[17] Justin later told *The Times* about this new vocal style he was trying out, struggling to work out how it would fit into his work, not yet happy or comfortable with it. He was experimenting with it on his own, singing along to Kathleen Edwards tunes in high pitch while he was driving, but as yet he didn't feel it had clicked.

As a forerunner to his next record, the one that would finally make his name, 'Frail Sail' was an invaluable trial run, and not just vocally. More so than any song before, the lyrics were more about the sound and rhymes of the words than the meaning. Though the opening lines made reference to his new interest in online poker and other forms of internet gambling –

"filling up your winnings here for spinning . . . you're killing, you're still in" – their rhythms and rhymes were more important to the song, loping along rhyming every other word like a dense rap verse. Glimpses of meaning were dotted across the tune, suggesting a couple discovering they're expecting a child in the asides of "I'm late now" and "I'm pregnant", a rock band connection in the line "our little pairs of British fans are leaving" and a sense of needing to up anchor and escape the pressure of the situation – "later on you can point and laugh at all the rest of us/When you pull out like a compass weight/Frail sail". But the images are so abstract, the words so often selected for their rhyme rather than their reason, that it's folly to attach any firm autobiographical detail to 'Frail Sail'.

'Game Night' continued the percussion apocalypse that closed 'Frail Sail', a 180-second assault of cymbal and snare drum heavy on the sibilance, an acoustic guitar picking out a melody akin to early Nineties cult folk mopers Red House Painters or Death Cab For Cutie. Combined with the song's continuation from 'Frail Sail', its three central lines, bawled in the same slurred manner as 'I Been Drinking', hinted at the previous relationship reconciled by circumstance, the day saved by improved fortunes: "Your wallet on the rise, no more tears inside her eyes, lay down your head".

Taking to a languid, misty and emotive piano and returning to his husky baritone, Vernon still managed to inject 'Easy' with a modernist folk edge thanks to the extraneous noises of pedals being pushed and piano stools creaking, the pregnant pauses and lengthening of bars and the beauteous funereal tread resembling Nick Cave's 'Into Your Arms' or 'The Ship Song', creating the same sort of ethereal stateliness achieved by Radiohead's 'Motion Picture Soundtrack' at a fraction of the cost. A study in romantic pessimism, the six languorous lines of 'Easy' find Justin predicting the end of an affair and pleading to be let down easy. It was almost as if he could scent his personal storm coming.

The featherlight, R.E.M.-style 'Liner' lightened the mood to 'wistful' with its pretty pastoral pace and indistinct lyrics like Justin half-forming the closest words to the sound he found himself making. It was a meaning-masking technique he carried over to the album's fulcrum, 'Song For A Lover Of Long Ago', a foreshadowing of the title of his breakthrough album and a song far more blatantly and directly about his lingering feelings for Sara Jensen* than the subsequent album that bore her name would be. Teasing dour arpeggios from his acoustic guitar, Justin seemed to chew on his words like they were drenched thick in molasses, as though the memories he was singing of were still so hard to swallow. He sang of a woman he just couldn't forget no matter how hard he tried to bury the memory of her: "I have buried you/Every place I've been/You keep ending up/In my shaking hands". The desperation and frustration of the song brought out sublime poetry, images of "the famous violinist playing in my gut" to portray the inner swell of heartache and his feelings summed up in the lines "rain you out of me/Shake the memory free/Can't squash the molten soul/Can't chase away the hole."†

"She's a person that was always in my thoughts," he'd say of Sara Emma Jensen some years later. "Whether she knew it or not, her memory took many years to get over. I never got better and finally I just had to say 'enough is enough'."[18]

Ironically, by pouring out his pain over this lost love here, he would to some degree exorcise that particular demon, the final minute or so of birdsong seeping into a silent room so perfectly capturing the sound of loneliness and regret – the atmosphere of missing someone – that he'd never need to tackle it head on again. When he'd next come to record an album this long-lost lover would have faded into rose-tinted history, become a symbol of indefinable loss, a metaphor for all the loves that didn't work out. His next album would be less about any particular girl in question, and more about his inability to let his memories of them go.

Hazeltons ended at a funeral. A modern a capella spiritual that eventually grew splays of ragged and raw guitar notes, percussion that sounded like a marble rolling around a tin can, monotone puffs of woodwind, xylophone tinkles and traffic noise, 'Hanna, My Ophelia' was amongst the bleakest tracks Justin had ever made, imagining the internment of a loved one. Since "rifles crack" at the burial it may well have been a development of the theme behind 'Redemption 1 (An Army Man And His Self-Discovery)' from *Self Record*, placing us at a military funeral, in the mindspace of the family who'd watched an uncle, son and brother go off

---

* Or perhaps another old girlfriend he's never spoken about.
† Due to the indistinct nature of Vernon's vocals other readings of the lyrics have been suggested, including "Can't squash those open sores/Can't chase away the hope".

to war. "Tears fall on my muddy feet/I quiver as the pulleys creak/As they lower you slowly into the ground" Justin wailed as his guitar made the noise of creaking pulleys and a chorus of rattles, plinks and clinks struck up a mournful kitchen-sink carnival.

But it was a bad time for Justin to be asking for whom these tiny bells tolled. They tolled for he.

★ ★ ★

Justin Vernon's life in Raleigh died like dominos.

First to fall was his health. Working his eight-hour weeks at the Rockwell restaurant was, he thought, the reason he suddenly felt lethargic, feverish and out-of-sorts, with this heavy, painful weight around his liver, "sat in my gut like a rock"[19]. He felt he must have contracted some sort of bug from washing the dishes. He began to appear sloppy, grumpy and uninterested in band rehearsals, partly due to his encroaching illness and partly because, as they began recording for a new album, the creative chasms within DeYarmond Edison yawned impossibly wide.

"I didn't know why I was frustrated," Justin recalls. "I was really lost; they seemed to be really found, like they were really sure of themselves about the kind of music they wanted to make. It seemed like, day by day, I grew less sure of myself – less and less sure, less and less confident, and less and less into what we were doing as a band. What contributed to the breakup most, out of all the variables, was me being dissatisfied, and them being dissatisfied with my dissatisfaction."[20]

Justin realised he was more concerned with pleasing his bandmates instead of focussing on what he was enjoying about the music they were making, and he resented the way they seemed settled in Raleigh. "The three of us, after living in North Carolina for a year, had really planted some roots and were really happy there," said Phil. "He just wanted to go back home and we wanted to stay there and that was it."[21]

One doctor suggested Justin may have Lyme disease, a common tic-born disease that causes fever, depression and fatigue. Further diagnoses revealed otherwise. Justin had contracted pneumonia combined with mononucleosis, also known as glandular fever. The mono had also come with the added pain of a liver infection. Justin was likely to be laid up for three to four months.

The first thing he did was quit his job. "I don't know where else I would've got it except from there, washing dishes," he says. "I remember quitting: I was just like, 'I'm going to be in bed for three months, I can't come into work.' And they were like, 'all right', and I never went back. That's the last time I ever really had a job."[22]

Then his other job quit him. DeYarmond Edison had spent the year heading off into ever more outré experimental territory, demolishing any sense of creative limits, and Justin wasn't enjoying the trip. "Everybody was getting sick of my songs,"[23] he said, and they were also noticing him zoning out during rehearsals, not caring to join in on the communal adventure. One Sunday at a practice session in the Fairall duplex Brad noticed that Justin was particularly absent and pulled him up on it. Hard.

"One day we were practising something I was just not into," Justin said, "and I said I just can't do this any more."[24]

By the end of the practice session, DeYarmond Edison were no more. "To cut a long story short, I got butted out of the group,"[25] Justin would tell the *Daily Telegraph*, and later told Grayson Currin, once he'd moved on to write for Pitchfork, "It really unravelled. It was the most intense breakup I've ever been through; I couldn't imagine going through something deeper because it was a 10-year relationship with multiple people. It just took time for that to heal."[26] Without him, Brad, Phil and Joe set about creating their own band, Megafaun.*

Back at the duplex, another domino fell. His relationship with Christy was disintegrating too. By the end of the summer of 2006, Justin found himself jobless, broke, thrown out of his own band, seriously ill and sleeping on the couch at his ex-girlfriend's apartment. Though decidedly awkward, the split was relatively amicable; Justin had been helping to record an album for Christy's band, Nola, before they broke up and he completed work on it afterwards. Likewise, Christy let him stay on in the duplex.

For several months as 2006 decayed towards winter, Justin took to his temporary bed. He looked after cats, both Christy's cat, Tony, and one that belonged to a friends' band that was off writing a new album in the South

* Some time later Justin would see Megafaun play a song called 'Find Your Mark' and believe it was written about this split. "I remember seeing Megafaun play 'Find Your Mark' and just weeping," he said. "I vainly feel like it's about me. I listen to it, and think, 'Fuck, I hurt somebody'. We're really, really close friends, but I still haven't asked them about that song."

Carolina swamps. He was drinking way too much: "I was like, I never wanna be in a place where I'm drinking because something hurts," he said, "but then I did that."[27] And his online gambling habit was reaching breaking point, culminating in a particularly crippling run at the internet poker tables. "I lost $220 online, which at that point was all my money," he mused. "It was a microcosm of the rest of the stuff in my life, like, yes, you are actually not able to control this."[28] He became obsessed with DVDs of a Nineties comedy drama set in Alaska called *Northern Exposure*, most likely because it reminded him of home. "That's beyond a TV show," he'd say, "that's my favourite shit ever. It's brilliant, I got so into the show. I was laid up really sick when I watched it; for three months I was really, really ill, and so I think maybe I was kind of screwed up on some drugs a little bit, but I entered the entire village of that show, it was so good."[29]

His illness worsened before it got better. A rash of poison ivy grew across his face and his spine became twisted, unaligned with the rest of his body. "It was really hard because my back was out the whole time,"[30] he said. But as profoundly miserable and incapacitated as he was, he still managed to spot a light at the end of this darkest of tunnels.

"I had a moment when I was lying in bed," he said, "it was almost like the sickness gave me a ticket to get out of there. I had so much time to think, to lay out all the maps, to figure out what it was that I really needed. I was so brutally unhappy. It was like ending a marriage but with four people. I knew that the only opportunity I would have to have more of that time was to escape to my dad's cabin."[31]

Of course, Eau Claire. Retreating from hardships, back into the arms of nature. He'd be comforted there, alone in his own space, being snowed-in a living metaphor for his isolated psyche. He set his heart on it.

It was a long, long drive though, and he was too ill to make it. Before he could run away he had to see off the fevers and chills, fight off the mono. And if one thing was going to get him through this lowest of times, it would be music.

He reached off his death bed, picked up a guitar.

And began to write the music of his life.

★ ★ ★

It's telling of where Justin's mind was roaming that one of the first ideas he set to work on was an a capella loop of a single rhyming couplet. "I'm up in the woods," it went, "I'm down on my mind/I'm building a sill to slow down the time".

"I made that sketch in North Carolina in an afternoon," he said of an idea that would eventually be called 'Woods'. "It keeps rewarding me to follow my own thing."[32]

Alongside the wilderness escape fantasy of 'Woods', Justin was also penning songs about his breakup with Christy, in the very duplex they shared, and playing them to her. One such tune was a faux-jaunty, upbeat bawler built around bright descending acoustic chords, handclaps and slapped beats. It sounded like a desolate soul wrenching himself into an upbeat mood, and its words were those of a man desperate to eke out what little love there was left in his life. "Come on skinny love, just last the year," he sang to her, "I told you to be patient/And I told you to be fine/And I told you to be balanced/And I told you to be kind . . . Now all your love is wasted/And then who the hell was I?/And I'm breaking at the britches/And at the end of all your lines".

The private renditions, they both claimed, were "awkward but bitter-sweet"[33]. Christy assumed that 'Skinny Love' was directed at her, but Justin would argue otherwise. "To say that 'Skinny Love' is about Christy would not be entirely accurate," he said. "It's about that time in a relationship that I was going through; you're in a relationship because you need help, but that's not necessarily why you should be in a relationship. And that's skinny. It doesn't have weight. Skinny love doesn't have a chance because it's not nourished."[34]

Indeed, Justin would claim the song had just as much to do with Sara Jensen and the knock-on effect their relationship had on his subsequent ones. "Part of the trouble with the old haunting love," he said, "is that it fucks with your future loves, and can damn and/or ambush your relationships. That's who this is about."[35]

"Skinny love is basically a metaphor for someone you like a lot but you're not all the way there; the love is frail," he said. "That song was written about all those girls I was with, and I sabotaged the relationships because I realised I wasn't as in love with them as I was with my first true love."[36]

His resolve on the woodland retreat set firm, Justin waited out his illness, gradually improving over the late summer months. By the time he was well enough to plan his move Megafaun were taking shape and it was time to make the demise of DeYarmond Edison official. A notice was put up on the band's MySpace page announcing the split: "Justin will temporarily/indefinitely be heading back west, recording and performing as himself," it read. "I am sure there will be new recordings from him in no time." The scars from the split would eventually heal – "It was weird for awhile," Justin said in 2008, "but we'd played in a band together for 10 years and we're like brothers. I talk to them pretty much every day."[37]

As a parting gift, DeYarmond posted on the page a final five-track EP, comprising the tracks they'd completed recording before the band dissolved. The *Unreleased EP* showed heavy influence from the Bickett Gallery residency. First track, 'Baby Done Got Your Number', for example, was an a capella spiritual of the sort that had characterised Justin's night at Bickett. The song took a traditional blues slant, telling of an unbalanced love affair wherein the woman gave far more than she got back: "Baby done got your number, she ain't got your name . . . baby done took your hand and you just left her shame", but it was the delivery that made it stand out from DeYarmond's usual output. Full of spirited handclaps, thigh slaps and gospel harmonies led by various band members, it reached a caterwauling climax as they stretched their vocal powers beyond their ranges to throw every ounce of passion they had into the singing.

Having adorned a new version of 'Song For A Lover Of Long Ago' from *Hazeltons* with high-pitched harmonica whines and feedback and bouts of creaking amp noise like a guitar having a nightmare. Closing the song with a minute of ambient found sounds in the same style as 'Hanna, My Ophelia', DeYarmond wandered into even more radical territory on 'Epoch', a sleepy charmer of a track combining Justin's fuzzed baritone with backing vocals from a static-strewn radio, distant strains of harmonica and piano distortion, languid banjo and tambourine taps to shiver-inducing effect. The track had even more of an Ophelia link, since it seemed to envision someone drowning, their body shutting down as they sank – "It's your sinking divide/Clock went cold and readouts die/Head ain't reading things right . . . looking up at the waves . . . surface gets further away/Settle and sediment sinks to clay". But, as in previous Vernon lyrics, the dead live on in the memories of the living. "There's a flicker in the cold," the second verse continued, "Second chance to have and hold/Out with the new, in with the old . . . they'll remember you weep/It's more than a dream". The old Vernon theme of devastation laced with hope showed no sign of abating.

That theme, and the watery imagery – another Vernon trademark by now – continued into 'Where We Belong', a choral banjo classic that, more than any other DeYarmond track, hinted that, had they stayed together, they were probably destined for the same level of alt.folk success as a solo Vernon would soon achieve. "Waves crash on a vacant pier," sang an artfully weaved choir of voices, "boats rock on a sea of fear/The tide is high, your hope still floats/Pull the anchor, cut the ropes", a scene of emptiness and decay that followed lines suggesting a sailor sent to war and the lover left at home placing their future in the hands of fate – "A call to arms, an epic right/The war's begun, I choose your side . . . Come back and it's meant to be . . . Return or not, it feels the same . . . Be still, let the journey bring/Calm winds and a song to sing". Besides finding faith and optimism in the bleakest of situations – in this case the sailor's lover watching a storm at sea – it was the chorus line that once more highlighted Vernon's mindset: "In the pines where we belong".

The gorgeous 'Where We Belong' was stretched out to over nine minutes with Brad's lustrous guitar phases and wails, after which the EP's last track, fittingly called 'Finale', saw DeYarmond Edison bow out with a minimalist swirl of Joe's avant jazz improvisation on banjo and caressed drums. It, like the EP, was full of promise and possibility, pointing to a vast array of musical terrain DeYarmond still had to explore.

But that bridge was burnt, and its ashes set to scatter.

★ ★ ★

Justin Vernon's leaving party – a low-key gathering at the Fairall Drive apartment the night before he planned to leave for Wisconsin in mid-September 2006 – was a subdued and tense affair. Though he was no longer bedridden and well enough to face the long 18-hour drive north, his liver still hurt* and a heavy emotional weight still hung over him. The MySpace DeYarmond announcement had added to his sadness over the split, not least because only days earlier he'd witnessed the first ever Megafaun gig in Raleigh, a reminder that his own musical exploits were in a rut. Sure he had some new songs, most of an album's worth, but he

* His liver infection would continue to cause Justin problems for the next two years.

didn't know how best to record them, and all of his other musical projects had wound to a close. He'd been working with Nola on their album for most of the year and though he was immensely proud of what they'd achieved together, later calling it one of "my most meaningful and fulfilling experiences as a musician"[38], finishing it had left a hole in him, creatively and emotionally. It was, after all, a big full stop on his relationship with Christy.

He'd talked to various local bands about joining forces on new projects, most seriously with Phil Moore and Mark Paulson. They were in a band, of local underground post-rockers called Ticonderoga and Justin had met them earlier that year, before his illness, after having seen Phil's other band Bowerbirds[*], play early in 2006. That show had a deep impact on Justin: "When I first watched them play . . . there are just these kind of tempos, slow downs and speed ups, the melody and Phil's voice, the strange and beautiful places he takes you with his lyrics . . . all the songs blew my mind. I went home, and that was the first time I thought about quitting music. Yeah, it really was, I really wasn't sure I could do it any more . . . I thought what I saw that night just may be better than anything I could ever do."[39] Before long DeYarmond had played Raleigh shows with Ticonderoga and Justin had become close friends with Phil and Mark, so when DeYarmond split Justin and Mark spent several late nights drinking beer, writing and recording songs and talking over the idea of Justin joining Ticonderoga. But the plan slowly disintegrated; Ticonderoga were busy building their own cabin in the woods of North Carolina, there were talks of solo albums rather than group efforts, nothing solid could be grasped. Justin was left with that lingering feeling of uselessness. "I had kind of given up. I remember seeing the Bowerbirds play, and basically thinking, 'Wow, I am nothing'. I felt very un-special."[40]

He didn't feel that he had yet created anything as meaningful as what he saw onstage that night. "DeYarmond Edison represented all the years of me being an imitator," he'd say, "borrowing other people's sound rather than borrowing the emotion or the introspection of the songwriters I liked."[41]

This 'un-special' Vernon nodded and chatted to friends around the grill at the gathering to announce his departure, clearly sad, feeling boxed in by

[*] A duo made up of Phil Moore and Beth Tacular.

Raleigh, itching to get on the road home. Until a guy approached him with an intriguing proposition. Ivan Howard was multi-instrumentalist and singer with The Rosebuds, one of Raleigh's local bands that were breaking out of the scene onto a bigger national stage having been signed to Merge Records. "I met Justin Vernon for the first time at Kings Barcade in Raleigh [at the first Megafaun show]," Ivan said, "and during our conversation, I asked him about recording and what does he think about home recording. He said, 'You should just do it yourself. I know you guys can do it. Besides, only you know what you want.'"[42]

Since then Ivan had been mulling over an offer for him. Recording sessions for The Rosebuds' third album, *Night Of The Furies*, had hit a rut of their own, after two producers had been and gone they were stuck, in need of some local expertise. Howard had heard good things about Justin's abilities recording bands over the years, so offered him the job of helping them complete the record.* It was a bold temptation, to work with a signed band, maybe rejuvenate his enthusiasm for music and it would only postpone his trip home by a month or two. Vernon agreed.

Working with The Rosebuds was a nourishing experience for him; they were the sort of inclusive musical collective he'd been used to back in his Mount Vernon days. He'd visit the band at the brick house where Ivan and his bandmate Kelly Crisp lived as a model of communal living. With Justin completing their crew they did everything together, making crepes for each other, feeding Justin sushi and Bojangles takeaway chicken and sitting down with him to watch episodes of *Automan* or *Freaks And Geeks*, shifting into the next room whenever inspiration struck where the recording set-up was waiting to take down whatever idea was floating around. Justin wasn't only taken in as a producer, mixer, engineer and part-time member of the band, a close friendship soon blossomed.

"It was a really inspiring time for us," Kelly said, "and the record we were making felt maybe secondary to how much fun we were having together. Whatever the spirit of creativity was, it was so strong that I don't think it left him when he left us for Wisconsin. It didn't leave us, at least."[43]

"A lot of our music isn't based on theories or chords," Ivan added. "It's based on a feeling. I think maybe that rubbed off [on Justin]."[44]

This new musical vent inspired Vernon, who began to concoct his plan

---

* Some sources claim this offer happened at the Megafaun show

for recording his next solo album. He'd been mainlining Springsteen's *Nebraska*, Dylan's *Basement Tapes* and *New Morning* albums and the early works of Elliott Smith, hunting out new ways to hone his sense of intimacy, and experimenting with his falsetto, working out how it could fit.

Then one afternoon in the duplex, as the Rosebuds sessions wound to a close, everything clicked.

A wrist-swinging sort of rhythm. Dark, yearning chords. Cavernous wails of distant electric guitar enclosing this tiny nugget of warmth in writhing whale-song. And the falsetto, double-tracked, finally settling atop the music like an unbroken snowdrift.

"I am my mother's only one," he lied. "It's enough."

'Flume' hit Vernon like a Damascan sunstroke. The music and vocal tones gelled wonderfully, the image-rich lyrics dripped from his lips, subtle, full of bruised colours and evocative of the sticky violence of love: "only love is all maroon/Gluey feathers on a flume . . . leaving rope burns/Reddish rouge". Alliteration caressed the verses as deeply as their submerged meanings, making the line "lapping lakes like leery loons" feel like the tongue-lolls of a man driven insane by his moon-like lover, drift-ing in a womb-like sky. Ironically, considering its lovelorn theme, he recruited Christy to join him on backing vocals and add drum-tapping percussion to the song's immersive second swell, and added a mid-section of amorphous xylophone strikes and serrated string buzzes created by an e-bow, a "magnetic field you put over the strings . . . It creates a magnetic field between the strings and the magnet, so it gets the string vibrating really, really fast. And then if you slam the magnet against the string, it gives it a break sound. The string itself doesn't break, hopefully. It's a very light vibration, but it sounds very violent."[45]

Listening back to what he considered at the time to be a part-finished demo, Vernon felt the tingles of a masterpiece.

"It immediately felt insane," he said. "I'd never done anything like that. It was this new falsetto thing that I'd been working on but never landed. It felt really scrappy. I'd been working on so many songs that spring, but nothing really gathered itself until 'Flume' came along."[46]

"'Flume' was the catalyst for the whole thing, and it feels like it still is the catalyst. That song, and what that song is, I really can stand beside: that is the first thing that this band has done and it seems like it will feed it forever. Because whatever's happening in that song makes sense to me, and it's still all unravelling for me from that song."[47]

"I knew I was talented, but I did struggle with not feeling unique," he added. "I tried for a really long time – 15 years of writing songs – and I was thinking I might have to think about not doing this. 'Flume' was the catalyst for my life right now. I recorded it, not at the cabin, but I was there already. I was ready."[48]

He packed his bags, vision complete.

"That was the song that made me leave."[49]

CHAPTER SIX

The Cabin In The Woods

"When I made For Emma, *it was my last chance to see if I could sit down and make something, for myself, that was beautiful."*

– Justin Vernon[1]

November 17th, 2006

I'M now technically back home. Although home is much more north than it has been for the last 25 years. The last few months in Raleigh, were . . . many things . . . trying, rewarding, hard, sad, exciting . . . Right now, I am just glad to not have a plan and to be able to concentrate on music. Not where to play it, not when, not with who; just music. And I have that now. Between that and digging, building, cutting, buzzing, sawing, nailing and splitting . . . my days are full up. As for now, in less than 20 hours, I will be sitting in the middle of nowhere, with a freezing nose, toes and fingers, at 5 a.m., watching the sun come up through the trees.

see ya, Justin[2]

The day the Rosebuds album wrapped up, so did Justin Vernon's life in Raleigh. He packed everything he owned into a U-Haul and his old Honda car, throwing his four-track, his old-model Mac and Pro Tools LE home recording rig into his car alongside the microphones that had been stored in there for a couple of weeks already, fired up the engine and hit the road northwards. It was an 18-hour drive, on the road right through the night, and he filled it smoking cigarettes, listening to maudlin tunes and thinking about the friends he'd left behind.

On the brink of a breakthrough: Justin plays a showcase for blog site Brooklyn Vegan at the Bowery Ballroom, October 2007.

Keeping it local – Justin at Eau Claire's Nucleus club, October 2007. AARON LANDRY

Everyone's a drummer; Bon Iver at The Turf Club, 2008. JOHN BEHM

stin Vernon: Snow Angel. D.L. ANDERSON

ext stop Wembley Arena – Bon Iver rock one of Brighton's tiniest stages at The Great Escape Festival, 2008.
LINOR JONES/REX FEATURES

Bon Iver's stripped-down stool section huddling up at London's Serpentine Sessions, 2009, (L-R): Matthew McCaughan, Mike Noyce, Sean Carey and Justin Vernon. ANDY SHEPPARD/REDFERNS

Master of Bon beats Sean Carey rocks out at Leicester's Summer Sundae Weekender at De Montfort Hall And Gardens, 2009.
OLLIE MILLINGTON/REDFERNS

'Non-stop eclectic cabaret at Gayngs' Last Prom on Earth. ANDY HARDMAN

The backwoods Wildman of Bonnaroo, 2009. MICHAEL WEINTROB/RETNA LTD./CORBIS

Rehearsing for Sounds Of The South in Durham, North Carolina with Sharon Van Etten, Brad Cook & Phil Cook, September 2010.
JEREMY M. LANGE

Freaking out to the Sounds Of The South in September 2010 as Vernon reinterprets Alan Lomax's field recordings with Megafaun, Fight the Big Bull and Sharon Van Etten. JEREMY M LANGE

...stin Vernon and Kathleen Edwards making sweet music at the Dakota Tavern in 2010. TANJA-TIZIANA BURDI

...ernon squeezes onto the stage alongside hip-hop's biggest ego at the Kanye West's secret Bowery Ballroom show in November 2010.
VALIK GOSHORN/RETNA LTD/CORBIS

Justin gets the concept of 'put your hands together' crowd participation slightly wrong with Gayngs in 2010. RYAN MUIR

"It was really kind of scary," he said. "I was afraid of what I was doing. But 51 per cent of me knew it was the right thing to do and 49 per cent of me was really aching and sad about leaving my best friends and this band was my identity. We all had girlfriends through the years, but we were really committed to each other."[3]

He spent the best part of a day on the road before pulling into Eau Claire to visit his family home. No-one was home. For five hours Justin stayed in his parents' house, weighing up his options. "I sat on my parents' couch, and nobody was there," he remembers. "I felt really claustrophobic. I knew just because I left a place I knew I didn't want to be, I wasn't heading toward a place that meant something to me, or was going to be good for me. I felt really super-empty, and was like, 'I don't know if I can be here. For the first time in my life, I don't have a real musical identity, and I'm really worried about that. Maybe I need to take some time and do nothing'. I had some music that I started to think about in the back of my brain, but at that point, I was still sort of depressed. It wasn't that I was sad; I was indifferent. It felt really odd to feel that indifferent and lost and unsure. I basically left that afternoon. I went straight up north to my dad's cabin because I needed to be alone. I needed silence. It was a necessity more than a conscious decision."[4] Home, he realised, wasn't where he needed to be. "I stopped for about five hours and I was like, I can't stay here."[5]

Over the coming years Justin would have many opportunities to ponder the reasons he got back in his car with his "junky old music equipment"[6] left over from the Rosebuds sessions and drove further north, to The Land, to his father's cabin in the woods. At times he'd consider it a running away, from distractions, from his situation, from himself. "I went because I had the opportunity," he told *Stool Pigeon*. "It sounded like something I always wanted to do. It may sound corny but I was just trying to escape myself. I really needed to locate where I was mentally. It was lonely sometimes but I knew I didn't want to be anywhere else. It was a bittersweet experience, but it was fine because I knew I had to be there for a period of time. I think when people have that peace and that ability to speak to themselves free of outside voices, chatter and phones, then you can approach yourself without distraction and it helps your mind."[7]

"The reason I went up there, first and foremost, was really out of necessity," he told Treble. "It was kind of a rushed decision. I didn't go up there thinking, 'All right, I gotta make a record.'"[8] "It wasn't exactly planned out," he said. "I moved up to the cabin to be isolated, and to enjoy myself."[9] "I went up there, because I absolutely needed it," he said to the Captain Obvious website. "Things had been chasing me, and I had been chasing too far from the things that I wanted in my life, in my cradle, my mind. I got up there to the space and the peace, the silence, and felt as if those voices you hear in your head had much more time to work themselves out. They aren't distracted by the doorbell, the phone, or your roommate walking in."[10]

"I needed somewhere to live," he told Drowned In Sound. "I didn't have any money and this place was free, plus it was in the middle of the woods, which was attractive because I was definitely going through a stage where I was sick of people and I recognised that I needed a change . . . I needed to clear a lot of cobwebs and extract a lot of things that were not good in my life."[11]

Other times he felt it was a sense of determination that drove him out into the wilds. "I was like, I'm going to do this," he said to *Mojo*. "I am just going to do whatever I fucking want. I'm going to sit around and drink beer, I'm going to do nothing, I'm not going to talk to anyone. It was kind of like laying flat on the ground, like stretching my back out and getting ready, or something. Just kind of shaking it out and allowing myself to adjust and kind of reel back from what I'd gone through, or what I was going through. I was all right with it. I had gained this weird confidence."[12]

Other times he put it down to economics. "I thought it was just a meantime sort of thing, an opportunity to escape the trap of society, to not pay bills, to play music and live really cheaply – but I ended up staying for months."[13]

Whatever his reasoning, a few hours after leaving his family home in Eau Claire, Justin's Honda wheels crunched over the familiar frosty leaves of The Land, and he pulled up beside the homely cabin. He didn't bother unpacking the recording equipment from the trunk, and wouldn't for a fortnight or more. Instead he brought the bare necessities across the icy path to the threshold and wrapped himself against the chill of the Wisconsin winter, burying away his bruised heart as if preserving it for hibernation.

Closing the door against the dead cold of the woods, Justin cracked open a beer and set about building a fire in the hearth. He marvelled at the fact that he'd arrived just as his dad had installed a toilet and a shower, as if knowing he'd be coming. Another beer and with the warmth of the fire immersing the cabin he drifted off, dreaming, no doubt, of the wolves.

The next morning, he set about using his hands in those hardy ways he'd been so frustratingly denied at the Rockford. He had gone there to find the focus of fending for himself, so he trudged out into the November snow in search of wood to cut. When he needed to go further afield in search of fuel he hopped on his father's tractor to head deeper into the woods, dragging logs up to the sawmill, reliving the handiwork of his youth, rediscovering himself. As the days went by he began rising at dawn, taking long treks out into the snow, revelling in the isolation, watching "frozen sunrises high up a deer stand".[14] By day he'd set about working on chores around the cabin, sawing and nailing wood into furniture or repairs. In the early evenings he'd drink beer and watch DVDs before turning in at sunset, working his way through entire seasons of *Northern Exposure*. He loved the familiarity of the snowbound hometown comedy, the photographic negative of the melancholy winter he was embarking on.

"I was just up there splitting wood, or nothing," he said, his music shunted to the back of his head. "It wasn't despair or anything, it was just like boredom. Whatever you do it takes a lot of time to get to a place where you can do it. Some people meditate, that's not for me."[15]

"I just went up there to turn my [life] around. When I was there, I was happy to be there, but it was lonely and sort of like, 'What am I gonna do tonight? Well, drink a half bottle of whiskey, I guess.'"[16]

But most of all, he pondered, picked apart his emotions, drowned within himself. "I unravelled up there," he said. "I unravelled a lot of shit – from a long, long time."[17]

"On a physical level, I would wake up to stoke the fire or get wood chopped to get it in the house to keep warm . . . I was about 25 miles from anything – even a gas station – and even miles from another home. The only thing you'd really hear is a slight howl from the highway 20 miles away and then maybe birds, but really it was so quiet. I had nothing but the sound of my own thoughts, and they were really loud when that's all that was going on."[18]

When he wasn't snowed in, friends and family would visit him at the

cabin. His father would stop by to see how he was and give him odd jobs
to do around the place, piling up lumber and clearing away brush. A friend
of his who'd found themselves in a similar state of emotional crash arrived
for a three-day stay; they indulged each other in their sadness, took lengthy
walks into the woodland and bared their souls over copious mugfuls of
coffee, chicory and brandy. His brother, Nate, was a regular visitor and
confidante too.

"It wasn't misery," Nate recalls. "We would hang out during that
time – and there were good times, and dark spots and turmoil. It was just a
time when he was figuring a lot of stuff out, and escaping from it made it
easier."[19]

Together, Nate and Justin went hunting to bag some deer for Justin to
live on during his time at the cabin. Over the three winter months he
spent up on The Land, Justin killed and ate two deer. "I understand why
people are repelled by the idea of hunters," he said, "there is a lot of
machismo involved, especially where I'm from. But at one point I decided
the most humane thing I could do would be to kill my food myself. That
deer fed me for the whole winter."[20]

Rather than make venison medallions, Justin would often cook up large
pots of venison stew to get him through weeks at a time. Cubing massive
amounts of venison, he'd brown the meat and add whatever spices came
to hand – cumin or even simply salt. Rooting through the cupboards for
leftovers, he'd make a soup base from whatever he could find, be it broth,
chicken stock or spiced water, then add potatoes, tomatoes, cheese, rice,
green onions and Amish egg noodles. Next he'd "let it get smooshy"[21] and
dish it out into some wooden bowls his father had made by hand. What
he didn't eat, he'd leave out on the cabin porch to keep cool for the
next day.

He'd call his storage routine "self-indulgent, lazy behaviour"[22] and, sure
enough, his outside larder brought unwanted diners to his door.

At 3.30am one particularly freezing night, he awoke to a scratching,
grunting, snuffling and the heavy thump of cushioned footfalls on the
porch. Easing himself out of bed in his underwear, Justin peeked out of the
window and caught his breath at the sight of a hulking dark creature
hunched over the stew pot he'd left out by the front door the previous
night. He was used to scaring off the turkeys and wolves that lived out in
the wilds, but a night-time scavenging assault from a wild bear was a

whole other level of potential disembowellment. Justin had returned to the wilds in the hope of restarting his life, now it looked as though it might end in some hideous stew-based re-enactment of *Grizzly Man*.

Chilled to the bone and "freaking out"[23], Justin grabbed the cabin's shotgun and set about trying to scare the bear off his property. "It was 3.30 in the morning and negative 20 out," he remembers, "and I was there on the porch in my underwear trying to shoo a bear off my stew. I had to kind of laugh to myself about that afterwards – just as soon as the adrenaline levels had dropped."[24]

★ ★ ★

December 6th, 2006
Tonight, I bury my past and powerbook in the new fallen snow.

Tonight, I will bury my powerbook in the snow. This seems (a) like a waste of money, even if it was a junker — I could at least sell it. (b) rather dramatic considering right next to the new fallen snow is a BFI co. garbage hauler. But, nevertheless, I will proceed . . . I still don't know exactly how to phrase what lesson I learned, and I usually don't care enough to follow through with my self learning to the point of coherently framing it in language, because at the core I know what it is I've learned; BUT, I do know that I feel new. I feel like dumping those bad songs and journal entry's was the best thing that could of happened. I am guilty of it, maybe more than others, but drudging our past around with us too much is of obvious badness, but here I sit in as old of a place as they come, with a new feeling . . . I'm putting on my boots and my mom's packer jacket she left up here and heading to the limestone bed for a little ceremony they call, renew.

Justin[25]

After three weeks of relentless isolation, Justin's mood took a turn for The Shining. His head was a swirl of "those weird conversations where, like, it's so quiet for so many days where it's actually starting to affect you."[26]

"It was all kind of hazy. It all sort of melted into . . . one day turned into another. I don't recall a lot of very concrete memories of it, because I think I was a little bit out of my head."[27]

Craving human contact, he began to edge into the tiny local community, a handful of houses, more a township than a town. An elderly couple called Dick and Sharon inhabited the house where Justin believed he'd been conceived 25 years earlier – Dick had recently undergone quintuple bypass surgery so Justin called by to offer them a hand splitting their wood. Over the following months he'd drive the log-splitter down to the house and help Sharon split and pile stacks of logs. "There was this time when the hot exhaust from Briggs and Statton was blowing on Sharon's purple sweat pants and I could see the exact shape or her calf," he wrote in his journal. "It was just a metaphor for how closely we were working together, with really having no idea about anything about each other. Touching hands as we hand off logs, unloading logs, logs that will heat their home the rest of the winter. One of us farted. I don't know who, she was moving too fast to notice."[28] No matter how intimate he was becoming with these strangers, though, he couldn't pluck up the courage to ask to go inside their house and see the room where he was conceived.

Eventually, after weeks of mind-warping isolation, Justin had nowhere left to turn but music. His surroundings were calling to him. "That space really did hand me a lot of ideas," he said. "Ideas I already had, but that I needed help with strengthening."[29]

He pulled out his old Mac to listen to demos he'd been working on before he left Raleigh. The laptop, full of old songs and diary entries, packed with his past life, fritzed, whirred and died. The dreaded computer crash no-one ever thinks could happen to them had happened to Justin, a metaphor for his deleted life. For two days he tried to rescue his lost files, putting the hard drive through extensive data rescue programs and unscrewing the machine down to its component parts, but it was, as his Creature Fear blog would confirm, "zapped clean. Washed completely of any trace of these things of mine. These 010110's of mine."[30]

It felt like fate tapping his shoulder. Flushed with the symbolism of a former life interred beneath winter's fresh blanket, like his life wiped clean by the whiteness, he took the laptop out into the woods and threw it into the snow. "It wasn't actually that dramatic," he'd later argue, downplaying the forlorn nobility of the gesture. "It was basically broken."[31]

But the act was certainly meaningful for Justin. "Every one of those songs had been written for years and were all written the same way about the same things," he said. "I felt like it really robbed me of all these personal memories – there were photographs – but it was really a metaphor for me that those songs were leaving. It was almost like somebody was saying, 'Dude, get rid of 'em. You don't need those any more.' Because it sounds like another person wrote those songs compared to the person that wrote the songs in *For Emma* . . . . At this point, I don't miss those songs at all . . . I sounded like I was wrapped up in my influences, where I had tried to sound like people who had inspired me to be a songwriter, rather than approach it myself with any sort of honesty or validation. I couldn't write beyond myself for years and years."[32]

Then one night, with an idea for "this choir-ish sounding thing, layers of vocals"[33] careening around his head, Justin could hear what it would sound like to write beyond himself. He went to the trunk of his Honda and pulled out his recording equipment at last. A battered Silvertone guitar, a Shure SM57 microphone and his four track. He took them up the cabin's poppel plank stairs to an upstairs room which would become his studio. Over the coming weeks they would be joined by wires and boxes, Nate's old drumkit brought from Eau Claire and various home-made instruments Justin would forge from whatever he found around the cabin. When his guitar broke, he'd trade venison with a local musical technician to get it repaired. But for the time being he had all he needed; a guitar, the icy enormity of the wilds and his innate need not to hate his life any more.

"I didn't go up there to make a record," he said, "but music was just part of the process of me ironing out that weird vibe inside me. I sat down and started working on the songs, layering vocals on top of vocals, trying to be a choir. . . . Almost every lyric on the album was written in that weird, subconscious back-door way . . . I wanted to have songs that live in one place."[34]

"I'd just found it impossible to have any sort of joy in my life," he expanded. "That's what that record was for me. But in your life it's like 'why continue to go down this path of not being happy?' I'm not sure why anyone would do that."[35]

This method of isolated four-track recording was unusual for Justin, but somehow liberating. "I didn't know what I was doing," he said. "It was very foreign. The landscape was definitely breathing on me. The cold, dry space of the woods gives you enough quiet that you can hear your own thoughts."[36]

"When I was alone, I think I shed all these guards that had always been up, all that periphery. It became like this very small internal dialogue between me and the microphone. It's so hard to be totally honest with other people – even with loved ones – but being alone, that difficulty fell away."[37] "I thought I was gonna quit music altogether," he said, "and so I was just making the music for myself."[38]

"By being at my dad's cabin, by myself, surrounded by woods, with no outside influence, that really helped me to shake loose a lot of things that'd always been there, and allowed me to access a lot. In that way, it really was a result of its environment."[39]

"I didn't have anyone to answer to, I wasn't in a band, and I didn't even know I was making a record," he said. "I was just messing around, trying to do something new because I'd sort of reached my wit's end on a lot of levels, life-wise, right around that time. I was just scraping my sub-conscious trying to find some sort of flame in there and it really worked for me to uncover some of that stuff."[40]

"Making food and creating songs, I was by myself, no band, with a very limited set-up that gave the whole thing a real four-track vibe, for me, personally. I arranged stuff very meticulously, because I had nothing but time. So all that fed into the way stuff sounded."[41]

One of the first sounds Justin wanted to explore was his own voice. Back in Raleigh he'd pulled out the Auto-Tune program being used by many R&B and rap stars at the time* and used it to write 'Woods'. Now he wanted to try the technology out on his new falsetto. "I realised that I have all of this information in all of those higher registers," he recalled. "All of a sudden I realised all of these female things that I was never able to."[42]

Working around tunes he'd written back in Raleigh, Justin also started expanding on his idea of concentrating on the sounds of words, writing lyrics that evoke a mood or impression through their rhythm, cadence or syntax rather than clearly spelling out an image. Over the tunes he recorded he'd sit and sing a wordless melody then, listening back, he'd try to work out which words the sounds of the melody were trying to become.

"I'd listen to them over and over and annotate what I guessed I was

* So much so that within two years Jay-Z would come out against the widespread prolifer-ation of the software on a track called 'D.O.A. (Death Of Auto-Tune)'.

saying," he explained. "I ended up feeling like I'd gotten to my real meaning somehow, by going through the back door that way. Excavating my subconscious."[43]

He'd expand at length on the process in *Treble* magazine. "I'd record a line in 'Lump Sum' then I'd go back and record a melody, and then if I liked the first line but didn't like the second line, I'd go back and record syllables of a melody. So I'd have the melody, then I'd double that with the new syllables. And it kinda sounds like jargon: two people saying different things.

"I'd do that for all the songs, then I'd go back and listen to them about 20 times and write down what I thought I heard . . . it was very freeing. I found all this shit, all this grudge and meaning in what I was singing, these syllables. It was weird to put them together and match them up to the sounds that I was hearing . . . Good lyricists are also people who just put words in good order 'cause they sound good together. So I was able to do all that completely unhinged, instead of having to make words that rhyme or whatever, and I was able to get lyrics that were born and meaningful to me in a way that was distant and new. It wasn't like I was pulling them out of my heart and putting them on a piece of paper."[44]

"I'm a pretty overt emotional person," he'd tell Captain Obvious, "and I think I get addicted to emotion and emotional context. So, if I have an idea . . . I usually am too quick to get to the point if I go in the conscious way. I usually set the song up, go in and try and get lost somehow . . . . in it, in sounds, and vocal shapes . . . And, I usually end up extracting some kind of lyrical idea that is more folded and obscure but somehow gives ME even more meaning to what I am feeling about a subject. I really actually learn a lot about myself writing in that way."[45]

"I've always been into the Springsteen thing, writing pretty literally and trying to tell stories," he said. "With these songs, I was creating sounds first. I would create a space for the vocals, then transcribe vocal sounds and listen to what it sounded like. I would get lyric ideas from the sound of the voice. And I was actually able to pull out more meaningful stuff, personally speaking, because of that. I would surprise myself by what I was singing about, just all these weird, subconscious melodies and sounds . . . I was alone, I had no rules, I had no band, I had no sound I sounded like, I had no one to answer to. I just felt a little freer. I went back to those days as a 14-year-old, working on an eight-track."[46]

Recording these new songs began to feel like a mission of redemption. Seven songs he'd describe as "an opus: seven songs that have succeeded to pull me through a hardened shell of myself, surprise me, entertain, impress and even heal me. They are me, and I am them, but, they sound nothing like I have ever really written before."[47] He dedicated himself to the recordings, working 12-hour sessions until two or three in the morning, sometimes forgetting to eat. During the day he might spread his time between the wood shop and the cabin, but when he sat down in his makeshift studio amongst "everything I love . . . a pile of old guitars, a mound of microphones, wires, chords, electric boxes"[48], he worked tirelessly, playing all of the instruments himself, re-recording each melody line and guitar part in intricate detail, overdubbing eight vocal tracks on virtually every tune, scavenging extracts of guitar parts from demos he'd recorded back in Raleigh. His aim was "to get them to blend and do the right thing, I just went over and over it until it sort of smoothed out."[49]

And soul-searching too. Vernon saw the process as a way to "challenge myself, in a very specific way, not like games, or exercises, but challenge in the sense of really trying to navigate way down into my subconscious, to find where my real aesthetic shit is. My art. Not my gross EGO self-expression stuff; that's the Springsteen/Dylan in me."[50]

"I was very much making a record that I needed to make," he'd say. "It was my last chance."[51]

Over Thanksgiving and Christmas of 2008, Justin took some of his new tracks back to Eau Claire to try them out on friends and family. "Once he said, this is the song, and what do you think?" recalls Justine. "Of course it was in his falsetto which I wasn't used to so I was kind of like, 'oh I don't know', but it was 'Skinny Love' and I loved that song."[52]

One night he recalled a time back in Raleigh, laid up in bed with mono watching endless DVDs of *Northern Exposure*.* He remembered a detail he'd caught hold of, an Alaskan tradition touched on in the plot. The episode had focused on the residents of the Alaskan town that forms the setting of the series as they witnessed the first fall of winter snow and came out of their houses to meet as an entire community in the town square. There, they hugged and kissed each other, hailing their neighbours with a

---

* Justin had become such a huge fan of the show that, when he saw the final episode with its emotional montage finale, he reportedly shaved off all his hair and cried for hours.

strange French phrase. "I was like, 'whatever that is, that's cool!'," Justin says. "So I would write it down."[53]

Justin first heard it as 'boniverre', but when he looked up the correct spelling of the phrase, he wasn't quite as impressed.

"I already knew what it meant to me," he said. "It was whatever those people said to each other. Then I found out it was French and I was like, 'Ohhh'. I'm not French, I don't want to bastardise this, whatever. Then I found out how it's spelled and it was sort of disappointing. I didn't like how it looked. It didn't have any emotion. Looking at it didn't make any sense. I wanted to look at it and feel something."[54] There was something niggling about the original French spelling, something that wormed away at his gut. "'Hiver' reminded me of my liver, so I dropped the 'h'."[55]

Justin first used the moniker Bon Iver in a letter he typed to Kelly Crisp of The Rosebuds to thank her and Ivan for taking him in a few months earlier and for being such good friends. "I wrote them a letter on my type-writer saying: 'Thanks for letting me work on your record. Thanks for letting me crash at your house. Thanks for being friends'." He said. "I signed off 'Bon Iver'."

Mis-spelt or not, the phrase struck a chord with Vernon. It meant 'good winter'.

"For me growing up here in the Midwest," he'd say, "it was a sacred thing. A lot of people run away from it or shy away from winter. It seemed very fitting to name the project after the winter that created the music."[56]

And that cruellest winter, for Justin, would soon become the kindest, most celebrated of all.

CHAPTER SEVEN

Blindsided

January 3, 2007

I reallllllly think I am going out of my head sometimes.

I'm watching re-run marathons of sexual victims shows and shows about sex in the city . . . I'm at least 60 miles away from anyone I love, sometimes more like 1500 . . . Today, instead of sitting in the recording chair and working from basically when I wake up till 2 or 3 in the morning (just because nothing fills time better than that for me, except maybe for sitting with people) I woke up, ate a piece of toast with mom's strawberry jelly, took a jog down the road and back, walked out to the woods to check on a deer carcass, ate a cheddarwurst cut up into pieces, watched a couple of these shows, teared up. In the afternoon, I took some shit over to the town dump . . . I took two truck loads, and after driving back the second time I parked by the pull barn and hitched up the log splitter. I drove it down the road to an older couple that lives down the road.

Dick just had quintuple bypass surgery but he helped me and Sharon split a large, huge pile of wood for about an hour . . . Sharon and I, were a well oiled machine . . . we just split and stack. Split and stack . . . I was leaving in the truck, when I suddenly heard myself say 'I feel good' followed with the retort: 'I feel great'. I punched on the CD player and, I know it seems unpoetic, Michael Jackson's solo version of 'We are the World' . . . My friends are a thousand miles away. I miss them. But here I am with re-run marathons and an opus. I'm okay. I'm doing okay.

Justin Vernon,[1]

When Vernon emerged from his cabin hideaway "looking like a caveman"[2] early in 2007, drawn by an offer from The Rosebuds to tour Russia with them, he didn't know the value of what he brought back with him. "I don't think I really had any clue what was going on while I was there," he said. "I was just there. There would be days when I would work on music that sounded really happy. Or I'd be really happy to be working on it. I think you can be jazzed about working on a really sad song if you're into it. But when I left the cabin, I don't think I felt renewed or 'done' or anything. I still felt sick, my liver still hurt. I was going back to North Carolina sooner than I thought, to work with The Rosebuds. It took me months and months to realise what I had accomplished up there musically, personally, all that . . . It's sort of odd to look back and see it as magical, because it felt like a lonely few months at the cabin, where I plugged in the laptop and fucked around."[3]

He hadn't fucked around entirely alone, though. That January, two of Justin's old UW-Eau Claire Jazz Ensemble I compatriots, Randy Pingrey and John DeHaven, had added tracks to the recordings, writing and recording trumpet and trombone parts over shots of whiskey. But the collection of songs he'd completed nonetheless felt decidedly Justin's own, another album he'd made ostensibly for himself, but one of which he was immensely proud.

"I think the biggest thing that happened out there was I managed to make peace with a lot of dark circles that had started to pool in different areas of my life," he said. "You know oftentimes you don't have the time or the strength to really deal with those issues or whatever. It's a bizarre feeling because for the six, seven years prior to that a lot of these demons had started to creep up and take hold of my life in a secretive way, so to actually face up to them was bold and kinda scary. I can't say the day I left I was like, 'well that was great', you know I was still pretty fucked up – maybe fucked up is a little strong – but a couple of months after that I started to realise what had happened to me up there. And during that time I also realised I'd made an album. Before that I'd thought I'd made maybe some demos, but as I gained perspective I realised I should make a record of that event."[4]

When he reached North Carolina again and started playing it to people, the magic in the first Bon Iver recordings gleamed through like sunlight off a snowdrift. It opened with the tune that had illuminated the project from the start. From its opening muted strums, 'Flume' rose from the speakers with a glacial grace, Vernon's haunting, high-pitched voice like ectoplasm drifting in a mist across the lens of the song, the buzzing of the e-bow and the cosmic echoes of guitar enclosing the song in a cocoon of intimacy from which burst chilling choral choruses of multi-tracked devotionals. As much as its evocative imagery was open to the listener's interpretation – the words like throbbing organs, warm blood in the snow – the sound of the track conjured visions too. A ghostly woodland cult singing a sacrificial campfire song. A pack of mountain wolves given human voices to howl at the moon. A feral woodsman communing with his smiling, swaying choir of multiple personalities over the insanities of loneliness, isolation and lost love. It set the wintry wood-shack atmosphere of the album perfectly.

Like all of the tracks on the album, 'Flume' would come to inspire reams of debate as to its meaning. Some believed it was a fictional ode to a dying or dead mother and the unanchored sense of grief at her passing, her photograph hung on the wall a constant reminder, keeping him emotionally unstable, marooned. Others put forward the idea that the journey down the flume represented Justin's difficult first love, the loss of the emotional protection of childhood and the transition into adulthood, the gluey feathers being the pieces of him that he lost – not least to 'Emma' – on the inexorable slide towards maturity, or the sticky fragments of love that stuck to him through the years. Here the "sky is womb and she's the moon" line was about how young this old lover had made him feel and how she still shone in his memory, even when his innocence had turned to confusion, an ungrounding and "reddish rouge" pain from the rope burns of romance, injuries sustained as he slid downwards, trying to keep his grip.

The interpretations flooded in. The line "I wear my garment so it shows" was suggested to define an emotional exposure, a naked vulnerability, a heart on a sleeve.* The idea of being his "mother's only one", some argued, was meant as a barb to the bandmates and girlfriend that had abandoned him, leaving him to find solace in his family alone and realising "it's enough". The "gluey feathers on a flume" were said to be the remains of the birds crushed by logs cascading down a water flume, and therefore Justin's sense of being one of nature's small and helpless victims of love's violent torrent. A universal spirituality was found in the sky/womb/moon

---

* It was also suggested to refer to a tattoo, of which Justin has many.

image, or a sense of self-love or rebirth; water was taken as a metaphor for love and the flume for its inescapable flood, his past relationships turned to emotional cascades. The "gluey feathers" were argued to be Justin's stick-on disguises or the plumage he lost while shifting from a pre-birth 'angel' to human form. The "rope burns" were quoted as evidence of possible suicidal thoughts.

Icarus was mentioned often. Freudian commentators equated the mother in the song with a recently lost lover, arguing that men are looking for the unconditional love and protection of mother figures in their life partners – and the 'death' here represented the breakup. Ecologists pointed to the moulting cycles of the loon bird as a clue, stating that the often solitary loon, which is flightless unless it has every single one of its feathers, sheds its breeding plumage in its mating pond in order to grow flight feathers to migrate – when discarded 'gluey' mating feathers occasionally stick to it in the mating pool, it will be stuck there for an entire year, its partner long gone, until it can shed its plumage again. Into this was read an image of Justin, homesick and incapacitated by illness, stuck in his barren mating pool in Fairall Drive.*

'Flume' became a song that people deeply related to their own experiences. Some, fresh from the tragedy themselves, read into it a song about a baby lost in pregnancy, the lyric a conversation between mother and unborn child, maroon the colour of our memory of the womb, the flume the birthing canal, the rope the umbilical cord, the child spending their entire short life 'moving in water'. Some heard a story from a pregnant girl's perspective, abandoned by her child's father. Many were certain the song was an open letter to Justin's mother, bemoaning the loss of childhood love; a few were positive it meant nothing at all, just a smorgasbord of pleasant vocal sounds to chew on.

The sheer volume of discussion would be testament to how much the music touched people, spoke to indefinable truths at their very root. "I've got so many incredibly touching stories from people with experiences they've had with the record," Justin would say later, "the fact that I might have had something to do with helping somebody through something or at least expressed something that was going on in their life, you know

* Another outré suggestion had the song being narrated by a young loon gosling, the "mother on the wall" being a stuffed bird on a hunting lodge wall.

that's why music exists."[5] It was generally accepted, though, that the phrase "only love is all maroon" referred to the scarring effects of love[*] and the sense of being cast adrift, abandoned and desperately alone, when a relationship ends. And in that sense, 'Flume' was about not only the five years of melancholic rut he'd felt in the wake of his first failed romance with 'Emma' but the fresh wounds of his breakup with Christy. It was about lingering feelings, a lover hoisted as out of reach as the moon but, even at an aching distance, still glorious and bright, affecting his emotions like the moon affects the lapping tides. And as such, one fascinating interpretation suggested it was the start of a linear story threaded through the album of Justin's downfall, seclusion, inspiration and slow recovery.

The choral idea that had inspired Justin to drag his guitar from his trunk back in December had become 'Lump Sum', the first tune written in the cabin and a song that opened with monk-like harmonies resounding around a virtual cathedral before giving way to a jaunty folk guitar, a muted beat and Justin's tripping falsetto, a voice like an icicle that occasionally opened unexpectedly into a cavernous choir. Again, speculation abounded about the truth behind the lyrics. Were the "cold knot" and "heavy stone" he sold an engagement ring? The "red horse" a Mustang car[†]? Perhaps the most fitting interpretation, and one in alignment with the album as a continuous narrative, is that the song is about his escaping Raleigh for the cabin, and his settling in there. The "cold knot" Justin sold, in this interpretation, was the loveless tie to Christy and the "heavy stone" the weight that settled him elsewhere. He'd languished "in my arbor, 'til my ardor/Trumped every inner inertia", his desire to leave finally surpassing his illness and his natural tendency towards inaction.

---

[*] The fact that maroon is the colour of dried blood hints that Justin was singing about the damaged after-effects of a relationship.

[†] Justin has never spoken about selling a car in order to make the journey back to Wisconsin. Other suggestions included the horse being a metaphor for war or a symbol of nobility and success. But a particularly satisfying, if unlikely, reading is that it's a reference to the 'horse latitudes', another term for the doldrums where Spanish boats transporting horses to their colonies would often become delayed by the lack of winds and the crew would have to push any horses that died from starvation or drought overboard. Hence "sold my red horse for a venture home/To vanish on the bow/Settling slow/Fit it all, fit it in the doldrums".

Hence his "venture home, to vanish on the bow", a shift of scene into which he put the entire "lump sum" of his hopes, the full balance of his future. At the cabin he found himself "settling slow . . . in the doldrums", imagining the scene as a sepia, filmic slice of history and waiting to see how the winter alone would change him: "balance we won't know/We will see when it gets warm".

'Skinny Love' sat third on the album, representing Justin's solitary thoughts returning to the loves he'd lost. A brave-faced review of the failings of his relationship with Christy, it laid bare the selfishness, impatience and inconsistencies of the affair. One verse he's begging his "skinny love" to "last the year", pouring salt on it to help the healing process or sour the soil and witnessing the emotional bloodshed beneath their mask of a relationship unable to do anything about it – "staring at the sink of blood and crushed veneer". The next he's pleading her to "wreck it all, cut all the ropes and let me fall", too weak to finish this shattered relationship himself. There were hints that the whole romance was based on lust ("suckle on the hope in light brassieres"), but the fulcrum of the song appeared to be that the relationship was too one-sided. Justin was a hopeless case, his "sullen load" too full, too damaged and broken by his past hurts to return Christy's love as fully as she offered it, and it was the couplet "I'll be holding all the tickets/And you'll be holding all the fines" that was pivotal to the song's meaning. Christy was paying the fines for "tickets" Justin had gathered from previous failed relationships, most notably the love that still haunted him from forever ago.

Even more than 'Flume', fans would see mirrors of their own worst times in 'Skinny Love'. Interpretations of the song ranged from characters struggling with bulimia, depression and self-harming issues to suicide tragedies, domestic abuse, infidelity, cocaine addictions and dealing with terminal cancers. 'Skinny Love' would become a receptacle for a myriad of hardships and self-hatreds, a cathartic balm on a generation's deepest wounds.

'The Wolves (Act I And II)', the first sign of Justin's own form of catharsis on the album, wasn't quite so dissected. Addressing an unspecified ex with the opening line "someday my pain, someday my pain will mark you/Harness your blame, harness your blame and walk through", this plaintive flicker of guitar and harmonising soul spectres – a wildwoods gospel – came on like a revenge fantasy, the "wild wolves" of karma coming to savage a lover who'd wronged him. Yet here Justin was slowly coming to terms with his heartbreak, striving for forgiveness – "solace my game," he sang, magnanimously promising to call her the next day to "send it farther on"* and offering himself as a selfless sacrifice, "swing wide your crane, and run me through". As the choir developed hints of a subtle Auto-Tune and percussion built from chainsaws, chopped wood and crackling drums in imitation of fireworks, the refrain of "what might have been lost . . . don't bother me" struck up, indicative of Justin finally letting his regrets and retributions go, leaving his ex to whatever fate may befall her. It was a song of bitterness but also of relief, redemption and rehabilitation. Although the coda of dislocated voices repeating "someday my pain" suggested it was hard to let go, 'The Wolves (Act I And II)' was a howled healing.

There were two ways to tackle 'Blindsided', the album's wistful mid-paced centrepiece. It was either a straightforward story, fiction or memory, of a character riding a bike to a rundown side of town one snowy night, crunching his way through the rubble of shattered wood and nails to crouch down and peer into a window to witness his partner cheating† and then, "blindsided" by "the agony I'd rather know", throwing himself into a nearby river as "the end of a blood line". Or it was a metaphor for Justin retreading damaged old ground and peering through a window of his own memory to revisit pains from his past, remembering a time he felt "I'm probably plight-less", just before being side-swiped by sadness. Either way, it was a beautifully brutal form of exposure therapy.

With the bears on his porch and the wolves in his head, Justin had had plenty of reason to fear creatures of his own that winter, and perhaps this was the inspiration for twisting the metaphor of being afraid of other species into arguably the most political song on the album. 'Creature Fear' was amongst the album's most rousing and sumptuous tracks, an unhurried, pine-festooned folk ballad backed with an incorporeal choir, evoking images of a blissful evensong at a chapel shrouded by evergreens. The song

---

* A suggestion to move on their relationship past the resentment phase, a promise to shoo off the "wolves" or perhaps a recommendation to go impose her cruel ways on some other guy.
† Another interpretation has the protagonist as an old man returning to his hometown to peer through the window of old friends or lovers shortly before death, the "agony" being realisation of his life having slipped past.

itself was less peaceful though – the verses seemed to tell of a broken and bloodied relationship and the choruses expanded the idea to a global scale. The first verse, "I was full by your count*/I was lost but your fool/Was a long visit wrong?", found the protagonist wonder what had gone wrong in an affair they'd supposed was a happy one, and later verses had him increasingly lowered and abused by his lover: "teased by your blouse/Spit out by your mouth . . . the soft bloody nose/Sign on the floor". It told of the hatred and violence that results from the clash of opposing mindsets, intentions or personalities, and the choruses took that concept of humans distrusting other, slightly different forms of human into the arena of international politics where "so many foreign worlds" were "so relatively fucked"† but "ready to reform". The line "so many Torahs" added the frustrations of religious differences to the catalogue of reasons that humanity was constantly fighting itself‡, but it all boiled down to "creature fear", the base, ignorant terror of anything unlike oneself. And Justin's humanist plea? "Don't let it form us".

Obviously, there were personal metaphors behind the political references if you were to look for them. The "foreign worlds" could represent the travel, excitement and possibilities the couple could have shared together. The "territories ready to reform" could be internal areas he'd happily improve to fix the relationship as he pleads with his lover not to let animalistic impulses define their relationship.** The "creature fear" itself could refer to a fear of exposing our inner selves to possible harm, much as any animal with a natural predator does everything it can to protect

* Being 'on a full count' is a baseball term describing a situation where a batter has two strikes and three balls, meaning that a third strike will send them out and a fourth ball will give them a walk. This gives the line a double meaning; he's both fulfilled by the woman he's with but also on edge, the relationship could easily go one way or the other, he could take a chance and swing at his hopes and risk losing everything or do nothing and win an easy but unfulfilling advancement.
† Some argue this lyric may in fact read "so ready to be fought".
‡ See also the line "seminary sold", referencing a loss of a spiritual base, and the possibility that "spit out by your mouth" could refer to Biblical verse in which Jesus spits out lukewarm Christians. These two lines, however, could be interpreted as using religious imagery to illuminate the relationship in the song, Justin's solid security or "seminary" being sold from under him and his being spat from his lover's life for not being to her taste, respectively.
**A reading supported by the protagonist, in the final verse, questioning if he himself was the cause of the conflicts and if he's ready to reform.

itself.* In this interpretation, Justin is calling for an openness and high-mindedness between the two of them, unbound by dumb primal instinct, an acceptance of life's possibilities, even in a relationship that is fundamentally flawed. Like much of the album's central section, it's part of the bargaining stage in overcoming his grief and loss, foraging in the entrails of his massacred life desperately fathoming ways to piece it together again.

'Creature Fear' bled into 'Team', a drum-driven instrumental of overlapping discordant guitars reminiscent of Sonic Youth and Death Cab For Cutie, winding its way to a whistling five-note finale that could support claims of a military leaning in the lyrics of the previous song. After which 'For Emma' returned to the theme of 'Skinny Love', unravelling his recent split and the effects that his lingering feelings for Sara had had upon it. A bold and determined acoustic rhythm struck up, joined by Pingrey and DeHaven's horn lulls and a spectral surf guitar, and Justin laid out his breakup in the form of a short script, set in a sunlit snowy scene, the stage instruction "(so apropos: saw death on a sunny snow)" giving a vivid sense of a tragedy about to happen. It seemed an impressionistic staging of a parting, "him" trying to preach a positive, motivational slant on their situation ("for every life . . . seek the light") and "her" distracted, curt and annoyed by the whole thing, wanting the affair swiftly buried ("forgo the parable . . . my knees are cold†). His retreat to the cabin was declared in the line "running home" before "she" gave him the advice "go find another lover to . . . string along with all your lies" (suggesting an uncertainty and inconstancy on the part of "him", in keeping with 'Skinny Love') and the song ended with a bittersweet conclusion. "She" – by now encapsulating both 'Emma', Christy and all lovers in between – comforted him with the compliment "you're still very lovable" while he looked back to the first love he'd lost and contemplated, having taken her advice to find other lovers, the tangled emotional roads he'd travelled ever since to try to reach some closure on it: "I toured the light, so many foreign roads/For Emma, forever ago". As the scene ended, the harsh sound of wind on microphone

---

* Commentators have put forward many other interpretations of the phrase "creature fear", from the fear of wild animals seeing their habitats destroyed by mankind to humanity's terror of living without laws and regulations and the fear of change or of not being loved.

† Also arguably a reference to prayer, since she's tired of and uncomfortable with his parable.

seemed to convey a weightless ruin of romance blown firmly away.

"There's a lyric in there that says 'I saw death on a sunny snow'," Vernon said of the song's opening contradiction, the metaphor for cold-ness filling what had seemed like a warm and sunny relationship.* "And it was very typical for a day up there in February. I remember there was a day before I left that it was minus 20F but the sun was shining and it was sort of a brilliant contrast. Whenever I sing this song, or perform this song that's where I am. When I'm singing, 'running home, running home,' it's sort of this repetitive thing that happens in the song. It's not as much about home, because I didn't know what home was at that point. That wasn't as established for me. My parents had a home. And I grew up at a home. But I was just running. These stories and this song all happen during the winter, because about February every year is when it gets really hard. And I think the starkness and the greyness and the lack of sun, and when the dirt and the salt sort of build up at the side of the roads, I think it's about time for the ground to start thawing and I think it's when people's hearts really start to give out. I think that's when you remember it the most."[6]

Its antiquated folk airs, lustrous horns and relatively direct lyrics made 'For Emma' an uplifting burst of brightness, an apology and letting go, like Justin throwing open his psyche's windows and clearing himself of the gluey feathers of his past loves before the album's slate-cleaning finale. 'Re: Stacks' was an airy, winsome folk rebirth, a declaration of a fresh start, as heralded in the first line, "this my excavation, and today is Kumran". Kumran, correctly spelt Qumran, is an ancient excavation site, as Justin explained. "It's referring to the excavations where they found the Dead Sea Scrolls. When they found them it changed the whole course of Christianity, whether people wanted to know it or not. A lot of people chose to ignore it, a lot of people decided to run with it, and for many people it destroyed their faith, so I think I was just looking at it as a meta-phor for whatever happens after that is new shit . . . That excavation, I love that because it shows how people really need to wake up and learn; they can choose to look things like that in the eye or they can ignore them and scoff at them or whatever. And that's how things felt to me, like a closing of an era. It felt like I literally got to be a new person."[7]

So 'Re: Stacks' represented a brand new era of enlightenment and

* The sun melting the snow could also be seen as the death of the relationship.

optimism for Justin – "everything that happens is from now on". But the song still reflected on his dark periods, comparing his life-altering experience to "pouring rain" and being "paralyzed" and relating it to the big poker loss that had plunged him to the depths of despair back in Raleigh: "I was throwing it down two hundred at a time/It's hard to find it when you knew it/When your money's gone/And you're drunk as hell". The stacks of the chorus, indeed, were poker chips and the racks the containers chips are transported from table to table in, the shifting rhymes telling the story of a man buried beneath the burden of his stacks and gradually offloading it, a reference to working through a depression. "In 'Stacks'," Justin himself explained, "there's a mention of gambling chips, and also how that is a metaphor for how things stack up. The chorus is very repetitive, but there are different lyrics every line. It's just a billion ways to say that things build up and it's impossible to break them down sometimes. You're just underneath it all."[8]

So the stacks were his emotions*, his "load" weighing him down onto his back, thrown down 200 at a time in a game he was bound to lose until it's all "unstacked"†. From there, Justin set about rebuilding himself. Picturing himself "twisting the sun I needed to replace" as if swivelling in a new light bulb of positivity in his life, he reflected again on the "rusted out . . . fountain" of his love and how "all my love was down in the frozen ground". He envisioned his sadness as a "black crow sitting across from me", dangling keys of false hope and "even fakes a toss" as if teasing him. But ultimately the song saw Justin slowly unloading his stacks of unhappiness – not leaping from beneath his burden like "a new man, or crispy realization" but "the sound of the unlocking and lifting away". Finally, after the agonies of 'Flume', 'Skinny Love', 'Creature Fear' and For Emma', he concludes that he's swept away enough of the emotional baggage of his past loves that he's ready for a successful future relationship: "your love will be safe with me". The journey of psychological submersion, excavation, confession, acceptance and renewal had reached a hopeful, liberating end.

---

* In a game of poker you commit your chips to a pot you hope to win, much as in a relationship you commit your emotions, but you run the risk of losing it all; drunken poker players often play more recklessly too.

† The repeated stacks reference could also refer to stacking his equipment into the back of his car to leave Raleigh, or stacking logs at the cabin.

Justin would sum up the song most concisely when introducing it at the Mesa Arena two years later: "This song is about knowing you have to understand when you're in a tough place, and believe that it's not going to last forever."*

Probably because of the restorative attitude her son takes on the song, 'Re: Stacks' became Justine Vernon's favourite track on the record. "I think it is a very beautiful song and I love the emotion in it," she said. "I especially like the part, "'there's a black crow sitting across from me, his wiry legs are crossed, he's dangling my keys, he even fakes a toss; whatever could it be that has brought me to this loss'. Even though there is sadness here, I think this song is more about hope . . . to me, it is not about getting over things and moving forward, it is about going through the sadness, taking some of it with you and being made whole because of it. I cry every time I listen to it."[9]

Justin himself, though, would come to tire of it a little. "I really like 'Re: Stacks' of course, but it's more of an explaining song, and every time I'd play the song, I'd feel like I was explaining the same thing over and over again. And not that that's bad – I think that song means a lot to a lot of people, but the song on that record I still respond to is 'Flume'."[10]

For such a personal record, recorded so privately about such private issues, it's understandable that Justin would give it a name that meant something only to him and one other person. *For Emma, Forever Ago*, like a monograph at the bottom of a goodbye note. Ultimately, though, the title would lead to him having to duck and dodge questions or delve even more intricately into his past to explain his decision. And to point out that the record wasn't a literal paean to Sara Emma Jensen, but a collection of songs around what she represented.

"It felt like something different," he'd say, "almost like I had set up some fake land or something. It was something outside, and something over there."[11]

"No-one will completely understand a lot of the things I had to say in that record," he'd add. "It's a story, not just about a person, but about what someone can do to the people around them."[12]

---

* He'd also introduce it at Illinios Canopy Club with the statement "This song is for anyone who's ever been at a poker table and seen their soul. Good or bad", claiming it happened to him around 2003.

"The album was more about me than anything," he'd tell Pitchfork. "Emma isn't a person as much as it's a place and a time."[13]

When pushed for details he'd cryptically admit that Emma was a real name representing someone from his past, but also that it wasn't her actual name and it also didn't represent any specific old relationship. "The record's not about her. It's about my struggles through years of dealing with the aftermath of lost love and longing and just mediocrity and just bad news, like life stuff. And in the [record], where the title comes from, the lyrics are actually a conversation between me and another girl, not this Emma character."[14]

"The story of the album, without getting so obvious, and internally personal, is about long gone, bruised, and pained love – about someone. The album was truly the one thing out of 100 things I tried to create peace around my . . . heart, for lack of a better word. It was actually more about me, than it was about this other person."[15]

He'd be at pains to protest that he hadn't made the archetypal breakup album too. "That is the most boring version of the story possible. Who hasn't broken up with somebody? Who hasn't broken up with somebody because they were still thinking about somebody else? Who hasn't wrote a fucking song about it?"[16]

"It's, like, six per cent breakup. Most of the record is about a love from very long ago. But there are many conversations in there between me and my most recent girlfriend, and we talk about this other third person from long ago. So, it's definitely not a 'breakup record' in that specific definition. It's more a portrait of seven years of my life, and how it unfolded in the end. It was a long bottoming-out – a really long, grey period – and, finally, at the end of those seven years, I started having some perspective on what I'd been going through, and that's what the story of the record is. My revelations and ruminations on that whole era."[17]

★ ★ ★

When Justin would allow the final notes to fade on his record and turn to the friends that he'd been playing it to – Ivan and Kelly of The Rosebuds, for example, or good friend Beth Urdang, who was one of the very first people to hear the record – he'd see a wide-eyed wonder, then an avid enthusiasm.

"I didn't know I made a record," he recalled. "I thought what I had was demos for a record I might want to re-record. I brought it down to Ivan from The Rosebuds, and he was like, 'Dude, these aren't demos. This is your record.'"[18]

"I played them [The Rosebuds] the record and they were huge supporters of it. I was like, 'I don't know what to do man. I don't know if this should be a band. I don't know if I should put this out. I've never been on a label. I've never toured. I don't know what the fuck's going on.' [Kelly]'s like, 'Dude, don't worry about it. Bon Iver – that's your name.'"[19]

Justin found the reaction to what he considered rough demos dizzying, but vindicating. It gave him confidence, proof that to make a 'successful' record all he really had to do was be true to himself. "It wasn't because I thought the record was my chance to be successful; it was because the record actually meant something to me, and I felt like I was actually applying myself. If you are yourself and you don't become successful, the happiness that you get from creating something that is that truthful to yourself should be enough to propel you forward in life."[20]

Back in Raleigh while rehearsing with The Rosebuds for their forthcoming tour Justin stayed on friends' couches or in spare bedrooms, spending periods staying with The Rosebuds and Grayson Currin among others, all the while starting to mix the tracks on *For Emma . . .* and exuding the vibes of a much happier guy than the one who'd fled Raleigh in ruins three months earlier. He took those positive vibes out on the road that February too*, playing guitar with The Rosebuds every night and sitting in the back of the van mixing his record every day. They headed to Moscow, where an assistant producer on Russia's first ever big-budget blockbuster, *Paragraph 78*, had heard The Rosebuds' 2005 song 'Boxcar', asked to use it in the movie and then flew the band over to perform at the premiere alongside Brett Anderson from Suede and The Stone Roses' Ian Brown in the coldest week of the Russian winter. It was an eye-opening experience, particularly when Brown spotted the star-struck Rosebuds crew across the lobby of the President hotel and raced over to help them carry their gear to their rooms and then joined them for breakfast the next day. The show didn't stop Justin doing a little sightseeing either, having his picture taken in front of St Basil's cathedral holding up a note reading

---

* Much to the relief of Ivan and Kelly, who were then playing down relationship issues that would eventually see their marriage split.

'To Moscow With Love, Eau Claire WI, USA, c/o Justin MCCIII & Tera' and rounded off with a peace symbol.

Then followed a tour of Europe and Scandinavia alongside The Shout Out Louds, where they unexpectedly found a wild, enthusiastic crowd dancing like maniacs to The Rosebuds⋆ and partied nights away on the SOL bus to Pet Shop Boys and Magnetic Fields, a chance for Justin to bond with The Rosebuds' touring bassist Matthew McCaughan. And finally a short tour of the US (which would include a two-night stopover in Eau Claire) on the way to a show at the Hot Freaks! event at Club De Ville at SXSW, the annual industry showcase in Austin, Texas, where Justin would meet Ryan Matteson, the editor of online music blog *Muzzle Of Bees* who would come to be a big supporter. Along the way, virtually everyone who heard the songs Justin was quietly working on was blown away, an avalanche of appreciation that Justin's insecurities could no longer bat away as merely friendly support.

"At that point, I thought the songs were just demos," he recalled. "I was only trying to mix them really, really nice to send out to a few labels to see if they would give me money to record a 'regular' album. But I handed a couple of my buddies a copy of the CD, and literally, after handing those out, it never slowed down. It started an avalanche and I had no choice but to put it out as a record."[21]

He began to start seeing *For Emma . . .* as a great personal achievement, the record he was subconsciously always meant to make. Though he'd need to be pushed towards acknowledging it by the enthusiasm of his friends for the album, deep inside he knew it was what he'd been working towards all those years. "I just knew that what I was doing was extremely honest. It was all the things I wanted my music to be, but yet it wasn't grand and it wasn't obtuse – it wasn't overshooting, it wasn't undershooting, it was precise. The lyrics and the way that I was able to extract and excavate emotion within me . . . I had a great victory just as a person. I overstepped countless obstacles by creating that record. And the record's a metaphor for the personal steps I [took]."[22]

Decision made; the record was finished. Now to filter it out into the world as quietly as it had been born.

⋆ The Rosebuds had no European record deal, so didn't expect to have as many fans there as they did.

CHAPTER EIGHT

Amongst People

SPRING break week of 2007 and, back home in Chippewa Falls from McNally Smith College Of Music in Minnesota, a music mad 19-year-old called Kyle Frenette sat in his room, like a million other music mad 19-year-olds that very same moment, randomly clicking through music blogs and MySpace pages, looking for something to love.

If you were to glance through Frenette's biography to that point, you might suspect fate or serendipity had some influence on guiding his mouse. He'd been a musician in high school in a band called Elliston and, after graduation, he and his bandmates decided to move in together to keep the band intact through college. Only to find the pressures of being away from home drove them apart.

So Frenette had put his energies into the business side of music instead, launching a label called Amble Down Records*, home to local acts including Daredevil Christopher Wright, Gentle Guest and Meridene, and it was for new local signings that he went hunting that day. Eventually, he came across something that grabbed his eye – an unusual name on a MySpace page, kinda French sounding. There were two new tracks just recently posted up. Frenette clicked on the first of them, a track called 'Flume'.

It was a click that would change his life.

"He posted two new songs, 'Flume' and 'Lump Sum' from that album," Kyle recalls. "I listened to them and they floored me right away. This was one of those moments that happen when it's like, 'What is this? I want to tell the world about this! This is incredible!'"[1]

The MySpace page had email contact details for the guy behind this

---

* Frenette also made spare cash working behind the counter at an Eau Claire coffee shop, Racy D'Lene's.

thing called Bon Iver. Justin Vernon, a familiar name; Frenette had been a fan of his solo and DeYarmond albums back in high school. Wasting no time, Kyle mailed him, explaining how inspired he'd been by the songs and how much he'd love to work with Justin on it. It turned out Justin had a whole album where those two tracks came from and he didn't have a label or manager. They also had not just a history but friends in common – Kyle was the piano student of Justin's best friend.

Kyle caught up with Justin's activities that spring of 2007. While preparing for another tour jaunt with The Rosebuds and Land Of Talk in May and June (including dates in Eau Claire), he'd hooked up with Mark Paulson of Ticonderoga again and had semi-officially joined the band, as announced in an excited post on Ticonderoga's MySpace page on March 29: "Shazam! Ticonderoga has undergone another transformation. Mark Paulson and Justin Vernon (ex-DeYarmond Edison, Hazeltons, Bon Iver) are now carrying the torch aloft, working on new music, and trying to get our third record done before Justin goes out with The Rosebuds on May 18th. It's been a strange and exciting transition, and we're proud to keep the Ticonderoga sailing on into uncharted waters. We'll be posting some new material soon to get y'all salivary glands a-pumpin', so stay tuned."

"Phil and Beth have become seriously important to me," Justin would say the following year as the project developed, "musically most certainly, but really as friends. Mark is honestly, maybe the best musical partner I've ever had; we've become really close, and musically, I just don't think I could be on a page more evenly with anyone as I am with him. Ticonderoga is still going. It was Phil and Mark's and Wes Phillip's band, and when that sort of dissipated, Mark approached me to join forces. So, it's been developing and developing. Now it's kind of like Mark's the centre of the band and the filter which everything goes through."[2]

Over the coming weeks Justin and Kyle came to the decision to work with each other, Kyle becoming Justin's manager. "I asked him what he wanted to do with [the album]," Frenette remembers, "and we decided to self-release it."[3] *For Emma, Forever Ago*, they agreed, would get its first release on Frenette's Amble Down records.

So, between Rosebuds tours and working with Ticonderoga, Justin and Kyle worked towards the album's release. Even with the official stamp of Frenette's label behind him, the project still had the home-made touch of his previous releases. Some of Gil's photography was selected for the album by designer Brian Moen, an Eau Claire drummer friend of Justin's, and Vernon family members were roped in on manufacturing duties.

"When he put out his first 500 copies of the *For Emma . . .* record, we put that together sitting up at the cabin, [a] bunch of us were folding and stuffing," Justine said, starting to get an inkling that this time Justin's life as a musician might be getting a little more serious. "People were watching him and reacting to him with all this admiration and this CD had barely been out. That's when I started to think 'hmm, I think he might be onto something here'."[4]

Meanwhile, word was gradually creeping around the blogosphere about this magical, soulful new folk music that had crept silently under the net. On June 1 Bon Iver received its first blog plug on My Old Kentucky Blog: "Justin Vernon was the frontman for a couple bands (Mount Vernon and DeYarmond Edison) in the Eau Claire, Wisconsin area, but has struck out on his own with a new project he's calling Bon Iver . . . Vernon sings in a perfect falsetto over sparse folk backgrounds on a lot of tracks, but opens it a bit more naturally on this one. You can hear the rest of the tracks at Bon Iver's MySpace. His debut album is called For Emma, Forever Ago and "was made on a pilgrimage to the woods of northwestern Wisconsin. With only guns, venison, firewood, a sears typewriter, and ancient musical equipment."[5]

The blog included a link to 'Skinny Love' and gave a plug for the album release show at the House Of Rock in Eau Claire on July 8, when Justin would perform two shows to his old hometown supporters, an all-ages set in the afternoon and a show for over-21s in the evening. Justin played solo, but not without a little hometown help.

"My first show I actually printed out lyric sheets to three or four of the songs," Vernon said. "I needed the voices . . . People were singing 'Flume'. People were singing 'The Wolves'. I think it gave me confidence . . . The song actually needs 80 to 500 people singing or whatever the vibe is of that room, it needs that fight."[6]

Eau Claire had welcomed Justin back into its fold like a returning hero. Despite returning to Raleigh to such a warm and appreciative reception, Justin had once more felt the draw of home. "The seasons are part of the reason why I had to come back here to live," he said, "'cos I think that I attached myself to that sort of spin and got so accustomed to understanding

119

and changing with it. It gave me this path that I could pick up and hold in my hands. I might be guilty of over-romanticising this town. There are some great things that I do here, like going to the bar, the coffee shop, these places that build their own history every day, and me being there and my friends being there – I get a lot of joy out of that."[7]

"I want to get to know every inch of this city, rather than getting to know a bunch of inches of any other city,"[8] he said, and expanded on the theme in a radio interview with 89.3 The Current. "It's a good way to get to know a place by knowing it for your whole life rather than moving on. And it can be a challenge sometimes. We're a small town and we don't have everything. At all . . . But it's also kind of the reason that I want to stay, sort of be a part of it, lend myself to it, or whatever."[9]

Eager to re-launch himself into the Eau Claire music community, Justin began playing with Brian Moen, the drummer with Eau Claire acts Laarks and Peter Wolf Crier, in a garage blues duo in the vein of The Black Keys or The White Stripes called The Shouting Matches. Giving Justin a chance to revert to his baritone blues bawl, they recorded a five-track EP called *Mouthoil*, consisting of raw battered drums, chunky blues riffage. Although they played no gigs and held on to the EP rather than release it, their cover of Son House's 'Death Letter Blues' was rumoured to be a stormer, Moen revelling in the primal power of percussion and Justin growling and hollering like the hoariest old blues survivor: "I got a letter this morning, I packed up my suitcase and I went off down the road . . ."

Over June and July, meanwhile, the Bon Iver snowball gathered momentum. As Justin began playing shows to promote the album the entire record was put up online as a stream and of the 500 copies of *For Emma, Forever Ago* that were initially printed up on Amble Down Records, only 17 were sent out to the press and radio, but these all made a splash. On July 27 two blogs tipped the record. Mere hours before going to catch Vernon support The Comas at New York's Mercury Lounge, the influential Brooklyn Vegan site providing downloads of 'Skinny Love', 'Blindsided' and 'For Emma' and likened the sound to various folk heroes: "The 'Skinny Love' song especially reminds me of Tim Fite. He also channels Chad VanGaalen, Wolf Parade, TV On The Radio, Neil Young, and a few others I can't think of. Mostly I just think it sounds pretty good."[10]

Simultaneously, Ryan Matteson's Muzzle Of Bees site put a more personal slant on the story. "I came to know Justin Vernon aka Bon Iver while slightly drunk and in the front row of The Rosebuds' blistering Hot Freaks set at SXSW," the post read. "It was during said performance that Rosebuds frontman Ivan Howard introduced Justin (then holding down guitar duties for the band) as a native of Eau Claire, Wisconsin. When you're a long way from home, had your share of Lonestar beer, and with good friends, that will earn you some easy respect and admiration from my entourage and I. Since that time I've kept in touch with Justin, and . . . through the course of our conversations he mentioned his project, Bon Iver, and how much he thought I'd like it. Fast forward to a few weeks ago when Bon Iver's *For Emma, Forever Ago* beautifully packaged compact disc arrived in the mail. Through countless listens it was apparent that the music, not our mutual home state, was the important part of this story. This album is a little bit folk and, at times, hard to pin down to a specific genre or type – but that's what I love about it. Expect this to be the release that takes everyone by surprise this year."[11]

Come October, it would be Vernon and Frenette that were taken by surprise. The local Eau Claire buzz around *For Emma . . .* and the trickle of online support had already made the record more successful than any of Vernon's previous solo efforts, steadily selling 200 copies of the 500 printed over the course of three months. But on October 4 it got the push that would send it stratospheric: a review on influential alternative music website Pitchfork.

"It came to my attention first," says writer Stephen M Deusner of the album's progress to the cult media big time. "I got an email from Amble Down in July and I really liked what I heard, so I pushed a few tracks forward and tried to push the album forward to my editors, who liked it as well. I thought [Vernon] was doing some interesting things sonically and especially vocally. It seemed odd to me at the time to hear somebody treat his voice that way, through all this distortion, and the lyrics I thought were very interesting. I'm kind of a lyrics person so that's usually what I go to, so to have something that's almost nonsensical and yet that evocative of this weird landscape, I thought was very interesting. Plus they were just really catchy, powerful and atmospheric songs so I fell into them from that point.

"Now I look back and I can see that he was doing some very interesting things with American folk elements and especially to have come out of

North Carolina, which now has this huge scene for that, and to have tweaked it even before the scene gelled that way is pretty interesting. It seemed a lot more eccentric than Sufjan and out of left-field, it did not feel like it was part of any larger thing. A big thing at that time was this super-orchestrated indie pop music and freak folk of Devendra Banhart was on the wane so I didn't think it fit into that because it was much more textured and much less naturalistic. The thing that struck me was how close his voice sounded to the guy from TV On The Radio and nobody ever got that, it sounded a lot like him, that was my main point of reference."

Was it unusual for an album with only 500 released copies to get reviewed on Pitchfork? "Yes, especially for a debut. By the time we ran a review in early October it had gotten enough of a groundswell that a lot of other blogs and stuff like that were noticing it, so it wasn't completely out of the blue but it is unusual."

The mark out of ten was mildly baffling – an 8.1, according to Pitchfork's thinly-veiled out-of-one-hundred scale – but Deusner's review on Pitchfork was emphatic in its appreciation. "A ruminative collection of songs full of natural imagery and acoustic strums," Deusner wrote of the record, "the sound of a man left alone with his memories and a guitar . . . Vernon gives a soulful performance full of intuitive swells and fades, his phrasing and pronunciation making his voice as much a purely sonic instrument as his guitar . . . Rarely does folk – indie or otherwise – give so much over to ambience: quivering guitar strings, mic'ed closely, lend opener 'Flume' its eerily interiorised sound, which matches his unsettling similes. It's as if he's trying to inhabit the in-between spaces separating musical expression and private rumination," Deusner concluded, "exposing his regrets without relinquishing them. His emotional exorcism proves even more intense for being so tentative."[12]

Though the Pitchfork review stopped short of foretelling the sort of impact the record would have on the alternative folk scene, which would surprise Deusner as much as anyone. "In retrospect, we didn't even give it that high a grade. It's an 8.1, which is good, but I think I'd give it a lot higher today, definitely a high 8 or a low 9 even. Most people would probably give it a ten. So for that reason I was very surprised and it's odd what people catch onto."

The response to the review, back in Camp Vernon, was instantaneous and overwhelming. Justin's inbox filled to bursting in a barrage of computerised pings. Frenette's phone rang with the ferocity of hell hounds scenting fresh blood. By 6 p.m. on the day the review went live, all 500 copies of *For Emma . . .* had been sold and Bon Iver was the hottest name in the blogosphere.

"That day was insane," Vernon remembers. "It tipped things over the edge. My manager was taking calls in the shower. I'd go for a piss and come back to 50 emails in my inbox."[13] "It just snowballed, took off," Frenette added. "I was fielding calls every day from interested people in the industry, wondering what was up, what our plans were, if we had signed a deal yet."[14]

Rather than leaping on the first offer to land in their lap, Vernon and Frenette decided to wait until the CMJ Music Marathon, an annual four-day industry conference event in New York City held each October, wherein hundreds of new bands play showcases in venues across Manhattan and Brooklyn while industry figures hijack cabs to race across town chasing the hottest tips and the coolest leads. Justin was busy producing the first Land Of Talk album that September anyway, and Bon Iver were booked to play one of the many showcases at CMJ 2007 – their iron couldn't be hotter, so they'd wait to see what the showcase would bring, barely a fortnight away.

Meanwhile, across the globe, one of the astute CMJ attendees was doing his research, plotting his route around the head-spinning plethora of potential new signings at CMJ 2007. And becoming one of the first to exhibit early signs of Iver Fever . . .

★ ★ ★

"I was doing some homework for the CMJ music event 2007," says Ed Horrox, head of A&R at 4AD Records in London since 2000, the man who'd signed the likes of TV On The Radio and Beirut to the label and worked with Scott Walker, Kim Deal and Kristin Hersh. "When you've got something like that that you're attending you usually do whatever you can in the weeks in the run-up to it to get your head around who's gonna be there and what's of interest. Whether it was on the CMJ player, they'd have an online jukebox or something or a track from everybody playing, I can't remember [but] we came across the Bon Iver music and it was clear that it was pretty great."

After hearing one track, Horrox hunted down the full album stream and swiftly fell for *For Emma* . . . . "I think there was some kind of band page," he says, "one of these online platforms for artists to get their music up and out there. Whether that involved making a donation or pay-what-you-want I'm not sure. I tracked it down from some website, whether it was his website or somewhere else. I heard a track or two, pulled it down, was listening to it within a week or so of coming across it, this was in September. Then obviously it became pretty clear pretty quickly that it was a very special record. What makes it special is the feeling you get from it. There's a gut reaction that's not cerebral, it's like 'fuck, I'm listening to this, I'm returning to it, I love it, I keep playing it'. Then you ask yourself what is it about it and try to understand it. For me, when I first heard it I thought 'this is a singer-songwriter record, this is something there's been a lot of'. There'd been a decade when there was a lot of singer-songwriters, from Will Oldham through Iron & Wine and on. There were many people who had been the singer-songwriter guy with the beard. So to a certain extent, when you do what I do, you're always looking for someone who's breaking the mould or doing something different, and in a way you thought 'I think I know what this is' and because of that you're disposed to maybe dismiss it. But it became clear very quickly that it was more than that, it was something else, and it's what makes music magical, that a person can re-invigorate a certain area."

Horrox was turned on by the soul inherent in Justin's falsetto. "It wasn't a million miles away from someone like Curtis Mayfield and he reminded me a little bit of Kip Malone out of TV On The Radio, who I was working with. I was hearing the soulfulness of those kind of vocals in Justin's falsetto. His falsetto certainly set it apart and his voice was crucial to what made it very very special. Voices are what usually make an artist special and makes them connect, and a lot of the bands you don't give a fuck about, it's because of the voice. If you listen to his voice on 'Re: Stacks', that quickly became my favourite tune, his voice on that is incredible and his lyrics are fantastic. I guess I wasn't asking questions about them, I was just enjoying them. Words and lines would float into your consciousness, something about that crow and 'my keys' in 'Re: Stacks'. He's imbuing this crow with human characteristics, it wasn't easy to understand what he was talking about but 'gluey feathers on a flume', that's describing the intricacies of a feather, it's kinda fucking good. With the second record he definitely went down a very impressionistic, poetic road where it's even harder to get your head around what he's talking about and he probably just put it together because it sounds good. He talks about the way he writes being a phonetic thing where he'll make noises and then try to find words from those noises. The first album, the words did rise up."

On the night of Bon Iver's CMJ show, the A&R interest had turned into a scrum. Word had spread like wildfire; Mute Records was keen to sign Vernon and Indiana's foremost indie label, Jagjaguwar, was hard on its heels. The industry interest at the showcase was intense and, juggling offers from a whole host of majors and independents alike, Frenette was beginning to see the benefits of having such a fascinating back-story to the project. "It always helps to have an intriguing and inspiring story to go along with a record," he said, "one that fits the aesthetic and people can latch onto."[15]

Horrox, however, couldn't make the show. "We had lots of artists playing at CMJ and our gigs fell at the same time he was playing," he explains. "I hadn't listened to it enough at that point to realise how important it was, so I prioritised our artists over him. So I missed him but while I was there I called his manager and said, 'Hey, I've missed you but I think it's great, I'm really very interested', and we started talking about a deal."

After impressing Justin by phone Jagjaguwar would eventually secure Vernon's signature for the US on October 29* but, in keeping with Justin's homely nature, it was the fact that Horrox made the trip all the way to Eau Claire to meet him face-to-face that helped seal the UK deal for Horrox. "I went to meet Justin in his home town of Eau Claire," Ed recalls, "which was a bit of a trek to get there, so I went. I don't think anyone else did that. I went to meet him, because there were other people who wanted to sign him, two or three people who were very focussed on trying to do it. It was a very very stressful time because the more I listened to it the more I realised that he'd made a masterpiece, he was clearly the most fully formed debut artist. Obviously there's a history leading up to that that's the reason why he was as fully formed as he was at that point, but for a debut record it was as good as it gets. I was starting to think of

---

* Frenette would claim that of all the labels chasing Vernon, Jagjaguwar most closely shared their ideals.

him in the same breath as people like Neil Young and Joni Mitchell, I was getting carried away and thinking that's how good he is, that this was going to be one of the best records the label's ever released. So when you're thinking that and you haven't signed him, you're thinking 'I've got to sign him!'

"We met, we sat down. I was excited about the conversation, with regard to the music. He took me to the bar, The Joynt. It's a great old American bar. We went there and got a pitcher of beer for not much and drunk that talking about Jackson Browne. I'd had an obsession with Jackson Browne recently and it turned out he knew more than I did, which was great. Talking about music, having that sort of conversation, it's inspiring, it's exciting and it reinforced any ideas you had about the guy being extremely well-listened. He was a scholar, he was a student of everything and it was fun. The music conversation was brilliant, then he drove me back to my hotel listening to gospel, he was playing some incredible gospel music in the car. It was everything you would hope it would be about a musical conversation. He was friendly, an extremely friendly man."

Ed's bold jaunt would endear him to the Vernon clan for some time to come. "I remember a night, I think it might've been his father's sixtieth birthday," he chuckles, "and we were at a gig in Dublin that he had played – it was a big gig, he'd grown quite big by that point, a few thousand people, and it was a bit of a party after the show for his dad or his mum, one of his parents, they'd travelled from America. He introduced me and his dad said, 'Is this the crazy guy that came to meet you in Eau Claire?'"

★ ★ ★

Meanwhile, Justin had been building a band for Bon Iver.

"One of the big problems was when I made the record, part of the reason why I thought I wasn't going to put it out was: how the fuck am I going to play these songs?" he said. "How is it going to sound good? How am I going to find people I can trust? . . . I was just like, 'I better book a show and just see what happens.'"[16]

Luckily for Justin, the first piece of the Bon Iver live puzzle fell into his lap in the shape of a drummer and backing vocalist by the name of Sean Corey, a Lake Geneva native, top of his class in the EU-Eau Claire jazz program, alumnus of Jazz Ensemble I and the drummer in a band booked to support him at one of his first Eau Claire shows as Bon Iver. Corey cornered Justin backstage before the gig and practically blagged his way into the band, explaining that he'd met Vernon in passing before and had become obsessed with the online stream of *For Emma . . .* when his Jazz Ensemble bandmates Pingrey and DeHaven pointed him in its direction.

"They weren't just good songs, they were great, interesting, unique; it's a beautiful album," said Carey. "So I spent two weeks holed up in my bedroom with laptop, headphones and notebook, and I wrote down all the drum parts and learned all the lyrics, melodies and harmonies. When the band I was in opened for Justin at his first local show as Bon Iver, I told him I knew all his songs and I wanted to play with him."[17]

Impressed by his skills and chutzpah, Vernon let Carey onstage to play three or four songs with him to a crowd of around 40 that very night, and by the end of the show Sean, having "nailed it"[18], had become the sole other member of Bon Iver.

With his mind set on a four-piece band to play the *For Emma . . .* songs, Justin knew exactly who he wanted on guitar. He called Mikey Noyce, his old guitar student from Eau Claire, then just 20 years old and 18 months into a course at Lawrence University. When Vernon called him out of the blue enthusing that he'd be perfect for Bon Iver's guitarist position, Noyce was uncertain whether to drop out to go on tour, and Justin only gave him a day to make us his mind. "He called me the next morning and said, 'Yes, I don't know how thrilled my parents feel about it but I'm in.'"[19]

Completing his on-the-road line-up by hiring his brother, Nate, to be his tour manager, Justin told his band he'd be operating an unusually egalitarian touring regime. Although at some shows Bon Iver would also have horn players onstage, Justin would concentrate on acoustic guitar duties while the remaining members would take on a variety of instruments as needed and every band member, Justin included, would get an equal share of the live revenue.*

The three-piece Bon Iver got to know each other playing shows around

---

* Justin was keen to make sure any potential band profits benefited his friends and local community as much as possible, even going as far as to hire an accountant in nearby Osseo rather than any out-of-town big-shot firm.

Eau Claire, including a Muzzle Of Bees showcase gig at the university's music hall on November 10, alongside The Selfish Gene and Common Loon and a support slot at the Nucleus club for Land Of Talk, whose singer Elizabeth Powell Justin had started dating. As a sign that he hadn't forgotten his old friends, Justin also played two shows with a reformed DeYarmond Edison that November at Eau Claire's Nucleus club, opening the night with a set as Bon Iver. Then they ventured further afield, encountering not just awestruck crowds blown away by the soul-baring intimacy of the *For Emma . . .* songs but also hordes of bloggers waving Dictaphones, keen to get Justin's views on the storm of hype building around him.

"I still don't expect anything to happen," he told one such writer that November. "I feel so fortunate. So lucky. In so many ways. But if it just petered out tomorrow, I'm too small-town of a person, I feel, to feel bad if I just disappeared. I've already received so many letters and such, enough for a lifetime of artistic fulfilment . . . I can't even measure it. I knew that when I finished making these songs up there, that I had done something that was more current and pure and honest than anything I had done to that point. I thought it was special in that way. The fact that others seem to understand, from different places all over the world makes me feel . . . well, like something good is happening in general."[20]

Ed Horrox saw the nascent Bon Iver line-up play an early show in Chicago that December. "I think, [they were] playing a place called Schubers," he says, "which is about a 200 capacity venue. This was the first time I'd seen him play, we were still working on the deal at this point. [It was] incredible. That was another moment where the significance of him as an artist and of the career he was going to have became clearer, as clear as it's possible to be. When you've got the record and then you see the live show and it's as good as that was – I guess it was still relatively early stages – it was fantastic, the musicianship was incredible. He had Mikey Noyce with him and Sean [Corey] and it was the first time I'd seen those guys, they were fantastic musicians, and his voice live was fantastic. They were all sat down, on that first record, for most of it. Until 'Blood Bank' came out, everyone sat down for every gig, which was interesting. It was different, there was something about that. There were people in the audience who were singing the songs. I'm not talking about when he asks the audience to participate, I'm talking about looking around me and, it tended to be young women, there were quite a few young women singing the songs. That was quite an eye-opener, like a 'there's something happening here' moment for someone at such an early point in the life of a record, to see people so into the music.

"I remember coming out of that gig and making a call to one or two people back in the UK, knowing I'd get their voicemails, but I had to tell them at that point when you've just seen the show and you're as excited as you are, sometimes you want to just share that, so I did."

Horrox's enthusiasm was part of the reason that his deal with Bon Iver was settled in double-quick time. "It all happened pretty quickly," he says. "Hearing it first in September, realising how good it was and making an offer within weeks, in October, meeting Justin in November and seeing their first gig in December. It was a pretty swift thing, the way those things unfolded. It wouldn't usually happen like that."

Hence, as the whirlwind of 2007 drew to a close with two record deals in the bag, Justin suddenly found himself relatively monied. His first cheque, at least, was enough for a deposit on a modest house of his own, firmly back on Eau Claire soil. On Boxing Day, after 18 months of sofa-hopping, sleeping on The Rosebuds' couch or up in the cabin, Vernon completed on a $76,000 bungalow a mere 80 yards from where he was born, which he decked out with a flat-screen TV and a PlayStation to spend the post-Christmas lull playing *Call Of Duty*.

"I buy records and play them in my house and I have a nice bed and that's about it," he said. "It's a huge thing, though, just to have some sovereignty and a roof over my head. It makes me feel almost like a real person at last."[21]

"My mortgage is less than half of people's rent," he'd claim. "I want to be able to write on my walls. I think that's the big thing . . . Just like quotes and stuff. Something I want to see every day."[22] Writing out quotes had become a big thing for Justin – in his pocket he carried with him a line from a Johnny Cash song, written for the veteran country star by Tom Waits: "I saw Judas Iscariot carrying John Wilkes Booth down there by the train". "You have experiences with art or phenomena that supersede your simple relationship with them as just a piece of art. They're more than that. That's just what those quotes are for me. They're big, they're important."[23]

And as the maelstrom of 2007 shifted into the January calm of 2008, rounded off with the major ego boost of having *For Emma, Forever Ago* listed amongst the Top 50 Albums Of The Year by Pitchfork, Justin needed to reconnect to his own phenomenon.

Over his best winter yet, the music of Bon Iver was calling.

★ ★ ★

Settled into his new home at the start of 2008, Vernon would have felt a million miles from the desolate dislocation of a year before. Within a year of his entire life falling apart, all his wildest dreams had come true. But it had also been a year since his creative impulse had been fully indulged, and his musical interest was freshly peaked by listening to Rickie Lee Jones' song 'The Horses', Steve Reich and Thomas Wincek's post-rock band Collections Of Colonies Of Bees. Indeed, the show he would play in Milwaukee that January with COCOB, who'd started life as a band called Pele on the Polyvinyl label, would be as pivotal to him as the Indigo Girls' gig he'd seen as a teenager. "They're just amazing," he told Pitchfork. "Their 'Customer' record that came out on Polyvinyl is . . . just noise manipulation, acoustic manipulation, but it's not tired like everything else you hear in that genre, in my opinion. It's just really beautiful. And then their new record ['Birds' is] super smart and textural and manipulated but it's got this soul in it. It's really, really brilliant . . . Their show in Milwaukee was just life changing. I literally told the promoter I had to wait 15 minutes before I played because . . . I just didn't want to play. It was just too good. Their live show for their new record is unreal."[24]

With such inspiration driving him, some material left over from the cabin sessions and new tunes whirling around his head, Vernon sat down once again to revisit the mindset he'd found up at the cabin, worried that he'd simply forgotten how to write songs any other way.

"I became very eager to explore what Bon Iver meant to me in the life of this project," he said. "I wanted to move forward because I knew it was about more than the one record I made. This was the chance to break out. I had the golden opportunity to make the record of my dreams."[25]

"When I sit down now and work on stuff," he continued, "I'm drifting toward the place that allows me to be more honest. And I think the way I did this is The Way − it's like a path or something. I don't want to re-create [*For Emma . . .*]. I just want to re-create the path and get into a place where I feel comfortable, and not think too much about what the lyrics sound like, or 'I better make this record sound very Bon Iver!' So many people's sophomore records sounds like that."[26]

What's more, he was acutely aware that the location of *For Emma . . .*'s recording was a vital part of its atmosphere. "The opportunity to create something like this," he said, "for a lot of people, only comes when you have nothing but time and you're by yourself. The longevity of the ideas – the way they came out in an intact manner – I probably only could get from being isolated."[27]

Knowing he wanted the second Bon Iver album to be a bold departure from the first, one of the first tracks Justin set to work on early in 2008 was a snippet of what he considered "a Civil War-sounding heavy metal song . . . sort of chaotic, dense, jarring."[28] He was intent on opening the next Bon Iver album with it in order to prove the project wasn't cemented in minimalist miserablism. "It's saying 'you will not tell me what to do, you will not dictate what I do as an artist'," he said, "I needed to thrash and chaotically deconstruct things that had become too plastic in my life. That's why it's called 'Perth', it's like beginning, it's like birth. There's a chaos to that and there's also a beauty."[29]

Though the song would hardly end up resembling Megadeth, retaining a certain gentleness even in its chaotic attack, it would be a bold, brazen blast of brass, military drum rattles, electric guitar splashes and choral soul screeches. The intensity of 'Perth' was such that just setting up the drums to record the initial takes took Justin five hours, at the end of which his hands were bleeding.

Characteristically, 'Perth' grew out of loss. On January 22, 2008, Justin was in the middle of three days of filming his first ever music video to accompany the release of 'Skinny Love' as a single that April. Typically, Vernon wasn't the star of the video; nature was. Heading out into the crisp winter scenes around Eau Claire, Justin and director Matt Amato set about filming lapping lake shores, icicles dripping from branches, rushing rivers, swaying grasslands and fields drenched in snow. A peaceful and idyllic three days that were shattered in the ring of a cellphone.

Amato's best friend, Hollywood actor Heath Ledger, had been found dead, accidentally overdosed on "a toxic combination of prescription drugs". Amato went to pieces.

"So I've got this guy [Matt Amato] in my house whose best friend [Heath Ledger] just passed away," Justin told *Rolling Stone*. "He's sobbing in my arms. He can't go back to L.A. because the house is under siege. Michelle Williams is calling my parents' phone. All this stuff."[30]

"We sat with bottles of bourbon around the fire and he grieved," Vernon recalled. "It was the strangest and most intense three days of my life."[31]

The trauma of the experience gave Justin not only the idea for the song but also the theme for the next album, and the fact that Heath Ledger was from Perth provided the opening track with its title. "It just sort of became the beginning of the record," he said. "'Perth' has such a feeling of isolation, and also it rhymes with birth, and every song I ended up making after that just sort of drifted towards that theme, tying themselves to places and trying to explain what places are and what places aren't."[32]

It would be some years before 'Perth' was finally completed however. And, in the meantime, there was a whole new storm coming.

CHAPTER NINE

In Demand

THE bigger the crowds got, the quieter they became.
Mid-January, 2008, Bon Iver played at St Paul's tiny Turf Club, performing *For Emma . . .* in its entirety, in sequence. Though the record, having sold out, was available only as an online stream, the crowd knew every word, mouthing along in a rapt hush, only bursting into full-throated song when 'Wolves . . .' reached its chant-along crescendo of "what might have been lost". As Justin finished 'Re: Stacks', solo and sublime, the room was thick with held breaths.

When he played Eau Claire's 100-capacity Nucleus club to launch the Jagjaguwar US release of *For Emma, Forever Ago* on February 10, sitting behind two microphones and playing a bass drum as he strummed, he faced a sold-out crowd that had queued around the block to get in since, as a café with a venue attached, the Nucleus didn't sell advance tickets. Justin was so excited by the turn-out he Tweeted a picture of the queue; before long he'd have his fill of queues.

When *For Emma, Forever Ago* hit the shelves just over a week later on February 19, wrapped in a sleeve of ice and mystery – a stark woodland scene obscured by a fine film of frost – America was as charmed as the Nucleus. Reaching a modest 64 on the *Billboard* Chart it was an Independent Albums Chart hit, hitting number four. The critics gushed: *Rolling Stone* and *Spin* magazine both reviewed the album warmly, and *Stylus* magazine described it as "an album possessing Elliott Smith's folk-tinged starkness and the analog-tape warmth of Samuel Beam . . . Vernon's music is stripped-down, uniformly quiet, and confessional, his clipped, cracked, Will Oldham-inspired lyrics not evidence of cabin delirium, but the work of an artist warmed by a creative glow that only pure isolation (read: freedom) can fully render."[1] When the album was released on 4AD in the

UK on May 12, when it would reach a highly respectable number 42 aided by iTunes making 'Skinny Love' a free download around the release, reviewers were even more enthused.

Uncut's John Mulvey ranked the album a maximum five stars, dedicating its Album Of The Month slot to the release and calling it "a hermetically sealed, complete and satisfying album . . . a record entirely predicated on isolation . . . so securely and so intensely in its own world – a world of snow and silence and long-percolated memories – that listening can seem like an intrusive act . . . a magical, hyper-real experience." Hearing echoes of Fleet Foxes, Dawn Landes, Band Of Horses and Howlin' Rain, Mulvey also appreciated the background noises of Justin moving round the room, the weather outside, even a police siren in the distance in 'The Wolves . . .'. "He seems to capture the performance with a forensic intimacy," he wrote, "while imbuing it with an extra, ethereal dimension."[2]

A *Mojo* review by Victoria Segal also gave a maximum five stars and Album Of The Month status and the accolade Instant *Mojo* Classic. "If you were told that it had actually been found by some folks from town who rode over to the cabin to check on its occupant after the spring thaw and found nothing inside but dusty wax cylinders and a note with the title scrawled on it in sooty ink . . . well, it wouldn't be so hard to believe," she wrote, praising songs "of rediscovery and redemption, of coming to terms with the past and getting to grips with the future . . . the quiet excavation of a painful past unearthing songs of stunning beauty. "This record wears its gloom very lightly indeed," she continued, likening the album to Elliott Smith, Iron & Wine, Smog, Tortoise, Calexico and R.E.M.'s debut album, *Murmur*. "It's easy to imagine him playing back the tapes and jumping at what he heard . . . the liquid imagery coalesces into a remarkably powerful whole . . . 37 beautiful minutes far away from the everyday. Isolation doesn't get more splendid than this."[3]

The *Sunday Times* review was another five-star ranking, relating the record to Willard Grant Conspiracy and praising it as a "minimalist masterpiece . . . the songs are relentlessly simple, sometimes barely there, and the meaning of the words is often similarly elusive until the vocal suddenly focuses round a burst of anger or frustration."[4]

Over the course of 2008 *For Emma, Forever Ago* would grow in critical stature. In the end-of-year round-ups the *Observer Music Monthly* would award *For Emma* . . . its Album Of The Year honour, writer Gareth Grundy describing it as "an uncanny snapshot of its creator's turmoil . . . the pitch might've been backwoods primitive but the sound was contemporary, all magisterial drones and vocals tweaked until they became spectral choirs."[5] *Uncut* also listed it amongst its albums of the year, commending its "insidious power . . . a suite of songs that had both a raw, immediate integrity and a ghostly experimental dimension."[6] *Mojo*'s albums of the year list claimed it had "become the album of 2008 that everyone felt they had discovered for themselves, adding an extra magic to the listening experience . . . something beautiful and true that will last for ages."[7]

Uncut's Bud Scoppa would pinpoint the moment Justin became an important musical figure, during 'Flume'. "His double-tracked falsetto abruptly multiplied into a celestial choir . . . in that moment, Vernon touched a nerve", the people moved by it "making the connection between this stunningly personal work and their own inner lives."[8] Later, some critics would suggest the album itself was a turning point in alternative culture, the moment when gender barriers in music blurred and sensitivity, delicacy, insecurity, emotional complexity, tenderness and vulnerability – everything the traditional rock'n'roller might consider un-masculine – became celebrated virtues.

Ed Horrox considers the reception of *For Emma* . . . to have been "'of the decade'. I think it's certainly top ten of the decade, one of the best records the label's ever released. I was thrilled, but the record was so good it started to become clear that people were feeling the same way you were feeling. Sometimes when you come across something that good you don't have that uncertainty that you sometimes feel when you're sharing music and hoping people like it. It's like 'if you don't like this, you're crazy'. You get that confidence with certain records, certain artists. I remember sharing the music with Laura Barton at the *Guardian* who wrote a think piece about music and how it can affect you and her life over a few days or a week and how obsessed she was becoming with this record. It wasn't a review as such, it was about the power of music, it was an amazing piece. I remember Justin once saying he doesn't read his press, he doesn't read his reviews. I think his dad did keep up with the press and did read the Laura review and did send that to him and said, 'You've got to read this one, I think it's a bit special.'"

"It feels strange," Justin said of the acclaim, admitting his thoughts occasionally strayed with fondness back to the calm of the cabin. "This is all such a beautiful big thing, but I'm kind of wondering if maybe it would be cool if it just slowed down a little bit."[9]

"It became clear that he wasn't interested in being famous," Horrox says. "He wasn't interested in being big, he was interested in making the right move creatively. That was what mattered to him. He didn't want to accept an offer that might make him a bigger artist, might help him sell more records because his choices would be based upon what he felt was the right thing to do creatively, to help his music and his band resonate with people. That's one of the reasons why he's such a great artist and why people care."

Jagjaguwar's Darius Van Arman also found Justin art-focussed. "For him it's really about the body of work," he said. "He's very careful about those decisions. And sometimes they are very anti-commercial decisions. He makes decisions that leave not only sales and fans but huge amounts of money on the table."[10]

To his Eau Claire scene-mates, however, the rise and rise of Bon Iver was a brilliant spotlight of validation on their small town. "Watching him grow bigger and bigger in the music world is amazing for Kelly and me," said Ivan of The Rosebuds. "He is like our very own Larry Bird out there that we helped unleash on the world."[11]

In the midst of all of the press coverage surrounding the album's release, detail after detail of Justin's hidden life emerged. He told Pitchfork about his and Elizabeth's ideas of moving out of Eau Claire, to Portland or the Yukon, and his dreams of scoring movies.

His record collection came under scrutiny too, citing Sam Cooke, Nina Simone and Mahalia Jackson as formative influences. "While I don't share her actual convictions," he told *Mojo*, "she is singing always in her conviction, towards the truth that is her own and showing it so well that you have no choice but to believe her. Also, when she sounds like she is in pain she is actually in joy."[12]

He even talked music equipment with Pitchfork. "Probably my favourite piece of musical equipment remaining is this National brand acoustic guitar, it's one of the metal dobro things, and it's from 1928. I picked it up from a dude at the music store, a guy that worked at this old place I used to give guitar lessons at. He gave it to me for 400 bucks and I restored it. It had been painted over probably five or six times and somebody had scraped all the paint off; it had this really weird rusty look but it's one of those guitars that you just play and it's, like, magic time – the whole room resonates. It's really beautiful, I love that guitar."[13]

The cold isolation of the recording sessions was a regular talking point, both the myths it had begun to throw up ("The stories got pretty wild," he said, "that I had killed a deer with my bare hands"[14]) and the atmosphere it had inhabited. Would it have been a different album, the *Guardian* asked, if he'd recorded it during the summer? "Probably would have been a bit more joyful, but it's weird, I find I get more heavily depressed in the summertime. In the winter, it's more like this lengthy, beautiful thing. It's more inquisitive; winter is a time of internal thinking for me."[15]

But besides the fascinating story behind the album, it was his intriguing, mysterious music that was most debated in the press, Justin openly admitting he was still learning about the songs himself as he toured them, that they still remained an enigma to him, they were full of dark corners he was slowly exploring night-by-night. He spoke about the effect the record had been having on its listeners; about the Scandinavian who'd claimed they'd fallen to the floor and wept the first time they heard it; the couples who were blaming it for their divorce; the man he'd heard of who'd been playing the record to his dying mother. "The music seems to be doing something for people in a serious way. I'm really happy but I don't know how much I have to do with that. I just feel lucky that I had the opportunity to take the time to do it. Maybe that's what this whole thing is about? That people want to be able to go to the cabin. People need to have the time to deal with their issues. Find sanctity . . . serenity."[16]

"I know that the record is responsible for that," he said. "I'm not responsible for that . . . I did down-deep know that it was going to do things like that."[17]

"There's always pain and joy to be explored, it's a matter of how willing you are to go there. The record is out there doing its own thing and it's cool to watch. Everybody makes it their own thing. The idea of disappearing and dealing with your life is something some people want. Other people latch on to the relationship side."[18]

He also claimed he intended to have a follow-up album completed within months. "I don't want to rest on these songs," he asserted. "I know too many musicians that have to tour on the same 10 songs, and they burn out. They get back to their house and they have no reason to write new music. They are music'd out."[19]

Admitting to a nagging sense of insecurity in his work, he nonetheless insisted he'd make the second Bon Iver record, if not actually isolated physically from humanity, at least entrenched just as deeply in his own world. "I think that I'll continue to make records like this. I'm not going to hire engineers; I'm not going to hire producers. I'm fully capable of doing all that stuff, and I'm just going to keep it within myself, under my control and surveillance."[20]

One awkward question kept coming up, interview after interview. Who exactly was Emma? Justin remained suitably cagey. "Emma is her middle name but we had split up long before I moved," he told *The Times*. "I called her anyway and she's pretty freaked out. But as I explained to her, it was never about her. The record was me finally stopping a terrible, slow spin that had been building for years. Me alleviating memories, confronting a lot of lost love, longing and mediocrity."[21]

"In any situation with lost love," he told Pitchfork, "I don't think it ever really goes away fully. You just sort of learn where to keep it."[22]

"I've had conversations with the people that the songs regard," he said, "and, while it can be uncomfortable or awkward, I feel like we're in a very celebratory, loving place."[23]

Indeed, as his album crept towards 300,000 sales, and 400,000 in the UK, Senator Russ Feingold declared himself a fan and his songs were snapped up to soundtrack TV shows. Indeed, amongst a flurry of Bon Iver syncs over the coming years, 'Flume' and 'Blindsided' were used in *One Tree Hill* and 'Skinny Love' featured in *Grey's Anatomy* and *Chuck*. Director Judd Apatow also asked permission to use 'Skinny Love' in his film *Funny People*, but Justin took too long to decide and missed the cut. He was wary of giving the songs too much sync exposure though: "The album became a pretty personal thing for some people," he said, "and I just didn't want to be a part of ripping some of that away for anybody."[24] Justin hinted at a state of mind most likely to upset his freshly cast fanbase: contentment. "I was very sad and very lonely and now my family's doing really well and I'm in love. What happens now? I've done things that I've never dreamt of doing and I've kind of ran out of goals. So I'm kind of super happy."[25]

For a reminder of Justin's more maudlin days, though, those who bought the album via iTunes needed only to listen past the nine tracks to a bonus song on the download version. 'Wisconsin' was a churchy ache of distant misty guitars, harmonic whirlpools and a typically evocative vision of a couple reacting differently to their split. She went wild, dancing on bars and flirting with casual encounters; he, stripped of everything, retreated to a home in a cold climate, a place of security that was always with him: "That was Wisconsin, that was yesterday/Now I have nothing that I can keep/Cause every place I go I take another place with me". There was a tangible sense of timelessness to the track, echoing Simon & Garfunkel's acoustic wafts as much as ancient madrigals and ultra-modern alt.folk. If anything was worthy of following 'Re: Stacks', it was this.

Meanwhile, Justin himself was busy living his dream, happily playing the saddest songs to the world. Even if touring the globe brought its own host of frustrations.

★ ★ ★

Justin rooted through his day bag one more time, desperate. The $300 he'd be pissed about losing, the credit cards could be cancelled, but he was only a month or two from having to fly to Europe to embark on his first Bon Iver tour there, so he urgently needed to find his passport. And as for the Polaroids of him and Elizabeth, those were irreplaceable.

After a thorough search of the back room at the Parish venue in Austin, Texas where he'd been headlining a daytime party for NPR Music as part of the city's annual SXSW music conference, he admitted defeat. He'd been robbed. While he'd been out in the main venue someone had crept into the dressing room and swiped his wallet – cash, cards, passport, photos and all.

The robbery only added to Justin's feeling of unease at SXSW 2008. He wasn't comfortable with the crush of people, crowding him to small-talk their appreciation of one of the conference's hottest names. And no matter how in-demand he was, he still felt chronically uncool compared to the industry hotshots filling his gig and grasping for his hand, he felt intimidated by the atmosphere. *The Times* newspaper was in town to interview him and report on his packed Parish gig full of people singing along, but he'd rather have gone and bought himself a taco, called his dad to help sort out a replacement for his stolen passport and kept out of everyone's way. The news from home that they'd had four inches of snow on a day that

Austin was basking in glorious sunshine roused him a little. "Every so often it's nice not to have to cope with snow," he told *The Times*.[26]

He'd been on the road for a few weeks; the tour opened on February 21 with Black Mountain as touring partners* and it was a draining, tiring experience. Bon Iver had no sleeper bus, so they were making regular 30 hour drives eastward between shows in Washington, Philadelphia, NYC and Boston, blaring out the latest Black Mountain CD the whole way† and stealing whatever snatches of sleep they could. What's more, singing falsetto every night was causing Justin vocal problems that he was struggling to deal with. When he reached New York's Bowery Ballroom, a key stepping stone on the East Coast live circuit that Vernon played on his way up the coast towards a date in Montreal, the *New York Times* appeared to spot the emotional strain setting in, picturing him "in retreat, seated, hunched over and surrounded by keyboards and amps and guitars".[27]

Nonetheless, the gigs themselves were a joy to him – sold-out shows across the country, everyone singing his songs back to him – and Justin was enjoying exploring the songs more as they went, finding new depths to the opaque visual imagery of the likes of 'Flume' every time he played it. "I'm still discovering little niches and corners to hide in," he said, "those songs are still mysterious to me."[28]

"[Playing the songs live] stirs up the elusive emotions, for sure," he said. "They're definitely stirring the same pot of feelings [as I had while recording], but I don't just associate those feelings with that time. They go from way before I made the album, to all that's come after. The songs become this experience that I've been sharing with my bandmates. We've been trying to erect these songs as these singular entities, these things that come alive and exist just for that night, just for that moment in which we're playing them. It's almost like the songs I wrote were eggs, and now they're the cracked eggs, flowing and running and we're chasing after them."[29]

The downtime, however, was more trying. At times, after days of continuous social interaction, Justin's natural solitary instincts meant that he needed to get away from people and be alone in the van for a while. "I do enjoy quiet the older I get; the more quiet time I have, the better. It

---

* Other acts Vernon played alongside on the tour included Phosphorescent (who replaced Black Mountain for the latter part of the initial Feb/March tour), The Hollows, Nordic Nomadic, Quest For Fire and, at the Chapel Hill date, Megafaun.
† Bon Iver particularly loved Black Mountain's 'Stormy High'.

makes the other rambunctious periods a little more meaningful. And vice-versa."[30]

And now that his passport was gone, he'd face the opposite problem. When the tour hit San Francisco's Independent Club via Arizona and the Southern Californian coast cities, he was annoyed that he had to sit in his hotel awaiting news of its replacement rather than visit Golden Gate Park; similarly, in Portland, Oregon, before a show at Holocene, he couldn't go drinking with his friends there for the same reason. He was missing out on seeing the towns he was playing in and missing opportunities to spend time with the people he loved.

Once his passport issues were resolved and Bon Iver made it to Europe in May for shows supporting Iron & Wine at the Forum and Jens Leckman at the Scala, things appeared to brighten. The buzz in the UK was already deafening and Bon Iver's first show in London, supported by Laura Marling at the 100-capacity Social Club off Oxford Street on May 19, was rammed to bursting. "It came about because at the time I was really making an effort to keep on top of new music in a way I don't do any more at all," recalls Jack Lawrence-Brown, the drummer of White Lies who promoted the night as part of his Chess Club label activity. "There was a demo of 'Skinny Love' floating about, or maybe it was the album version, and he hadn't been to the UK yet. I went with a cold email to their booking agent and said 'how much? I love the track'. We booked it possibly three or four months in advance of him coming over and by the time that show came around he was actually a big deal and he seemed a little nervous. It seemed like a good venue for him to do that. I remember having my phone going the whole day for guest list and saying, 'It's just not gonna happen, it's full'. "Obviously it was going to sell out in a matter of minutes and it's got a really great vibe, you're really in the face of the audience. He did that thing, I think for 'Wolves . . .', where he comes out into the crowd and does the song completely acoustically without any microphone and it was just amazing. I was stood with my friends who I put the show on with and I thought, 'This is probably the best show I've ever put on here, he'll probably become a massive act'. I briefly chatted to him, he was such a gracious guy and his whole band were so sweet. To cram them onto that tiny little stage, you can't hide anything behind that and that's why everyone realised when they were watching that show that he was definitely the real deal, he can do everything he can do on the record but it's so much more immediate and exciting."

Similarly, in Paris the band played a tiny gig for an audience of 40 in an apartment in Abbesses emptied for what was called a Take Away Show, playing without amps or PA and using only instruments the organisers from La Blogotheque website had bought for them that afternoon – a melodica and glockenspiel, a minuscule toy piano. Rehearsing 'Flume' in a child's nursery – complete with tinkling toy piano refrains and an experimental interlude of guitar harmonics, knocks on the piano lid and rocking toys; and taking their stripped-back version of 'For Emma' all the way out onto the street, chasing a group of startled, if not terrified tourists through a cobbled square to sing it at them. It was a show Justin would describe as "incredibly special . . . a highlight, not just of the tour, but of our lives"[31]

Ed Horrox remembers a UK show on June 4 at St Giles Church in London that had an equally intimate impact. "It was really early days," he says, "he was building that initial first few fans, and this gig came at the end of that European run. It was relatively ambitious for that first run, it was a 400, 500 capacity space. It sold out and the excitement that people were feeling around that time, because it was clear by then that it was really special, meant that the atmosphere in the room was incredible. At the end of the show Justin and the guys came into the middle of the audience with an acoustic guitar and possibly sang 'For Emma . . .'. The audience sang along and that was incredible. So good live, lots and lots of great shows. A lot of joy in the room, a lot of very happy people having very moving experiences because the music was so good and he and his band were so good. A record that meant so much to people delivered live in such a profound, moving way that it was pretty emotional stuff."

Even though they were playing sold-out shows in Europe, their accommodation was sometimes borrowed. "I've got fond memories of the band staying at my house on the first tour," Ed recalls. "Justin in the attic, Mikey on the settee in the kitchen and Sean on the settee in the front room. All of the guys had their heads in their computers listening to music."

When Vernon returned home to Eau Claire after the first bout of touring to support 'For Emma . . .' he was keen to cement his links with the local artistic community. Having been turned on to the 'pocket party'

– the art of playing in houses and apartments, one of his first moves was to visit the house on Main Street in New Auburn where his author friend Mike Perry* was in the process of moving out. Over the previous five years Justin had spent many evenings in the house, making an album with Mike and having barbecues, and Mike had been a rock for Justin during his darker hours. So to mark Mike's departure he and a few musician friends paid a visit to make "an audio record of the house . . . we sat in the empty living room, in its magnificent reverberant glory and played a song that Mike wrote, called 'Sweet Edge Of Time'. It's safe to say this is one of my favourite songs. It's about waiting in the pines of Rusk and Chippewa counties, for a girl, until the sweet edge of time. We played numerous times, which was good, because it was too short to take in the energy of such a historic moment, for me . . . I felt like it was really special to be able to say goodbye to his house with him."[32]

He also reunited with Wisconsin itself. "Made Hobo's on the fire last night," he wrote in his Blobtower blog. "Banana Peppers, Perry's Pig's Bacon, Potatoes, Goat Cheese. Slept in Tent. Woke up. Stoked embers. 70 degrees and breezy. Made breakfast Hobo. Perry Bacon, Eggs, Potatoes, Sharp White Cheddar. You absolutely cannot fuck with Wisconsin summer. Fuck."[33]

When he wasn't reconnecting with old friends or spending the annual long weekend camping with his family on what's known as Sather Weekend, keen to remain the old down-to-Earth Justin he'd been before the tear-away success of *For Emma . . .*, he was inviting people over to his bungalow or hitting the YMCA to play basketball. "Nothing else seems so fluid," he said of the sport, his prime form of exercise. "It just shakes everything out. It's so good for your mind, because you don't think like you usually do. Your mind relaxes into this instinctive, reactionary zone. It's beautiful."[34]

When Vernon set out for two months of further US dates from July to August of 2008 he decided to take a small piece of home with him. So he asked Bowerbirds to support, and the party was suitably stoked. From the first show at Detroit's Crofoot Ballroom through 23 gigs in Canada,

* Author of *Population 485*, a book that, according to Justin's Creature Fear blog of June 19, 2008, "most specifically and devastatingly defines my admiration and deep relationship I have for and with Northwestern, WI."

Massachusetts, Maine and beyond, there were swimming pool parties in the early hours, massed choral versions of Rihanna's 'Umbrella' and a new drink called Yahtzee invented by the combined touring posse, swelled by sound engineer Brian Joseph and a new member of Bon Iver in the form of The Rosebud's touring bassist Matthew McCaughan. Each night Bon Iver would join Bowerbirds onstage to play a track called 'Lovin's For Fools', a glorious burst of vocal harmonies accompanied by a single acoustic guitar.

And the crowds, on this jaunt, had ballooned beyond all expectations. These were theatres, cinemas, churches and galleries rammed with hushed expectation and rapturous receptions. "I saw him at the 2008 Pitchfork Festival [in Chicago on July 20]," Stephen M Duesner recalls, "which was remarkable because he was on the smallest stage there and it must've been the largest crowd that he had played to at that time. I was backstage and I could see the crowd, an enormous crowd going back, I think they booked him on a smaller stage not realising how many people were there but he had a bigger crowd there than the headliners did, and they were all singing along with him. He's just got this enormous smile on his face, you could tell he was moved by this experience of having so many people singing along. I don't think he had any idea it had gotten that big yet."

In his breaks between live dates, though, Justin's guitar was rather less use to him. "I was writing and recording in the windows of time snatched between tours in support of *For Emma . . .*," he said. "When I finally came home to hunker down for a solid stretch there was a feeling of solid ground and an opportunity for liberation waiting in the space for me."[35] But he was finding that he couldn't write on guitar any more. "It feels really awkward," he claimed, "I need to be there working with the computer or looking at the tape or doing something with layers for me to get an idea that feels comprehensive out."[36]

"Somewhere along the line, I forgot how to write songs," he told *Rolling Stone*. "I couldn't do it any more with a guitar. It wasn't happening."[37]

"I didn't forget, I just couldn't write with a guitar any more," he said. "It wasn't speaking to me. I had to locate a new sonic space; people talk about their 'magic guitar' that they use to write songs – I don't have one of those any more – it takes more. It takes the studio and the gear and the microphone to have it sound the way that I need in order to write a song."[38]

"You know how there are people who have their guitars and they give them names like 'Old Blue', and it's like there are songs hidden in there or something?" he said. "Well I'd just lost that. I didn't have a guitar that did it for me any more. I had to go into the studio setting and find something that would help." His solution was to feed his electric guitar straight into the amp without any pedals to get the soft and dry Motown sound he admired, then mould the sound via pre-amps and a variety of microphones. "Then you get to a point where all of a sudden you're in that zone, the sonics of it are singing what you want the song to be, and it starts to write itself. No song really just got up in its fully finished form until many things were added to it. It's kind of a constructionist vibe."[39]

Deciding he didn't want his happiness to influence the next Bon Iver album and feeling like he was growing up and changing faster than at any time since he was a teenager, Justin vowed to "let it permeate"[40], to give himself a chance to listen to the ideas in his head and make sure he was creating the music he was meant to create. His strongest idea for following up *For Emma . . .* was to recreate the environment of the first album, to make the project a series of locations oozing their music. "I've had a lot of ideas but what I'm trying to do as a conscious move is I want to go in and record and write at the same time again," he said. "I mean I won't go to the woods or any crazy shit like that, but . . . I also like the idea of making a record rather than a bunch of songs. I want to do it all in the same time period so the songs come from a similar place."[41]

So instead of concentrating on the follow-up to *For Emma . . .* , in June Vernon completed a four-track EP that he'd started alongside the first album up in the cabin and finished at various apartments, studios and hunting lodges in the gaps between tours. It would be called *Blood Bank*, the title track recorded during the *For Emma . . .* sessions but left off the album as Vernon felt it didn't sit comfortably with the rest of *For Emma . . .* . "As much as *Emma . . .* is about the cold," read a Jagjaguwar press release about the EP, "the *Blood Bank* collection is about the warmth that gets you through it. You can feel the air move. Like a fire you've been stoking for hours and finally got to sustain itself, the heat blisters your face while your back is frozen solid."

The fictional story behind *Blood Bank* certainly didn't fit anywhere in the narrative arc of *For Emma . . .* . It told of a couple meeting at a blood bank, becoming snow-bound together in her car after their visit and starting an affair there. With its sense of familial warmth (the woman exclaims how similar the blood bags of the guy and his brother look "even in their plastic little covers", emphasising the closeness of both family and the 'brotherhood' of humanity at once) and its uncharacteristically happy ending (having kissed in the car, the couple are pictured many years later hearing their children stirring on Christmas morning), it was a dislocated scene from the gradual healing process of the album, although fans did read tribulations into it. They questioned why the pair were at the blood bank in the first place, and what was the "secret" that "fucks with your honour" and "teases your head", coming up with theories of terminal illnesses, pregnancies, paternity tests and the narrator having an affair with his brother's wife. All testament to the deep analysis Vernon's words were inspiring but the music, a cosy fuzz of electric guitar and non-falsetto pop hooks, was just as distanced from the *For Emma . . .* material, exuding warmth and positivity. "It just didn't seem to fit the story and lineage, I guess," Justin said. "So I just sort of surrounded *Blood Bank* with three other songs that were very different from one other, and they all kind of came together as a palate cleanser for the last record."[42]

First among these additional tunes was 'Beach Baby', a tangled saunter of slide guitar and maudlin acoustic that looked back to an idyllic tryst on a beach with an old girlfriend, from the perspective of a narrator watching her leave him.* A glint of deep-seated bitterness undercut Vernon's requests to the girl: "don't lock when you're fleeing/I'd like not to hear keys" and "tell your lucky one to know that you'll leave". Once the girl is gone, making no sound in the lock as a knell to the relationship, Justin reminisces about a bout of beach love-making, "put a tongue in your ear on the beach/And you clutched/Kicking heels". It was the pessimistic yin to *Blood Bank*'s fairytale yang.

The EP closed with two divergent experiments. First 'Babys' was an insistent and often discordant stream of high-range piano chords hammered out in the vein of Steve Reich's 'Music For 18 Musicians', over which Justin wailed a distinct ode to procreation. "Summer comes/To multiply," he sang. "I'll probably start a fleet/With no apologies . . . my woman and I know what we're for". Though there were hints that the life of a successful touring artist was possibly turning his head in the segment of the song where the chiming pianos cut out, leaving Justin's voice naked

* A true story, according to Vernon's live introductions of the song.

and exposed ("the carnival of scenes grows more and more appealing"), 'Babys' was a reiteration of Justin's homeliness and grounding, as well as his distant background in avant jazz. Finally 'Woods' took his experimentalist nature forward: an a capella piece fed through Auto-Tune to create a different, computerised form of haunting, a techno-mist of harmonising robot voices reciting four self-explanatory lines, written in his bedroom in North Carolina shortly before leaving for the cabin. "I'm up in the woods," the voices repeated 11 times, each round a more elaborate concoction of ghost-in-the-machine vocal whines, "I'm down on my mind/I'm building a still/To slow down the time". The still he was building could have referred to his alcohol intake or his need for quietude, and probably both, but either way 'Woods' was the perfect bridge between Justin's work on The Land and the new avenues of experimentation he wanted to explore with Bon Iver.

"When you crank Auto-Tune," Vernon explained, "you can use it really subtly, which is most of your pop radio vocal, to have a more accurate, normal human-sounding thing, but when you crank it up it just becomes this robotic thing that's no longer your voice . . . And much like all the vocals for me with this Bon Iver project, which was much different than anything I'd ever done before with the high singing and sort of femininity, that was just an experiment that I kept layering, and I was using another thing called Harmony Engine which you can get deeper vocal tones in."[43]

Some online bloggers criticised Justin for using Auto-Tune, however. "All these bloggers are going, 'Auto-Tune is evil and people in the folk realm shouldn't use it'," Justin said. "This has nothing to do with anything. It was inspired by an Imogen Heap song, it's not a comment on [Auto-Tune-leaning artists]. And even though blogs are tastemakers and have exalted a lot of bands that went on to become successful, there's this clique mentality that just . . . Look, if you like Bruce Springsteen, like him. Don't wait for somebody to tell you it's cool again to like him."[44] "This for me was a way to extend my voice or to experiment with different techniques, or just sounds," he said. "It was really freeing for me to do, and I'm really happy it's the last song on the EP."[45]

And to continue that exploration, Vernon was about to build himself a whole new home base.

CHAPTER TEN

The Veterinarium

T HE animal bones were the first to go. The remains of the sick pets and unsavable roadkill that still littered the 10 acres of ranch around an old veterinary clinic out in Fall Creek, south-east of Eau Claire, were gathered up and respectfully disposed of. Then the gangs of friends and band members would descend, a dozen at a time, to help with carpentry, removing old stainless steel surgery tables, fill in the old enclosed swimming pool attached to one side of the clinic to make a main recording room, or already start work on records amidst the wreckage and destruction.

Justin Vernon finally had the means and assistance he needed to build the creative music hub for the Eau Claire music community that he'd dreamt of since a teenager. Back then, his vision was of a shared old house full of music, laughter and inspiration; now he was watching a fully furbished professional studio, office and living space coming into shape around him. He'd call it April Base Studios and, for the next few years, all of Wisconsin would seem to revolve around it.

Justin and Nate, between them, had bought the disused clinic for $250,000 in 2008 and, excited to be a part of Bon Iver's idyllic musical commune, local bands rallied to help construct the perfect HQ. They filled in the pool, put felt on the walls and laid the new recording room with hardwood flooring that Justin had bought from a local middle school's gym in St Paul, Minnesota for $200 from Craigslist. Operating tables were torn out to make way for a production office and through a glass window from the recording room, a control room was created, where a huge wooden table sagged beneath the weight of Vernon's computers. The control room was Justin's personal den, slowly adorned with a cornucopia of memorabilia: a range of guitars hung on the walls between an enormous relief map of Wisconsin State, snapshots of Vernon's friends and an array of large oil paintings his father had painted in the Seventies during his research into the religions of the East – he dubbed the paintings "wild turkey people". Later, as the recording of Bon Iver's second album progressed, these paintings would be joined by the Gregory Euclide artwork commissioned by Vernon for the sleeve of the album; an isolated cabin in an icy landscape of real-life leaves and wood flakes. A glowering reminder of the origins of Vernon's new empire.

With visions of turning April Base into his own version of Dylan's Big Pink studio where his legendary *Basement Tapes* were recorded with The Band, Justin also set about constructing accommodation for the coteries of bands and artists that would come and go. A deck was built out the back of the clinic, a fireplace opened up in the front room and 12 sets of two-bed bunk-beds were put together by hand, allowing up to 24 sleepover guests. To give the place the ultimate homely feel he'd even rescue two cats from an animal shelter, the two-year-old Flo and six-month-old Melmon, and let them have the run of the place, batting at computers and constantly having to be shooed away from urinating on the Astroturf protecting the recording room's wooden floor.

"They are just weirdos," Justin said. "Totally mutt cats, but they have a lot of love and hunt and play outside. They live the high life. I'm really into my pets. They are a good thing to have around for your brain. It's good to take care of something other than yourself. I can't really have a dog with my lifestyle."[1]

"It's woody, it's comfortable, it feels like home," Justin said of the ranch. "It's not a sterile studio setting."[2] "It's a unique space and destination; it's our home out here. [It's] been a wonderful freedom, working in a place we built. It's also only three miles from the house I grew up in, and just 10 minutes from the bar where my parents met. When I finally came home to hunker down for a solid stretch there was a feeling of solid ground and an opportunity for liberation waiting in the space for me."[3]

When Justin returned from the last leg of his *For Emma . . .* tour in Europe he was tired but bristling from the experience. In September, as a single of the album's title track was released, he'd played at the left-field End Of The Road festival in the UK, blown away not just by the reception he got from the mud-smattered, welly-wearing UK festival crowds but by the setting itself, "a magical wonderland, set in the English woods, with white pianos in the middle of light/art installations in the forest"[4] and hanging out with Kurt Wagner from Lambchop. Bon Iver hung out with Bowerbirds in Amsterdam and watched punk kids juggling outside their dressing room window, soaking in the peaceful Dutch vibes even though his blog admitted "there can be days that are lonely out here". In Berlin, September 28, a short walk from the Berlin Wall, he lounged beside a river bank scrawled with the graffiti'd slogan 'I LOVE YOU TOO' and listened in raptures to the Land Of Talk album he'd helped make: "it stirs me, it makes me want to crush sh★t, it makes me LOVE rock music; find hope lining the strings of anger."[5] In Groningen, Holland on October 4, he was just as thrilled to find himself sharing a bill with John Hiatt at the Take Root Festival.

And on October 20, April Base still a focusing fuzz in his imagination, he arrived back in Eau Claire and threw himself back into town life, hitting Racy's for coffee, Egg Rolls Plus for carbs, The Joynt for cheap pitchers and the open country roads to suck in the Wisconsin fall air – "driving in the sun, the sumac red trees and golden mazes".[6] That weekend Vernon attended Sean Carey's wedding, sealing a blessed year with a fairytale kiss.

As he set to work buying and renovating April Base he knew there was nowhere else he could possibly set up his musical headquarters. "I definitely feel more closely knit to the fabric of people around here," he said. "This is where I'm from and it's where I plan on staying. It's so nice when you're a musician to feel like the fabric of an entire community, rather than just a part of a community of musicians. To come home and know that there are loggers and there are people that are actually doing hard work. Not that I don't work hard. It's just cooler to feel a part of that."[7] "I'm cool with being part of something bigger than me," he added. "That's what that house feels like as an opportunity."[8]

Even amidst the rubble of renovation, Vernon was itching to christen April Base with its first creative endeavours. He hatched a plan to record the Ticonderoga material he'd recorded as a split single with Bon Iver, but the scheme never came to fruition. At Halloween, with "bon fires" raging in the back garden, he set to work on his first remix offer, a reworking of Lykke Li's 'Dance, Dance, Dance', a slinky soul pop song that the pair had performed together around a fountain in LA in September as part of Lykke's series of online videos featuring herself performing with guest bands in unusual places and situations. Their video had Justin slapping his thighs with sleigh bells and wailing backing vocals and the Bon Iver band playing accordions and providing close harmonies as Lykke cavorted around with a plastic horn. "That was really fun," Justin declared at the end, and he was determined to capture the frivolous pop-up party vibe in his remix.

But his main ambition was to get the Eau Claire collective rolling, and he started by tying up loose musical ends. His first collaborative target was Thomas Wincek, whose records 'Customer' and 'Birds' with Collections Of Colonies Of Bees had had Vernon in raptures all year. He and Wincek had a smattering of old material they'd written together back in 2005 before DeYarmond Edison left for Raleigh, and Justin was keen to revisit it, revisioning it through the lens of the glistening sonics he heard in Collections Of Colonies Of Bees' latest offerings. Likewise, Wincek was excited by the idea of getting his avant electronic mitts on Justin's new Bon Iver aesthetic. "When I heard *For Emma* . . . I think people were hearing something different than what I was hearing," he said. "He got that comparison to Iron & Wine, but I always thought there was something weirder and more atmospheric about Justin's stuff."[9]

With COCOB – Wincek, Jon Mueller, Chris Rosenau, Daniel Spack and Jim Schoenecker – joining Justin at April Base, they became a brand new group, The Volcano Choir, and set about constructing an album that fall, the first of many April Base group projects. "It was a weird chance just to be a lead singer," Justin said. "Not having to do anything on the guitar, and not having to write any of the music, just sitting on top of music feels really good."[10]

The music they made together, pieced together into a nine-track album called *Unmap*, was a swirling, urgent post-rock stew. Justin's falsetto half-formed words, drifted across vowels, hiccupped over hooks, often acting as an instrument on an even footing with the others. Collections Of Colonies Of Bees provided driving, looping rhythms, dashes of cold electronics and galactic swirls of sound. 'Husks And Shells' opened the album with a deceptively familiar atmosphere for Bon Iver fans – a choir of heavenly male harmonies forming impressions of words over a sweetly plucked guitar. But Wincek twisted, reversed and looped these cabin atmospherics into an unsettling but beautiful machinated take on the *For Emma* . . . sound, an electronically manipulated deconstruction of folk music backed with the high-pitched 'beat' of a digital alarm beep. Then

'Seeplymouth' left familiar ground for more adventurous waters. It had an airy, repetitive sampled note as a backbone very similar to that at the foundation of Sufjan Stevens' 'Dear Mr Supercomputer', around which span cloudy organ chimes, weaving guitar trebles and fuzzy rock riffs, like a meshing net of noise. The appearance of Justin's voice calmed the growing maelstrom, seemingly cooing "all is summer" to a cascade of cymbal and military beats, but the relentless motoric gasp soon struck up again, joined by whines of machinery and a tumultuous noise collage resembling a subway train crashing, very slowly, into a Death Cab For Cutie gig.

After which, 'Island, IS', with its bright looping snippets of guitar creating a catchy electronic short-circuit melody and its comprehensible lyrics, felt like a radio hit. Justin was fascinated by Wincek's way of con-structing sounds, the way he'd take a snippet of Chris Rosenau's guitar and chop and loop it upon itself – or "cut it up and reassemble it", as Wincek would describe it[11] until it was barely recognisable, sounding more like a repeating flashback of a guitar, haunting the machine. It was a method Justin would learn a lot from, and try to incorporate into his next Bon Iver album, and for 'Island, IS' he brought one of his own Bon Iver techniques to the table, creating wild impressionist lyrics from the sounds that fell from his lips, drawn out by the tune. There was little sense to be gleaned from lines like "come and serve it with an omelette/And you're on it with the carpet/You solved it, said you're corporate/Set your orbit, set your coffin/Said it's often that your old fits/Are your old tits on your hard drive", let alone the earlier lines about catapults, the Reeperbahn and "a harbour mind in turpentine", but that wasn't the point. The point was the immaculate gelling of Rosenau's flittering micro-loops of butterfly guitar with Justin's circling rhymes, creating music that was as close to the intri-cate simplicity of nature as Vernon had yet come.

'Dote' was a far darker prospect, a drone of sampled monkish humming speckled with scatterbeats and awash with ambient industrial fuzz and Justin's paranormal wails, sparking images of cruel factories haunted by long-dead workers set on sabotage. Its deafening buzz finale gave way to a bout of metallic bouncing at the start of 'And Gather', a two-minute piece that developed into random clapping and esoteric synthetic meanders, held together by bursts of quite enthralling Beach Boys harmonising that was actually one of the album's more accessible melodic highpoints, despite the formless language. 'And Gather' sounded like a modern update of one of *The White Album*'s more avant garde moments, and made for the album's playful, brotherly centrepiece, the human heart at *Unmap*'s core. You could practically hear the giggles and bear-hugs.

'Mbira In The Morass' was an experimental free-form jazz noise painting of the kind Justin had indulged in before with DeYarmond and on his solo albums, but with a distinct, spooky mood and antique blues homage ingrained. As the Volcano Choir clattered random percussion out of bells, metal lids, chimes and what sounds like the creaking springs and winch of a jack-in-the-box turned scarily slowly, discordant toy piano chords and ghoulish plucks of taut strings, most likely played on an mbira*, made a contorted, mutilated melody. Over this Justin gave his best impression of Billie Holiday singing 'Strange Fruit', lacing this chilling four minutes with images redolent of the dark Deep South, demons and death: "beneath the willow . . . wild dogs around me howl and the moon burns my hands . . . fall at the lake, you're all alone". Like a werewolf's lonesome wail at a blood red moon, 'Mbira . . .' was the Portishead that only the seriously disturbed could dance to.

'Mbira . . .' was the first time since introducing his *For Emma . . .* falsetto that the soul element of Justin's voice had come so blatantly to the fore, an element that Ed Horrox believes would come to influence a new wave of electronic soul experimentalists. "There was a lot of soul in what he was doing, and I think that became clear later in his career. Other artists recognised that – people like James Blake, who sound a lot more like what you'd think of as a soul singer, were massively inspired by Justin."

At just over a minute long, 'Cool Knowledge' was almost like Volcano Choir catching themselves accidentally writing a pop song and stopping before anything too commercial happened. An ambient vocal drone was joined by a growled human bass beat and solid rock drums. A barbershop melody struck up, warping itself nasally out of tune like dive-bombing stukas as if to offset the conventional pop verse that Justin was singing behind it. Then the voices cohered into stirring harmony and the track stopped abruptly, just where the killer chorus would usually have been. Volcano Choir were never going to give their listeners such easy, basic pleasures as a traditional song structure; instead, they shift gears into 'Still',

* An mbira is an Eastern and Southern African instrument made of metal keys attached to a wooden board.

a reworking of 'Woods' from the *Blood Bank* EP with added organ drone, babbling brook guitars, metallic string taps and electronic glitches. Beneath Justin's Auto-Tuned vocals, Volcano Choir slowly built a cinematic cacophony of cavernous guitar echoes, pounding drums and resounding gongs that was anything but 'still'.

This mind-bulging post-rock parade closed with 'Youlogy', another experiment in classic blues and avant garde jazz, but where a eulogy looks back on a life worthily lived, 'Youlogy', in keeping with Volcano Choir's musical pioneering spirit, looked forward to one. A single oscillating whine and a few banjo plucks formed the backing to a modern spiritual, Justin's Billie Holiday voice singing grandiloquent snippets of soulful Americana – "my time, so long, look down that long, lonesome road where you and I must go" – expanding into distant gospel choirs as it floated through a melody inhabiting the emotionally charged space between 'Amazing Grace' and 'The Star Spangled Banner', and thus a melody intrinsically evocative of pride, honour, hardship and nobility. Despite all future lows or financial woes ("dollar man knocking on my door"), 'Youlogy' predicted that love would carry us through. A heart-warming human end to an album of cold, crisp, crystalline invention.

The album, which would reach number 92 in the *Billboard* chart on its release in September 2009 on Jagjaguwar, was a grand launch for April Base, bedecked with further cause for celebration. Amid the flurry of activity around the recording of *Unmap*, work stopped to avidly follow the election of Barack Obama as President, and share in the nation's tide of pride the following day – Justin posted a picture on his blog on election day standing next to a large US flag, and wrote "This is our time. We are entering our Golden Age. When we look back at this when we are old, we will know it as the time when America got its transfusion; with the red blood of the fore fathers of this young country and true patriots running through us again . . . Happy Election Day. Eau Bama".

Vernon had other unfinished business. In December 2008 The Shouting Matches finally played their first ever gig at the Eau Claire House Of Blues, Vernon glorying in the rough electric charge of his guitar and the deep, warm snarl of his natural voice. Those local fans unaware of Vernon's pre-Bon Iver work were blown away by the sheer muscle and thrilling brutality of the show, although The Shouting Matches' *Mouthoil* EP, despite much public demand, was still on the back burner where it had been placed to concentrate on Bon Iver's rise, and it wouldn't see the light of day for the foreseeable future. Unlike the track he began working on around this time for an AIDS charity album with Aaron Dessner of The National, a band he'd bonded with as his star had ascended, and who had seen immense potential in him.

"I think Justin's the Neil Young of our generation," Aaron's brother Bryce, also a member of The National, would say. "I'd go further, because he's combining good songwriting and very adventurous sonic production in a way that I don't think anyone else is doing. Usually, bands that are good at the sonic envelope are missing something in terms of writing actual songs. Justin does both things incredibly well."[12]

As the end-of-year magazine polls of the year's best albums rolled in, most featuring *For Emma . . .* in prominent positions, and Bon Iver rounded off 2008 with a final single from *For Emma, Forever Ago*, 'Re: Stacks', and a solid stint of live shows: in Dublin, London and the larger US cities, he found himself graduating to big theatres and music halls, seated venues of several thousand capacity. In NYC he was booked to perform 'Skinny Love' on the *David Letterman* show on December 11, a huge platform for exposure for upcoming alternative bands and a performance that Bon Iver watched that night on the screens of a bar next door to the 1,500-seater Town Hall where they were playing, insisting the jukebox was shut down and high-fiving each other and clinking beers as their individual close-ups appeared onscreen.

With a final gig at Eau Claire's State Theatre as a thank-you to the local fans who'd stuck with him throughout his rise, Justin ended the year in a state of serene shock and appreciation for the success that had landed in his lap.

"I feel extremely grateful and lucky and fortunate," he said. "There are so many things that have happened this year that, if any one of them had happened before, just one thing in one 10-year period, I would've considered myself lucky. So, it's been like this shining year, where the magnitude of it has been both constant and immense. I'm more than I can measure happiness with. I've gotten more than I've ever dreamt of. It's crazy. I think that all those years playing music, I never felt like it was hard, or like I was struggling. I was just happy playing music. Then, all of a sudden, this happened, and it far exceeded everything else I've ever done added together. I'm still reeling from that."[13]

Justin was, however, acutely aware of the weight being placed on the mythology of *For Emma, Forever Ago*, soon to be declared amongst the best albums of the decade by both Pitchfork and Stereogum, which ranked it number 29 and 11 respectively. "Whatever was special about that record got mystified into vapour at some point, almost beyond repair," he'd say. "It just got convoluted until it became bigger than what the original point was. I think what people reacted to was that someone made the choice to do that with their time but I also think people kind of made up what happened. Which is fine and romantic, but again there's a danger in mystifying things beyond truth. It's a problem with anything, like when they mystify the story of Jesus or whatever."[14]

He was already formulating ideas about the manner in which he wanted to create his next Bon Iver album though, and also the band he dreamed it might one day become. "The way I could see doing a band thing is if I was looking to put together like an orchestra," he postulated, "like two drum kits, five guitars and a French horn. You know if I wanted a specific vibe that I couldn't get by overdubbing stuff, and that's something I think about a lot 'cos I don't want to get into habits."[15]

The habits he meant, of course, were the need for isolation and misery in order to create universally moving songs. What Justin had to figure out was how to let that same inspiration come without the need for personal suffering. "Not everything in my life happened in those three months," he realised, "you live your life and you realise it's not that important."[16]

"I wondered about it for a second, you ask yourself the question: 'do I have to suffer to do this?'" he told *Stool Pigeon*, referencing his Religious Studies thesis on 'The Problem Of Evil'. "It's like 'why do good things happen to bad people?' and all that stuff. Then you get to the question of whether artists have to suffer, and it just seems to be a bullshit circumstance. Sadness just happens to be the easiest thing to get at, and that probably has to do with your brain or something. It's the easiest thing to realise that you're alone."[17]

"Part of what *For Emma* . . . meant to me was that it was an element of change," he said. "An autumnal sort of recycling of spirit or something. And I knew that what I had to do for the next album was simply make a record for me. And that it would be successful even if it sold five copies or no copies and I just gave it to my friends. That would've been successful to me."[18]

"I liked the process," he said of his cabin days. "I also don't want to recreate it, or invest in it as itself. I want to just take my attitude at the time and try to extend it, which basically means to keep growing and changing – two things I forgot to do from about the ages of 19 to 25. But, I have other stuff, folded down, and around in there, that I'll just try and excavate."[19]

The excavation would be a long one. There was just so much other stuff about to fold around him.

★ ★ ★

Sat at April Base early in 2009 – either alone for weeks on end or surrounded by bands and friends building beds, renovating rooms or filling the hallways with new music – Justin struggled to find a writing method that worked for him. It was almost as if there were too many possibilities, too many songs flying around waiting for him to catch hold of.

"I didn't feel like there was something I need to say any more," he mused, "which [gave] me a new-found freedom . . . that I never had before. The feelings are still rumbling away, but I don't know what they mean any more. I mean, I used to write songs like Neil Young or Springsteen, and who's to say that's not as personal."[20]

"I've always wanted this much room to work," he added, "but it is daunting. There were definite days where I felt like 'well, all right, I'm just going to have to try one of the hundreds of combinations of things in this room right now'."[21]

To kick off his writing process, he took inspiration from the way that Thomas Wincek had created the Volcano Choir tracks via his "glitchy, do-whatever-you-want vibe". Open to cutting, chopping and looping sounds to carve out the sound he heard in his head, Justin began writing by forming a soundscape rather than relying on a melody line, in the vein of the Volcano Choir sessions. He spoke of "de-construction/re-construction. It wasn't altogether different to *For Emma* . . . – that was the biggest change that I'd gone through sonically, songwriting wise, so the process didn't change that much between then and now – I just wasn't using an acoustic guitar as much. On this record I allowed myself to go in to a different zone . . . there was this vast, vague landscape you could go in to and not have any real idea what's going on, but somehow, at the very same time, know exactly what's going on."[22]

"The songwriting was sort of a part of some subconscious ramblings and attempting to discover new sonic space," he'd explain, "just trying to explore some new sonic space with different instruments and different ways of recording those instruments and seeing what I could come up with that way . . . Matt McCaughan and Sean Carey, I think, were there more in the beginning for me to help flesh out some of the drum parts. But I was playing some drums; I was playing some bass and keyboards and things like that, and also just experimenting with vocals the whole time."[23]

It would be a slow and painstaking process. Every song on the distant vision of a second Bon Iver album would take a year to complete, from start to finish, and Justin would only write 10 in total. The first to come (besides the already underway 'Perth') was a song called 'Minnesota, WI', a waft of saintly slide guitar and plucked banjo that Justin felt should be about his childhood and would ultimately grow the sort of jazz horns he'd first worked into Mount Vernon. Then, for four months, nothing. One lush and romantic early piece (eventually called 'Calgary') took the form, in Justin's mind, of a wedding vow to Kathleen Edwards, the folk singer whose songs he'd first sung his falsetto along to in the car, and for whom he clearly had great admiration and grand intentions. Should he ever meet her.

"I would always try to write songs like her," he'd later say. "I was never that good."[24]

Distractions flew thick and fast. There were press duties to perform to mark the January 20 release of *Blood Bank* for a start, and the inevitable questions about the pressures of following up *For Emma* . . . . "It does feel good to get something out, because it's been a while," he told about.com. "But it had nothing to do with pressure, because the only real pressure comes from me, really wanting to do it. People will have expectations, I know that. But I won't hear them, and won't allow them into my, um, 'worry centre'. I just don't think that's a good way to make music, with that sort of stuff in mind . . . A really powerful thing to do, if possible, is to not care about that; to go to a mental place that's only about making the music you want to play. I plan on shutting down that more 'aware' part of my mind . . . as my first album shows, a lot of it's about being in the right environment. I've got a house in the country, now, and out here I've got a little room set up, and I'll probably make it down there. I haven't thought about what's going to be on it, or what it's going to sound like. Eventually, I'll just sit down and fire off an album."[25]

"I was cool about it," he'd say of the pressure. "It didn't get to me. I just knew that I couldn't fail myself, that's all. I felt happy with *For Emma* . . . personally because I'd worked so hard on it and I let so much of myself subconsciously sink into it. I knew that I couldn't do anything less than that this time. That was the only pressure. I didn't feel any of the other stuff."[26]

Then there were more, ever greater numbers to digest. The *Blood Bank* EP hit the Top 40 in the UK and an incredible number 16 on the US *Billboard* chart, the same week that, on January 26, it was announced that 'Skinny Love' had hit the upper end of the countdown for the best 100 songs of 2008 on the Triple J radio station in Australia. A success cemented by Justin's first Australian tour that January, beginning (as his next album would) in Perth before wending across the country for a week, climaxing in four nights in Sydney, one of which was at the renowned 1,200 capacity City Recital Hall. The tour supplied at least one bizarre 'fan' encounter, as Justin described on his Blobtower blog: "A man just walked out of a coffee shop I am sitting outside of in a town at the eastern most point in Australia. A place of healing. He looked nervous, and came up to Nate and started to say something; I assume something like 'tell your friend after he takes his ear things off, you tell him. . . .', I could tell the way he was pointing at me and talking to Nate. So I took my headphones off and he said to me, almost as if he had a lump in his throat; this man was *notably* normal, 'just take it for what it's worth. im telling you. I don't want to clean up any body else's messes in this life. Okay?' Why did he tell me that?"[27]

And, most vitally, there was April Base's community of creative musicians to cultivate and encourage. Remembering his summers at jazz camp, he likened April Base to "a summer camp for friends that believe in the same stuff I do. We're these adults who get to continue living those weird childhood dreams of staying in a place and making records. It's cheap. It's easy. It just makes sense."[28]

Between the end of Bon Iver's Australian tour in January and the start of their scheduled summer dates and festival slots in May, Justin had four months to work on his own material, and collaborate with the Eau Claire music community, both home-made and external. On April 19, for example, Justin donned a white suit to join his old school jazz band once more, at a fundraiser for the Eau Claire Memorial High School Jazz Ensemble I's forthcoming trip to New York to compete in the Essentially Ellington Competition. The focus of the evening was the music of Duke Ellington and his peers, which the ensemble performed in their own early set – songs by Ellington, Juan Tizol and Benny Carter – before Justin joined them for the second half. Teasing the crowd with an instrumental take on 'Lump Sum', Vernon crooned through Ellington's 'Rocks In My Bed', Nina Simone's 'Since I Fell For You' and Ella Fitzgerald numbers 'Bewitched, Bothered And Bewildered' and 'Miss Otis Regrets' before pulling out one of his own songs, a rapturously received jazz take on 'For Emma'. By the end of the night he was dropping the falsetto and finger-snapping through Sinatra's 'The Lady Is A Tramp' and strapping on a guitar to play Mahalia Jackson's 'Satisfied Mind'. A live album of the event, titled *A Decade With Duke*, would be released in December, but it was a night that vibrated through the memory of anyone who saw it all year.

As did the pummelling African drum troupe who marched in front of Bon Iver and across the front of the stage as introduction to the rousing and ecstatic cover of Cole Porter's 'Don't Fence Me In' when Justin took the stage alongside The National, David Sitek and, centre-stage, David Byrne at New York's Radio City Music Hall on May 3 during the Dark Was The Night AIDS benefit show organised by Red Hot Organization. The show was the culmination of Justin's involvement with the accompanying *Dark Was The Night* compilation album*, a collection of songs and collaborations donated by a plethora of alternative superstars including The National, Grizzly Bear, Iron & Wine, Sufjan Stevens, Byrne, Feist and Death Cab For Cutie's Ben Gibbard.

Justin's contribution was two-fold. First, he gave the charity a brand new Bon Iver song for the album, 'Brackett, WI', a denser, grungier track than the *For Emma* . . . and *Blood Bank* material, all deep, distorted electric guitar thrums, Springsteen organs and a basement aesthetic lifted by Vernon's trademark angelic bursts of lush layered harmonies. The title directed us to the song's meaning like a rusted road sign: Brackett is a town just south of Fall Creek of just a few houses, a bar, a post office and

* Released February 16, 2009.

an abandoned school – so small the roads in and out were ripped up to widen the highway into Eau Claire. Just the sort of place Justin might drive through and see as a metaphor for an abandoned and wasted love, and so the song went: "Here we are rebuilding roads/Right by roosting towns/It's just like the love/The one that's never been enough". Peppering the song with images of the abandoned town – the first verse describes swings with their "bending ash"* seats worthy of old photos – and its mourning residents undertaking "the business of sadness" that's now the town's main trade – "And Fred had it wrong, Macy/Hon, he had it burned/now the curve in the county/Is Nana's urn" – Vernon conjured a place of loss and decay, but one he was "rebuilding roads" to, as if the "love that's never been enough" was worth revisiting. Indeed, having returned to it the chorus suggested Justin never wanted to leave – painting himself as a horse being held in sway by his lover's "twitch", he swore he'd "die along the ditches" if set free.

Vernon's second contribution was the track he'd written with Aaron Dessner especially for the project, 'Big Red Machine'. The track marked Justin's first chance to get fully orchestral, merging his wintry atmospherics with The National's knack with a keening chamber orchestra, welding together around insistent stabs of one-note grand piano. A delicate and elegant piece, its indistinct and impressionistic lyrics could be read to refer to sex, love, death and AIDS, as many other songs on the compilation did; the big red machine of the title representing the human heart beating its sorrow for "so many killed" by the disease and learning to endure the suffering of both illness and the fleeting nature of life – "the earth is only sand, fucked up and puked up in dismay". 'Big Red Machine' was a vital stepping stone for Vernon as Bon Iver, a sign that he was shifting away from personal dissection and introversion towards tackling grander universal themes.

The first major influx of musicians into April Base, meanwhile, also occurred in the early part of 2009. Justin heard from Ryan Olson, who was working on a collaboration with two members of Minneapolis sadtronica act Solid Gold, Zack Coulter and Adam Hurlburt, their new band working out of Olson's bedroom in Minneapolis. The idea of the

---

* Observant students of Vernon's lyrics will notice the start of an ash motif in the song here, culminating in the singings of autumn and the ash in Nana's urn.

band he was calling Gayngs sounded pretty intriguing – in love with Seventies and Eighties AM radio he planned to make an entire album of songs influenced by the layered synth choir of 10cc's 1975 number one hit 'I'm Not In Love'. "We just wanted to start playing some soft-rock music," Olson said. "I'd been listening to a shitload of 10cc and I was just like, yeah, I want to do something like this. Zach [Coulter]'s always had just a crazy awesome voice . . . We came up with a band name, and then the Friday after that Zach came over to my house and wrote what would be 'The Gaudy Side Of Town', the first song. The only rule was, I just wanted every song to be 69 BPM, so it could be seamless."[29]

It was just the sort of off-the-wall idea Justin was keen to explore, and when he heard that Brad, Phil and Joe from Megafaun had been roped in to contribute to the album, Vernon had all the more reason to get involved. He offered to add vocals to the songs and mix the record at April Base and by summer Gayngs had swapped their HQ from Minneapolis to Fall Creek and the halls of April Base filled with excited musicians and rang with soft rock cheese. Justin loved the chance to strap on a guitar and play squealing cock rock solos which Ryan would then drench in delay and drop into tracks in a cut-and-paste style that would influence Justin's own writing process over the coming years. While working up the sonic palette for 'Calgary', for instance, he would record the keyboard parts and then paste them over and over again onto the track to get the required effect.*

"Deciding to mix that Gayngs project was probably like the dumbest business move I ever made on paper," Vernon admitted, "but it taught me so much about how to mix my new record. Every time I've mixed a project, it's always taught me a lot more about how to hear music. So doing the Gayngs thing and doing the Volcano Choir record, all that stuff equally shared in the current information going into the new record."[30]

Plus, he loved the way Gayngs tackled such uncool music with a sincere love of the genre. "Gayngs is exploring this space that's fun, and there is such a difference between fun and funny," he said. "Olson is legitimately and sincerely into weird AM radio, and that was his whole idea with the

* Even then Justin wasn't happy with the first incarnation of 'Calgary'; it wasn't until the snare part was introduced that the track clicked, giving Justin the inspiration to write the guitar lines and bridge.

project. I deal with the folk-singer, guitar-guy scene, and he deals with this sense that people think he's a joke, which is much worse. Gayngs is not an ironic thing. It was in us."[31]

"It wasn't a joke for too long," Olson agreed. "It's definitely got a sense of humour to it, but it's not a joke album. It's not a Weird Al record."[32]

Over the course of summer and autumn of 2009, more and more acts found their way to April Base* to add contributions to the first Gayngs album, *Relayted*. Before they knew it Gayngs was a collective of 25 musicians including Ivan from The Rosebuds, Mike Noyce, Har Mar Superstar, Megafaun and various members of Doomtree, Roma di Luna, Happy Apple, Lookbook and Leisure Birds. It was a dream come true for Justin, who'd always hoped April Base would be like one big free-for all creative party with all his oldest Eau Claire friends.

"It was like being back in high school," says Solid Gold's Adam Hurlburt of one particularly populous three-day recording stint. "None of us had been in the same room together since high school. So it was just this insane experience. The music is sort of tongue in cheek, in a way. You know how you're not supposed to slap the bass, that's not cool any more? It's like just totally ignoring any social faux paus, slapping the bass and making it sound corny as hell. It was just this insanely fun three days, staying at Justin and Nate's house and doing that record and having so much fun with it."

"It's the most innocent thing you could ever think of," Vernon agreed. "There's a bunch of people not trying to do anything to make you impressed. They're doing it because it's fun."[33] The sessions also brought the concept of the 'guilty pleasure' to Justin's attention. "It made me realise how sounds had become political. It's not cool to have certain sounds on your record and I had no fucking idea. Like, I didn't even know that I was supposed to apologise for listening to Bruce Hornsby. It's dumb to meddle in those kind of questions, like, 'Is this cool or not?' I really don't give a shit about that stuff."[34]

"Typically, what happens is," Stef Alexander, aka POF, explained, "[Olson] has a skeleton of a song, which is a drum beat at a certain BPM, and maybe a couple little sparse synthesizer notes. And then, from there, he'll invite like two or three different bass players to come and play on top

---

* And to some sessions still held in Olson's apartment in Minneapolis.

of it. He'll listen to it and go through and cut out the awesome parts, and then put them in where he thinks they should be. And then from there, he gives it to the vocalists to see what they want to do with it. And a lot of people came, and the same thing happened – they sang a bunch of parts, and they sang a bunch of words, and he cut it up and arranged them into what the song would end up sounding like. So a lot of people who are on this record didn't know exactly what they did on the record until after – like, 'Oh yeah, I remember doing that.'"[35]

Relayted – essentially Olson's baby – would take a year of recording and mixing from start to finish before being completed, but the result would be an edgy updating of AOR. That first tune, 'The Gaudy Side Of Town', opened the album, based around a fuzzed-up human beatbox backing, Sade jazz synths and sultry Eighties soul saxophones, Justin adding a slinky wail of the title. Polite bursts of rhythmic static and modernist electronic fidgets kept the track lodged firmly in the 21st century though, a distant, less cartoonish cousin of Gorillaz, and it drained away to a bleak metallic wasteland march that became the cracked and desolate soul pop of 'The Walker', a kind of Dire Straits mood piece being bombarded with fire-crackers. Again, the closing minute of the track shifted mood; a warped deep-baritone rap bled into a sparkling icicle pop synth melody and Gayngs' most blatant homage to 10cc, a cover of Godley & Creme's 1985 hit 'Cry'.* The Gayngs version was distorted into a more sluggish drawl than the original, but otherwise captured its widescreen anguish and multi-layered vocal miasma perfectly.

Swapping between brittle piano stabs, Seventies soul organ, flamenco guitar and Kenny G-style saxophone, 'No Sweat' was an ominous and inventive soul ballad that pasted the misty vocal choir of 'I'm Not In Love' to trip-hop atmospheres and a lusty soul bellow to devastating effect. Just as devastating, in a very different way, was 'False Bottom', which seemed to find all 25 members bashing, blowing and beating away at their instruments full whack for the first minute, before a tribal rhythm and stuttering mechanical wail took control of the melee and guided it towards a danceable coherence.

---

* If Olson's intention for 'Cry' was to pay tribute to 10cc's 'I'm Not In Love', it was slightly off – the latter track was actually written by 10cc's other songwriting partnership, Eric Stewart and Graham Gouldman.

'The Beatdown' proved that Gayngs' mission wasn't just to emulate 'I'm Not In Love', they wanted to dive inside its rich sonic fug and frolic with wild futuristic abandon. The hyper-speed vocal Smurfs pioneered by Kanye West, the ethereal psychedelic world music of Animal Collective and MIA and the post-rock oceans of drone and distortion of Volcano Choir were all thrown into the stew, enclosed within a pulsating bubble of 10cc homage. This was exhilarating stuff, music focusing far beyond its quasi-comic concept, and as 'Crystal Rope' returned to the Eighties with its synthy slap bass and distorted cod-funk reminiscent of the yacht rock of Hall & Oates, Jan Hammer's 'Crockett's Theme' or Peter Gabriel's 'Shock The Monkey' – albeit attached to a deliciously downbeat gospel glisten capable of tugging the tightest heartstrings.

Descending into a marching band beat, 'Crystal Rope' segued into 'Spanish Platinum', a laid-back track coming on like Chris Rea in a wind tunnel, all canyon rock riffs, undulating saxophones and whistling dust-land sound effects. An Auto-Tuned Justin showed up towards the end, lilting a languid verse of incomprehensible sweetness before giving way to backwards guitar solos and a coda of buzzing electronic entropy. Thankfully 'Faded High' got the party started again, hitching itself to the Eighties revival bandwagon that had been gradually taking over electronic music for the whole decade in the wake of Daft Punk's *Discovery* album. But 'Faded High' was rather more ambitious than the three minute electro rehashes of The Human League, Roxy Music and Fleetwood Mac's 'Everywhere' that were becoming the norm. Clocking in at seven and a half catchy-as-hell minutes, it began as a subterranean NYC post-electroclash party pop tune full of amorphous she-bot vocal chants and wailing hair-rock guitar, and gradually pulled in more and more disparate influences: R&B, glitchtronica, shoegazing meanders and a sparkling psych-folk interlude led by Justin.

'Ride' took a more ambient hip-hop turn with its reverberating pianos, R&B clicks and galactic MIDI whines and the album wound up with 'The Last Prom On Earth', the smooch at the end of the universe. A futuristic prom scene full of romantic phase washes and Auto-Tuned backing singers, smacking of Psychedelic Furs, Billy Ocean, Barry White and a glitterball-speckled slow dance at the end of a Brat Pack flick, it included a spoken word declaration of undying love worthy of the cheesiest R&B and an air of ultra-fresh nostalgia. It closed an album which would eventually garner Album Of The Year plaudits* and be described as treading the "line between schmaltz and sincerity, between parody and earnestness"[36], although you suspect the fact that they managed to persuade Kevin Godley to appear in their recreation of the original face-morphing video for 'Cry' when it was released as a single was a far greater validation for Gayngs. A band that might have started life as a heartfelt homage from a dedicated trio to the MOR mush of their youth, but ended up as a gang-handed invigoration and celebration of lost AM arts, remoulded for the Animal Collective generation. "The most scintillating and daring record of the year so far," wrote *NME*'s Anthony Thornton, "Buy it. Play It. Get beaten up for being different."[37]

With such crazed larks and inspired music emanating from April Base, it must have been a wrench for Justin to drag himself away. But, come May 2009, The Road called again. Twenty-nine dates starting with some warm-up theatre shows in the US and a smatter of shows in the UK and Germany – one at an indoor festival called All Tomorrow's Parties held at a tacky Butlin's holiday camp in Minehead – before the festival season kicked off in earnest.

For the next three months he'd zig-zag across the Atlantic almost weekly: from the enormo-fest of Bonnaroo Festival in Manchester, Tennessee, to the sedate environs of the Serpentine Sessions in London's Hyde Park and back again for a string of dates in Utah, Colorado and California. July 25 he was in England for the kiddie-friendly Camp Bestival festival, on August 7 he was in Chicago to play at Lollopalooza, on August 12 he was in Oslo to hit the Scandinavian festivals. There was a solid stretch of European festivals to cover towards the end of the summer – Pukkelpop in Belgium, Haldern Pop in Germany, Summer Sundae in London, Lowlands in Holland, Green Man in Wales – but perhaps the most satisfying run of shows on this summer 2009 tour were the three in California mid-July. At Santa Barbara's Grenada Theatre, Fresno's Tower Theatre and Saratoga's Mountain Winery, Justin played alongside The Indigo Girls, finally part of the gig that had changed his life aged 14.

In songwriting terms, though, the tour was a frustration. The sounds he was creating for the next Bon Iver album were constantly stirring around the back of his mind, needing to be excavated, but he could do no

* *Relayted* was voted Album Of The Year by *Guardian* critics in 2010.

166

on-the-road recording, he needed a studio environment to work up his soundscapes. He had the bare bones of the songs in place but he was "looking for texture". "With all the touring and distractions going on, I would get a sound together but I wouldn't have time to work on it," he said. "So I sat on the road with these sketches and saw how they revealed themselves emotionally."[38]

Instead, he wrote lyrics, working on the words for 'Calgary' every day while on tour and grabbing any spare time between gigs and Gayngs sessions to settle into his April Base studio nook, ram on his headphones and let the sounds he was making suggest words to him. "I actually worked on the lyrics on this album for much longer," he said, "over the course of years, to get them right, and to get them right seems strange because they always read like I've just stopped in the middle of writing. But, somehow, each song is complete in that way."[39] "I had to work backwards in a way, the lyrics sort of came as the melodies and songs came together."[40]

"With this new record, I attempted to build odd landscapes that you could exist in that had weird feelings but also cool-sounding words," he said. "I really wanted to go deep – I went as far as writing out words on the page and making sure they looked good, reading-wise."[41]

"I've made this weird choice to write songs from this more subconscious place. It's kind of deciding on basic brain boundaries, to only come up with lyrics that come super weirdly, or just by sound, and I've learned enough by doing that to end up writing songs that mean something in a more elusive or opaque way, that makes it prettier."[42]

The songs were still elusive, unformed; like 'Perth', 'Calgary' and 'Brackett, WI', they seemed to be cohering around places, each song redolent of a city, a building, a place in history or a geographical metaphor for a state of mind. But to make the second Bon Iver the masterpiece it needed to be, he'd have to flip his working method completely, from micro to macro, from hermetic to expansive.

And the key, the spark, would come in the form of the most unlikely phone call ever.

CHAPTER ELEVEN

Pure Fantasy

THE rap superstar awaiting his response, Justin mulled over the strangest offer of his life.

Mid-January 2010, Eau Claire deep in the clutches of mid-winter, April Base as cut off as a coffin. Would he leave this freezing hub, his comfort zone, his home, and fly off to Hawaii to record music in the ultimate luxury with some of the biggest names in rap lounging around the top-of-the-range studio?

"I was in New York in January and I got a call from my manager," Justin said, "and he said Kanye West wanted to maybe use 'Woods' as a sample. I was like, 'Yes'."[1]

The trip to Hawaii, however, Justin had to give a moment's thought.

It wasn't that he was wary of collaboration by this point. Besides his work with Volcano Choir and Aaron Dessner, his live appearances with David Byrne and the ongoing recordings with Gayngs, he'd also recorded a song in 2009 with rising multi-instrumentalist singer-songwriter St Vincent called 'Roslyn'* for the soundtrack to the latest instalment in the *Twilight* movie franchise, *New Moon*.

"I don't know those films and the little bit I've seen was pretty unwatchable," Justin said of the sync. "And, to be honest with you, I said no to that because I don't really jive with that shit. But, the next day, I was working on this song and I thought 'Shit. This sounds like a fucking emo-vampire-song.' I was feeling really weird about it, but driving down this country road in the middle of nowhere I saw this farm girl and she had iPod headphones in; she was wearing a *Twilight* T-shirt and I decided: 'I'm doing it.' People don't read Pitchfork or read music magazines to hear

---

* Coincidence or not, in keeping with the place name theme of Justin's songs at this point, Roslyn is the town in Washington where *Northern Exposure* was filmed.

about bands – I heard about Dinosaur Jr for the first time because of *Wayne's World 2*."[2]

Revolving around a spectre of acoustic guitar and mist-shrouded throbs of slide guitar, there was certainly something supernatural about 'Roslyn', St Vincent's heavenly wisp melting effortlessly into Vernon's many-headed vocal chorus. Mirroring a scene in *New Moon* where heroine Bella leaps from a cliff's edge, the song seemed to tell of a woman's suicidal plunge, "Dancing around/Folds in her gown/Sea and the rock below/Cocked to the undertow/Bones, blood and teeth erode/They will be crashing low". He even slipped in vampiric images for the full *Twilight* effect: "Wings wouldn't help you . . . when did this just become a mortal home?" With a song on the soundtrack of one of 2009's biggest teen-friendly movies, it clearly wasn't concerns of mainstream commercialism that gave Justin pause, the rapper still on the line.

Nor was it a fear of immersing himself in the darkest of themes. Towards the end of 2009 he'd also collaborated on a folk opera concept album by Anaïs Mitchell called *Hadestown*, the hour-long story of Greek hero Orpheus' travels through the underworld to rescue his stolen lover Eurydice. Mitchell had been working on the project for three years before coming across the perfect voice to play the role of Orpheus.

"I got asked to open one of Bon Iver's tours in Europe," she says. "The very first night of the tour, when I heard Justin sing 'Re: Stacks' in this beautiful hall in Newcastle, my heart exploded, I thought, 'He HAS to be Orpheus.' I wrote Todd Sickafoose [the producer] and Michael Chorney [who wrote the score]: 'He is the Orpheus of the century!' But I had to have a stern little talk with myself that night, I was like, this guy doesn't even know you, he's already doing you a huge favour having you on the tour, you can't ask him now, you might weird him out, wait till the end of the tour and THEN ask."[3]

On only the second night, though, Anais made her move. "We were on a ferryboat from Scotland to Norway and I had a couple glasses of wine and I couldn't bear it any longer, I'd been thinking about it all day, I just blurted it all out in a rush, 'the opera, the record, will you please, please, please be Orpheus?' And Justin just said, 'Yes'."[4] *

* Also on this European jaunt, Justin stopped off in Prague to visit Trever Hagen, keen to stay connected with his oldest musical collaborators no matter how big he got.

Though most of her work on *Hadestown* took place in her Brooklyn studio, on Justin's request Anais travelled to April Base "in darkest winter" to record him singing the part in his natural baritone. "I'd teach him the melodies, then go out of the room and cook or read or whatever so as not to weird him out by hanging around," she explains. "I'd hear him from the kitchen, but just one part at a time, one line at a time, so I was pretty clueless until he'd say 'OK!' and I'd run back in the room to hear the symphony of harmonies and countermelodies he'd created. He's such an intuitive guy, he hears everything in his head, I think I saw him go to the piano ONCE to work something out. There was this one song where he sang some syllables, not words exactly, just sounds, they definitely weren't part of the lyrics, and I was like, 'hey man umm . . . what are you saying there?' and he said, 'I dunno! It just felt right' and I was like, 'OK we'll keep it!'

"I love the idea that Orpheus, the son of a muse, able to make stones cry and milk flow from virgins' breasts with his singing, is able to sing with many voices at the same time. When Todd and I went through Justin's vocal files back in Brooklyn we came up with little names and numbers for his different voices, 'cos they're so different, his low ones are so manly and sensual, and his high ones so ethereal and emotional, and the combination, to me, is a very Orphic thing, emotional manhood, I love it."[5]

Hadestown, which also had prime roles sung by Ani DiFranco, Greg Brown and The Haden Triplets, would become a critical hit, scoring maximum marks from reviewers at the *Guardian* and Drowned In Sound. So plunging into the depths of darkness wasn't a concern to Vernon as he considered the bizarre offer. Darkness sold.

No, Justin's only worry was the idea of dislocation. He was just settling in to working on his own album at April Base and, while he was very keen to snap up this new offer, he wondered if Kanye West might come to record in Eau Claire instead.

"Can't you see if he wants to come here?" Justin laughed. "I don't know why I said that. It was kind of dickish."[6]

Dickish or not, Kanye agreed. A flight was booked, Kanye was coming to Wisconsin in January, the rap royalty state visit of the century. "He was literally on his way," Vernon laughs, "and we were like, do we have to make the beds? Should we order pizza? We don't know what to do!"[7]

Inevitably, the Wisconsin weather intervened. A snowstorm saw

Kanye's flight cancelled, and there was nothing for it but for Justin to head to Hawaii and party rap megastar style. "He called the next day and said, 'Why don't you just come here? It's, like, nice.'"[8] "We ended up talking for a half hour about music and how we were fans of each other and *Avatar*. It was a really pleasant, easy-going conversation between two people that are pretty psyched about music." How had Kanye heard of Vernon? "This guy Jeff [Bhasker] who plays keyboards and writes a lot of the music with Kanye told me he showed Kanye my shit. He's like, 'My fucking girlfriend wouldn't go see Kanye play 'cause she went to see you at Town Hall in New York. I had to find out who this asshole was so I looked you up.' But I think [producer] No I.D. had something to do with it, too . . . [Kanye] was like, 'I like how you sing so fearlessly. You don't care how your voice sounds. It'd be awesome if you could come out to Hawaii and hear the track, and there's some other shit I think we could throw down on.'"[9] "I surprised myself by not being nervous or apprehensive," he said. "I said, 'When should I come out?' And he was like, 'How about tomorrow?'"[10]

The clash of genres held no fear for Vernon. "Genre is not important to me. I liked Kanye's music so it made sense for me to work with him, even if on the outside it seemed odd. Working with him wasn't difficult and it wasn't challenging because it wasn't my music, it was his."[11] "It seemed like a match made in heaven to me," he added. "I've really been a huge fan since 'The College Dropout'. Working with him made a lot of sense."[12]

The scenes he encountered when he reached Kanye's compound studio in Oahu, Hawaii were the stuff of a stoner surf bum's dreams. In what the *New York Times* would describe as a "luxury sleepover", Kanye West was piecing together what would become his fifth studio album, *My Beautiful Dark Twisted Fantasy*, surrounded by a swirling collective of rap's biggest names – Rick Ross, A-Trak, Jay-Z and Nicki Minaj would wander in and out of the studio at random – and Kanye's 16-hour working days would be punctuated by breaks to go jet-skiing or play basketball. Staying at Kanye's house on the island, Justin would shoot hoops and share breakfast with him, amazed to find him so down-to-earth and knowledgeable about Vernon's music. "He was into what I was doing; he would sit me down and talk to me about the lyrics to *Blood Bank* and I was like, 'Who are you, man?' He's a good fan and just like anybody. He just gets put in to a rap

171

genre; he is a rapper and he wants to make rap records, but he's smart."[13] "I think he liked that I had a similar emotional approach to music, and that I used Auto-Tune as a kind of texture. It made sense."[14]

Inspired by how "chilled, concentrated and hard-working"[15] Kanye was, the first week that Vernon spent at the Oahu studio was spent exclusively working on the track that Kanye had forged out of his sample of Vernon's 'Woods', called 'Lost In The World'. "He plays me the track and it sounds exactly like how you want it to sound," Vernon recalls, "forward moving, interesting, light-hearted, heavy-hearted, fucking incredible sounding jam. It was kind of bare so I added some choir-sounding stuff and then thicked out the samples with my voice . . . We were just eating breakfast and listening to the song on the speakers and he's like, 'Fuck, this is going to be the festival closer.' I was like, 'Yeah, cool'. It kind of freaked me out."[16]

With Justin adding new vocals to the crunching hip-hop rampage that Kanye had constructed around his sample of 'Woods', they bonded firmly over that first week of working together. "He's such a spirited dude," Justin said. "We would have political conversations and there'd be all this arguing back and forth. No one else there was afraid to say anything. I think he's very aware of the person he is, and I applaud him for that. It takes a lot of strength just to *stay* how he is amongst all the shit that he's subjected to. But I found him extremely like a bro. You could talk to him about whatever."

The pair exchanged viewpoints and ideas, shifting each others' perspectives a little. "Kanye hates the word 'humble'," said Justin, "and after I spent time with him, I don't use that word any more. He got really angry with me and asked me, 'Have you ever looked at the definition of that word? It's borderline self-loathing'. It really made me think. I don't want to be humble. I want to have humility."[17]

"After that first week he was like, 'I want you to come back'. So I came back a few weeks later and it was the same kind of thing, throwing ideas around – there are a bunch of other songs I'd just throw down on, write a little hook, whatever. In the studio, he was referencing Trent Reznor, Al Green, the Roots – the fucking awesomest shit. It made total sense to me."[18]

On his second trip to Hawaii, Justin requested a separate studio to work in "because I'd do so much overdubbing to get my ideas out. So I ended up recording in this tiny back room, and then Kanye would come back and listen to what I came up with, and then we'd work on changing the lyrics. We'd just sit there and collaborate. It was fucking fun, man . . . some of the stuff I was doing with my voice was more weird and instrumental – basically building what would sound like a synth part with vocals. I felt very much like a session musician, and that was really cool, too."[19]

Another brand of freak-out Justin encountered was having rapper and Maybach Music Group founder Rick Ross smoke joints throughout his recording sessions. "Rick Ross would just be sitting there a lot of the time while I was working on shit, on a piano bench right behind me, smoking blunt after blunt after blunt. In between takes, he'd inhale and then say real quiet, 'That was good, homie.' I'd be like, 'OK! I'll keep going!'?"[20] "I was literally in the back room rolling a spliff with Rick Ross talking about what to do on the next part of a song. It was astonishing. Kanye came back and was like, 'Look at you two guys. This is the craziest studio in the Western world right now!'

"There was one night where I was in the control room with the engineer and John Legend was in the sound booth singing along to something that I did. It was just like, 'Holy shit, man. There's John Legend in there singing like a motherfucker."[21]

Over three week-long trips to Kanye's Hawaii complex, Justin recorded vocals for around 10 more tracks for Kanye's album, of which one made the cut. After verses from Kanye, Jay-Z and Nicki Minaj exposing their inner beasts, Vernon's treated metallic voice took the final verse of the pulsing tribalist 'Monster': "I crossed the line/And I'll let God decide/I wouldn't last these shows/So I am headed home". Four lines that, along with his Auto-Tuned treble on 'Lost In The World', would grant Vernon a whole new level of crossover credibility, make him the indie rock name to drop in hip-hop circles.

But besides the rap kudos, what Justin took most from his visits to Kanye's studio was a sense of creative openness, a joint effort. "I watched how they were willing to see so many ideas through and allow the weirdest things into songs," he recalled. "Things that might not work initially, but that you could ultimately twist and contort into working. I watched them direct more than I watched them play."[22]

From the Kanye and continuing Gayngs sessions, Vernon realised that anything was possible in his music, and that collaboration was definitely preferable to isolation. So back in April Base, cushioned from outside pressure with only the Gayngs album mixing and a few Bon Iver live dates to get in the way, Justin filled the studio with all manner of instruments to use on the record, opened his mind to every genre from Bruce Hornsby to Charlie Mingus and Oxford shanty-folk troupe Stornoway★ and knuckled down to the second Bon Iver album, taking a far more open-armed approach, both stylistically and in terms of allowing other musicians in. Amongst the first to be invited to contribute were pedal steel guitarist Greg Leisz, Arcade Fire saxophonist Colin Stetson and saxophonist Mike Lewis.

"I think in that way I was emboldened by seeing how Bryce and Aaron [Dessner] work in their life and also how Kanye worked: 'I want that – get that. I want an 80-piece orchestra – get it'. And I guess I was just like: 'Oh, I can see now! I know my two favourite saxophone players in the whole world, so why don't I get them in the same room?'"[23]

"I brought in a lot of people to change my voice," he'd tell *Rolling Stone*, "not my singing voice, but my role as the author of this band, this project . . . I built the record myself, but I allowed those people to come in and change the scene . . . I always had a dream to be that sort of student of Neil Young, one of those people who can sit down and write a song and have it be this full statement and sound good. I just don't think I'm as good at it as those people, frankly, and over the last few years, I've adapted."[24]

"I like getting other people's brains in the process," he added. "I've brought other people in to help me try to change the landscape. I already knew what I wanted from them – it's more like me trying to author or direct."[25]

In all, over the course of 2010, Justin would work with 10 other musicians: Leisz, Stetson, Lewis and Sufjan Steven's brass player, C.J. Camerieri, added musical passages; Noyce, Carey and McCaughan provided vocals, Wincek and Schoenecker from Volcano Choir did the 'processing' and The National's orchestra guy Rob Moose acted as string arranger. Vernon flew musicians in to Eau Claire from around the country to help him work up the sounds in his head – the warm Neil Young distortion fuzz he

★ Whose debut album *Beachcomber's Windowsill* Justin's blog claimed he'd had on repeat for days at a time.

wanted for 'Perth', redolent of the sounds he'd helped Land Of Talk construct, or just letting the pleasure of making music with the best players in the world sweep through him. "It was more about just exploring feeling in general rather than some specific hook-up that I had," he explained.[26]

"Bon Iver is often equated with just me," he'd say, "but you are who surrounds you, and for [the second album] I wanted to invite those voices as musical catalysts."[27]

The big name collaboration offers didn't stop pouring in either. In February 2010 Peter Gabriel had released an album of orchestrated covers of songs he admired on an album called *Scratch My Back*, the concept being that he would ask the acts he'd covered to cover one of his songs in return for an accompanying album, *I'll Scratch Yours*. One of the songs he covered, with immense opulence and grace, was 'Flume', and Justin was accordingly invited to cover one of Gabriel's songs in return. As the likes of Radiohead, Neil Young and David Bowie dragged their feet over recording one of Gabriel's songs, he instead decided to release double A-sided singles on every full moon in 2010 as the covers came in, and on March 30 Gabriel's lush version of 'Flume' hit independent record stores backed with Vernon's gorgeous take on Gabriel's 'Come Talk To Me', a six-minute slab of glorious bombastic pop full of bagpipes and tribal drum cavalcades that Justin had brilliantly reduced to banjo, synth and glacial harmonies without losing any of its powerful melodic impact, adding muffled drum circles, Soweto guitars and strings to create a sepia memory of the original. Despite being so busy with his own album and side projects, Vernon simply couldn't turn down the chance to work with the true legends.

There was one megastar Vernon very publicly declined to work with though. On May 14, shortly before Shouting Matches performed another rare show in Altoona, Wisconsin*, the entire cast of Gayngs gathered together for their first gig, the CD release show for *Relayted* at Minneapolis' First Avenue venue, billed as The Last Prom On Earth. Ramming the stage with contributors to play the entire album in order, plus a final cover of Howard Jones' 'No One Is To Blame', it was like the indie psych circus had come to town – balloon drops, prom decorations and a free-for-all, punch-drunk atmosphere. It was "more like a play than a

---

* On May 29, rumoured to be the band's last ever show.

regular show," Olson exclaimed.[28] "We've got a shitload of balloons, a shitload of gossamer, a shitload of streamers. We're just going to try to make it as gaudy as hell. Try to fuck that place up."[29]

Throughout the carnival show, diminutive local Eighties funk superstar Prince stood in the wings, angling for an invitation to join the band onstage. But Justin, and the rest of Gayngs, simply ignored him. "I'm a huge Prince fan," says Justin. "But I've never told anybody this. When I heard he wanted to come, I thought, 'fuck that'. Like, he doesn't know how to play our songs. He's a good musician. He's probably the best guitar player ever. But Gayngs is already hanging on by a thin thread, and this was Gayngs' 'Last Prom on Earth' show. I'm sorry, but it doesn't matter who you are. I just didn't want our time to be eclipsed. And, like, everybody's gotta suck Prince's dick, because he's Prince. We didn't need Prince to be there . . . He was standing right next to my brother on the side stage. Mikey, who plays in Bon Iver, too, talked to him and said, 'Hey, man, use my amp. Plug in.' I was just drinking Pabst. I was indifferent. It's not my show to run. We definitely didn't tell him he couldn't come up there. But I think we fucked up and didn't roll out the red carpet or something."[30]

And with the music now pouring out of Vernon at a far more tumultuous rate, he sure didn't need Prince piggybacking on his talent . . .

★ ★ ★

Fast-forward, as so much of Justin's life had, to winter. Alone in an empty studio room at April Base, Justin listens to the playback of the last vocal take, hangs up his headphones and weeps. Bon Iver's second album was complete, ending as it had begun, with 'Perth'. Once he'd regained his composure, a more celebratory stamp would be put on the finishing of the album: a cork-board was hung on the studio wall pinned with Polaroids of everyone who'd worked on the album, in the centre a piece of paper with a lyric from Lucinda Williams' 'Fruits Of My Labor' scrawled on it: "I FINALLY DID IT. I GOT OUT OF LAGRANGE".

"She sings this line ''cause I finally did it baby, I got out of La Grange, got in my Mercury and drove out west'," he'd explain. "She's actually explaining the end of something which is actually the beginning of her life. When Lucinda got into the Mercury and drove out west, she was burying the stranger inside her."[31]

Vernon's own road had been long. Three full years since he'd first immersed himself into 'Perth', his alchemy of soundscapes honed and heated in snatched days, weeks and months between his vast array of offshoot projects. The final months of the album's creation, over the second half of 2010, had been no less busy. So busy in fact that, in the summer of 2010, it was clear that Bon Iver had gotten big enough and global enough to need more hands on the management decks, to bolster the organisational and decision-making end of the project. So Nate, who'd now moved out of Eau Claire to Minneapolis, stepped up to a co-manager role alongside Kyle.

Nate had had a formidable swathe of projects to oversee. In June, Vernon contributed a cover of 'Bruised Orange (Chain Of Sorrow)' to a John Prine tribute album, *Broken Hearts & Dirty Windows: Songs Of John Prine*, for which he also wrote sleeve notes; his cathedral choral effect slipping effortlessly onto Prine's misty mountain folk in what Justin would describe as "top of the list" of his life's ambitions. In September, with just a week's rehearsal, Justin was invited to join Megafaun for a series of three shows at the converted church venue Hayti Heritage Center at Duke University in Durham, North Carolina, to cover songs from a series of 1959 field recordings of classic blues and folk tunes by ethnomusicologist Alan Lomax called *Sounds Of The South*. Backed by the jazz big band Fight The Big Bull and accompanied by folk chanteuse Sharon Van Etten, the shows – all recorded for an as-yet-unreleased live album – were a richly rewarding chance for Justin to play with old friends and honour the American roots music he loved, as well as further proof that collaboration was now his most comfortable form of musical expression. "Vernon took a soulful lead vocal on Fred McDowell's 'When I Get Home'," wrote one reviewer, "backed by a heavily bearded trio of R&B-style backup singers who might consider a side career as 'ZZ Pips'."[32]

Then there was the chaos of Gayngs' first ever tour that September, to mark the release of *Relayted*; 10 dates over September and October, a touring dervish of clashing and merging musical tastes that bowled its way towards disaster. After nine successful shows straddling the States from Chicago to Nashville via Boston, New York, Washington and Toronto, it was due to wind up with a celebratory set at Austin City Limits festival on October 10. But at 4.20 a.m. on the morning before the Austin show, the band noticed that their tour bus had gone missing, along with all of their equipment and on-the-road personal possessions. The driver was out of contact; they reported the bus stolen. But the next day the truth emerged; since the band were a few days late in paying the $6,000 bill for hiring the bus, the owners had told the driver to bring it back to base in Nashville[*], where all of their stuff was now being kept. Feeling, as they put it, "insanely bummed out", Gayngs cancelled their show at ACL and Justin flew to Nashville to settle the bill.

"While it is totally 'Gayngs' to not pay bills," Justin wrote on Blobtower, "we were given no warning of our gear being taken and it was absolutely our every intention to pay our bill. Matter of fact, me and Lewis just paid it. In person. In Nashville. Flew there this morning. None of that changes the fact that our gear WAS stolen. And taken hostage. And caused us not to be able to play. Gayngs' feeling were fucking totally crushed; and tears were shed when we had to cancel what was possibly our last show ever."[33]

More successful was Volcano Choir's first ever tour, in the wake of Justin guesting on a track set to appear on the debut album of Wincek's latest band, All Tiny Creatures. 'An Iris' featured Justin's electronically treated, lower-register vocals careening over a math-pop swirl of chopped-up guitars, itself inspired by the Volcano Choir project. "Volcano Choir was kind of a catalyst because I saw how well those songs were working with vocals," says Wincek. "I started thinking about vocals and began asking my friends, who happened to be great vocalists, if they'd be down with recording for the album. Sometimes, I'd give them a little direction and say where I wanted to go with it. Or other times, I'd just let them go off. Justin was one of those people."[34]

The Volcano Choir tour of 2010 would frustrate US fans of the band since, for their first outing, they opted to play only in Japan. Arriving on November 5, they performed four rammed shows, two in Tokyo's O-West club in Shibuya and two more in Nagoya and Osaka, with Volcano Choir billed as support for Collections Of Colonies Of Bees. Their set consisted of seven songs from *Unmaps* and an encore of Collection Of Colonies Of Bees' 'Flocksill', played by Wincek triggering his loops

[*] The owners, CJ Star Buses, claimed to have given the band 45 minutes to remove their gear from the bus before it was driven away, and said that none of the band took them seriously.

live onstage. "With Volcano Choir, we really had to think about how to pull that off," he said. "In Volcano Choir's live set, I'm actually playing loops, triggering them on the keyboard. I couldn't do that in Creatures."[35]

Back from Japan*, November 2010 saw Vernon thrown back into the hip-hop big time. With New York abuzz with rumours, on the morning of November 23, previously unannounced, tickets were put on sale for a tiny show at the Bowery Ballroom by Kanye West taking place that very evening. Within minutes the tickets were gone and, come sundown, the queue to get in snaked around the block. Those with tickets faced a three hour wait to get inside, and some were even turned away as the monumental guest list – major celebrities like Spike Lee had to queue an hour or more; only P Diddy was swept past the queue without a pause – supplanted their spaces.

Running on hip-hop time, the crowd were kept waiting until way past midnight for the show to begin. When it did, with Nicki Minaj, Rick Ross, John Legend and Kanye himself in the wings, the first voice through the speakers was the unmistakable Auto-Tune trill of Vernon hovering over the spoken-word intro of 'Dark Fantasy', the opening song on *My Beautiful Dark Twisted Fantasy*, sounding nothing short of gargantuan. As the show wound its way through the entire album, Vernon was a regular presence. "Time and again, the stage belonged to Vernon, whose eerie falsetto ran through song after song," wrote the *New York Times*. "Vernon was transformed, supremely confident alongside a multiplatinum superstar, sometimes even eclipsing him . . . Vernon began ['Lost In The World'] a capella – for more than a minute it was a pure cyborg hymn, with Vernon, the self-described 'introspective, emotional country kid', singing about being up in the woods, while the crowd hooted and whistled. After the song, Justin Vernon, the pride of Eau Claire, Wis., and Kanye West hugged and walked offstage together."[36]

Of all the disparate tours, gigs, recording sessions and projects that he embarked on in the latter half of 2010, though, three were particularly close to Justin's heart. First was the burgeoning idea of his own record label imprint, funded via Jagjaguwar, that he was planning to call Chigliak. Initially he'd use it to release albums that he'd loved through the years

---

* Having filled his Blobtower blog with pictures of the strange things he saw there, including a Terminator eating spaghetti.

but had been lost through the cracks. And one in particular stood out.

"There's this band called Amateur Love from Eau Claire," he told Pitchfork, remembering the album that had so moved him back in his DeYarmond days. "They put out a record and it probably sold like 500 copies – it was like this electro-pop thing with a Neil Young or Paul Westerberg-quality songwriter, I shit you not . . . Amateur Love is going to be the first record I put out. It's like a 'lost records' thing and I'm encouraging other people to send in records of their local heroes – totally unsigned shit that never went anywhere but is incredible."[37] "There will be cool bonus material, songs never released, videos," he added in Eau Claire weekly music magazine *Volume One*. "But mostly that fantastic album on wax. As a whole."[38]

"[The] objective of that label is to put out unreleased or recorded but lightly distributed local music," Justin's dad, Gil, said. "I think that's neat to see. There's great fortune and wealth involved. I think he's looking back to music that inspired him or [through] lack of better luck didn't find its way to broader exposure so he's reaching back."[39]

And second, an email exchange that, for a time at least, got him the woman of his wildest proposal fantasies.

In Autumn 2010, a mutual friend played matchmaker. They suggested that Justin and Kathleen Edwards might make sweet music together. Emails were swapped, the suggestion of Justin producing Kathleen's fourth album dropped.

At their first sessions in November and December, at both Edwards' studio in Toronto and at April Base, the pair found they were musical soulmates.

"I was talking to Justin about the direction I wanted to go in fairly early on in the recording process," Kathleen said. "He was somebody that was able to finish my sentences when I was trying to describe what I wanted to do, and for the times that I couldn't articulate it, he really helped . . . There was never a shortage of ideas with Justin. He was quick at throwing down four or five parts and tinkering with them in a way that really allowed me to produce the songs while he produced some of the musical ideas based on stacking and creating sounds on two or three instruments at one time."[40]

Whether he wooed her with 'Calgary' or not, within weeks of meeting Vernon and Edwards were a couple. Though Edwards lived in Toronto and Vernon in Eau Claire they vowed not to let more than a fortnight go by without seeing each other, and recording for Edwards' album *Voyageur* shifted to April Base to help the relationship run smoother. Kathleen, it transpired, found Vernon's work just as alluring as he found hers.

"You can place yourself inside his songs and his music, because he leaves space for you," she said. "I mean this respectfully, but most of the time I have no idea what Justin's songs are about . . . This intense connection people have with him, I'm deeply, deeply jealous of that."[41]

And finally, around Christmas 2010, his parents moved out of Eau Claire, shifting out to Hudson, a 60-minute drive west. His brother, Nate, had already moved to Minneapolis and his sister to St Paul's so, just as everything in his life appeared to be reaching a satisfying cohesion, he felt suddenly unsettled.

"I'm the only one left in Eau Claire. And I know that I have roots here now with this place, and I know that I can come back here, but I wonder, am I supposed to live here? And so in a way it feels kind of late, but I think that I'm ready to have a stare in the face of me and this place and wonder if I should be here still."[42]

That winter's night that Justin laid down the final track on the new Bon Iver record*, the array of dizzying achievements he had to look back on made him break down and cry. Although he would delay mastering the album for a fortnight more in order to make it as perfect as possible, he certainly felt he'd finally put a full stop on his grandest work yet.

Through the studio window and Justin's teary eyes, a snowstorm was brewing, readying to bury Eau Claire in another glistening winter.

For the first time since Bon Iver was born, his back had stopped hurting.

* A post to his Blobtower blog featuring a snapshot of a microphone and the legend 'the end of a very long, good chapter' suggests this was December 22, 2010.

CHAPTER TWELVE

Melic In The Naked

APRIL 16, 2011, Palm Springs, Nevada. Lounging around the pool of a cul-de-sac bungalow with Ryan Olson, Har Mar Superstar and various members of Gayngs, enjoying the lull after headlining the Mojave Stage at the Coachella Valley Music And Arts Festival the previous night midway through Gayngs' second bunch of live concerts*, Justin lifted his shades and welcomed a new face. A journalist flown out from the UK. It had begun.

Having opened his album up to his fellow musicians, now it was time to open it up to the world.

As before, Justin took an inclusive, hands-on approach to the press. He took *Uncut*'s Alastair McKay – his visitor in Palm Springs – to his favourite local diner, King's Highway, where the waitress sings show tunes, and chatted about the Gayngs shows ("With Gayngs I feel like I get to throw on sunglasses and fuck around"[1]), his habit of getting to bed at 9.30 p.m. for the duration of his time at Coachella and his nagging inner fanboy: "I was a bit star-struck when I saw Ian MacKaye at catering yesterday. It was like 'oh shit, that guy's my fucking hero'."[2]

Later he'd chuckle amiably to other writers about the two shows he'd play on the Sunday night at Coachella 2011, the first joining The National for 'Terrible Love' and the second an appearance hoisted high on a white cube pedestal in a white suit, swathed in pyrotechnics and surrounded by half-dressed feather-clad dancers as a guest at Kanye West's G.O.O.D. Music headline set, with Kanye himself lowered onstage from a crane. "Sunday night at Coachella with just the 80,000 people watching us," he

---

* A primarily Texas and West Coast 10-gig schedule this time, in two sections; they started back at First Avenue on March 6 before making up for their cancelled Austin gig with several SXSW shows in the city and then, after their one-off Coachella appearance, Gayngs hit Portland, Washington and California in May/June.

said. "That was pretty wild."[3] "He knows my scene. He knows I can't dance and shit. But I showed up and they were like 'uh, you should probably put on some of these white clothes'."[4] "They gave me a bunch of white clothes and just said, 'Go up there.' It was surreal; it was cool to be a part of that big of a visual production but I'm not capable of constructing something like that for myself."[5]

To those who asked, he waxed lyrical about the first (and, to date, only) Volcano Choir shows in the US, in Minneapolis and Milwaukee that March, and about his reunion with DeYarmond Edison at Fader Fort at that year's SXSW festival, their first show together in seven years. "This is our college band," Justin had said as he and Megafaun took the stage to play only three songs – Bonnie Raitt's 'Lovers Will', Carole King's 'You've Got A Friend' and the DeYarmond original 'Set Me Free' – watched, bizarrely, by P Diddy from the side of the stage. Also at SXSW 2011, Justin had met rising UK post-dubstep/soul singer James Blake and got on like a shack ablaze, swapping emails over the spring about a potential collaboration.

"You know when you've got good friends where you don't see them for a while, but it's kind of the same?" Blake said, "It kind of reminds me of somebody like that. We've talked about music and stuff and played together, it's been quite nice."[6]

To the writers who came to interview him in Eau Claire that spring, Justin was even more accommodating. The *New York Times'* Jon Caramanica was driven around Eau Claire in the Honda CR-V that Justin had borrowed from his mother, Justin taking him to the local meat market, Mike's Star Market, to pick up the deer Gil had killed back in November 2010 and had stored there, all the while Vernon explaining how he was arranging his tour dates for the new album so that he wouldn't be out of town and miss the hunting season. *Spin*'s reporter was taken to The Joynt and for pizza at Justin's favourite Eau Claire restaurant, and granted access to April Base – cats, polaroid pinboard and all – where Bowerbirds and Kathleen Edwards were recording, Dan Spack was converting an upstairs room into an extra studio and the second Shouting Matches album was underway.*

---

*Justin's plan was to release the new Shouting Matches album, made by Vernon, Moen and Phil Cook, and the unreleased five-track EP at the same time – a plan yet to come to fruition.

Chicago *Time Out*'s correspondent was given a guided tour of Eau Claire, from the favoured eateries of Pad Thai and The Nuke to the apartment in town Justin was now renting overlooking the Chippewa river, his home since April Base became too busy for him to have any personal space there, and the abandoned building he was planning to turn into a live music venue and study centre he was going to call Union College after a women's college that had once stood on the same patch of ground. His interests as a local developer led him to an interest in local politics, finding an affinity with the ideas of 'active rogue' John Morgensen, an Eau Claire developer known for converting historic buildings into restaurants and apartments, as a means of achieving real change in Eau Claire. He saw himself, he told local magazine *Volume One*, as a similar sort of Eau Claire activist. "I believe that Eau Claire is such an opportunity. It represents 'middle' America in every way, and I want to think that isn't a lost thing."[7] And *Volume One* knew just how active Justin was in local affairs since it was founded by Justin's friend Nick Meyer and Justin had taken time out to help shift the magazine into its new office downtown, building shelves and installing himself into a spare room to make videos of Eau Claire graduation ceremonies or highlight compilations of local sport team successes. "Like if the high-school football team had their banquet, I would make a 45-minute film with highlights and put awesome music in it."[8]

He chatted about the phone call he'd had from Neil Young that spring requesting a collaboration he was trying to fit in, and the phone interview he'd conducted with Fugazi's Ian MacKaye for *Under The Radar* magazine which had turned on another moral light: "I was asking him a bunch of questions, and long story short, he comes around and says, 'I'm not an expansionist.' I've thought about that word for the past three days, and thought that you can just choose to do what you want, versus what there is this magnetic pull in the industry for you to do. It's not like somebody's fault or some conspiracy. People just fall into knowing they should make money, and they do forget about a bunch of other stuff."[9] He grinned at the memory of playing on the Jimmy Fallon show in February, his first promo TV appearance for the new album booked so early that his band were still in rehearsal for the summer tour and he had no album tracks ready to play so, to a nationwide audience of millions, had to perform a 'Calgary' b-side and covers of Bonnie Raitt's 'I Can't Make You Love

Me' and Donny Hathaway's 'A Song For You' with Phil Cook on piano. He bemoaned the fact that he'd become a workaholic, unable to rest whenever he got home from tour; claimed that he finally felt he was discovering "my own zone" after years of "trying to spit out John Prine influences of whatever"[10]; enthused about the expansion of his live band to a nine-piece, one of whom was trombonist Reggie Pace whom Justin met while working with Megafaun, and explained his idea to only tour for four weeks at a time so as not to succumb to homesickness.

"If I was going to decide exactly what I want to do, I'd play two shows a month for the rest of my life," he said. "But making the record, that I would sign up for every time."[11] And, as usual, he gushed forth on the pleasures of rural living ("My house is next to farmers and I like being outside, splitting wood, mowing lawns or hauling shit around. But following a pattern for a pattern's sake is like bad death for me."[12]) and small town anonymity: "I can just be a person in this community and not really feel extra special or anything. I like going to The Joynt and Racy's. I feel like a person there."[13]

"I think what's even more rewarding then the 'fame' or whatever you want to call this that's going on with him," added his mother, Justine, "is the fact that he's just Justin. I mean when we talk on the phone or when he's at our house or it's Christmas time, we're all just the Vernon family hanging out."[14]

When Justin wasn't answering flippant questions like who he'd still like to collaborate with (Bonnie Raitt and Tom Waits, since you ask) and what his Desert Island Disc would be (*John Denver and The Muppets: A Christmas Together* because: "What other disc could help you deal with the notion of death better in that situation!?"[15]), and was probed a little deeper, he was more intimate and open than ever. He admitted that fame and touring had lost him friendships, and even delved into his feelings of inadequacy at turning 30 that April. "I had just turned 30 and was dealing with a lot of self-deprecation in the discreet comparison of other people," he disclosed, "like when you think of what your parents were doing when they were 30. I was thinking, 'Shit, I haven't prepared'. But I realised I had done a lot, and the things like Kanye were other external compliments."[16]

But when the tapes began whirling, one topic was on every journalist's lips. The new Bon Iver album.

"*For Emma . . .* was this black and white thing," he told *Uncut*, "it's a

185

record of an event in time, and it's past, it's forever ago. This is like the present – it feels more colourful and inviting . . . it's a little bit like taking a drug."[17]

"I knew I had to search for the right album and let it come to the surface . . . this album really snuck up on me when I needed it,"[18] he told *Q*, and expanded the point to *The New York Times*: "Those are the only 10 songs I wrote in the last three years, I had to go looking under rocks."[19] On the album's lyrics, which he described as being "so unspecific that I'm not actually going to use words that have specific meanings"[20] and even more about the sound of the words than on the first album, a technique inspired by 'Loaded At The Wrong Door' by Richard Buckner, he hinted "there's finding love, not needing love, and then there's sleeping with your buddy's girlfriend . . . I'm not really asking you to hear what I'm saying too much, because I would have spoken the words harder . . . It was important for me to discard the storytelling aspect of it."[21]

"The music that has always resounded with me – and art as well – is when it feels a little bit like it's coming from a person," he expanded. "And it's coming from a visceral place. A place that is maybe trying to explain something that isn't explained yet. And I guess that's what I was trying to do, and by trying to write songs in a subconscious way, I've ended up with something I'm pretty proud of that I didn't know I was capable of doing . . . the songs on the new record, they all mean something to me. But they all can kind of change and trick me and trick people. Not 'trick'. But the song isn't trying to say something so obvious that it's like law. Like all things, those kind of boundaries need to change."[22]

There were also clues that the real life pain behind the *For Emma, Forever Ago* songs had dragged on in the constant singing of them. "It's such a weird thing: People sing sad songs and then they have to sing them all the time."[23]

"By no means am I in a race to be in some kind of genius list or anything," he said, "but I think what's important is trying to expand your palette and your ability to express things. And with this record I was like 'I don't need to be sad'. I mean, there's some grieving on there, but it's more like I'm grieving sadness. Like a 'goodbye loneliness'-type thing. I'm not gonna invite that shit into my life if I don't have to."[24]

Although the album had initially been rejected by his label when he first handed it in, claiming it didn't sound professional enough, the remix the

We're gonna need a bigger cabin… Justin jamming in April Base studios. Note the markings from the school gym flooring.
LL ALKOFER/POLARIS

Upping the head-count, Bon Iver's new nine-piece line-up premieres at the Celebrate Brooklyn show, 2011. RYAN MUIR

Don't stay in college, kids: Mike Noyce, 2011. RYAN MUIR

DeYarmond Edison reunite to dazzle Fader Fort at SXSW, 2011. ROGER KISBY/GETTY IMAGES

Making molten harmonies with Volcano Choir, (L-R): Thomas Wincek, Justin Vernon, Chris Rosenau, Jon Mueller, Jim Schoeneker, Daniel Sack. CAMERON WITTIG

The Shouting Matches in a more harmonious moment. GRAHAM TOLBERT

"A photo shoot walking in the wood? If you say so…", May 2011. TURE LILLEGRAVEN/CORBIS OUTLINE

A shouting match in progress onstage at the Coachella Valley Music & Arts Festival in California, April 2012, (L-R) Brian Moen, Justin Vernon and Phil Cook. KARL WALTER/GETTY IMAGES FOR COACHELLA

Hep-cat shades a-plenty for Vernon at the New Orleans Jazz & Heritage Festival in April 2012.
LEON MORRIS/REDFERNS VIA GETTY IMAGES

Who the hell is Bonny Bear? That'll be this guy, at the 54th Annual Grammy Awards, LA. PICTUREGROUP/REX FEATURES

Waving farewell to Bonnaroo 2012, (L-R): Michael Lewis, Justin Vernon and Colin Stetson. FILMMAGIC/GETTY IMAGES

Bon Iver using Mike Joyce as a human banjo in NYC, September 2012, (L-R): Matt McCaughan, Colin Stetson, Sean Carey, Reggie Pace, Justin Vernon, Mike Noyce. ROGER KISBY/GETTY IMAGES

Shrouded in arena theatrics in Berlin, November 2012. ANNE-HELENE LEBRUN/REDFERNS VIA GETTY IMAGES

label did on the album wasn't as good as Justin's original mix, so he was justifiably proud of his achievement.

"I'm not an egotistical person but I'm very proud of this new record I made," he argued, "precisely because I did figure my stuff out, and I think the music is better as a result. Not to take away from the last one . . . I'm proud of that still, but it's a different thing – it's like black and white, charcoal-ash compared to this album where it feels I'm starting to use colour."[25]

And then, they asked, what of the title? The stuttering eponymy of *Bon Iver, Bon Iver?*[*]

"It's called Good Winter, Good Winter," Justin said, "but it's not about winter; we're putting it out on the Summer Solstice – that's sort of the beginning of life, of the longest life there is, you know. But it's also wishing 'good death' to this place – this Bon Iver, Bon Iver. But this album is more about dealing with joy as it comes – inviting it in."[26]

"It's almost like you're saying 'happy death, Bon Iver' because you're inviting change. You can look at winter a couple of different ways. You could see it as a metaphor for death or life, or as the end of an old cycle and giving in to the new cycle with spring. It's meant to be ambiguous, because I didn't want it to be boiled down to one single idea. I don't think anything really can be."[27]

At first sight *Bon Iver, Bon Iver* would seem as wintry and isolated as its predecessor, coming adorned with a sleeve painted by Gregory Euclide of a wood cabin in a winter wilderness landscape made from real leaves, twigs, snow and dirt.[†] "[I'm] accepting winter is a big part of the album," Justin said. "It's the all-knowing thing, it's more constant than sleep. Everyone deals with it and everyone is in it. It's about what winter means, what everyone goes through, not just the season but the death of anything, the birth of anything. Winter equalises everybody. There are different classes of people, different types of people, but winter is the one thing that levelled off everyone I grew up with. There's a certain resilience to Mid-western people. They like to complain about the winter but at the same time, they get through it and that is endearing and enduring . . . it

[*] A rumoured working title of the album was *Letters For Marvin.*
[†] Euclide made two films of the artwork being constructed, which were posted on YouTube.

forces you to have a certain humbleness. It doesn't allow you to feel in control of much, especially from January to March."[28]

And in May 2011, Vernon would feel that lack of control sweep over him once more . . .

★ ★ ★

Vernon couldn't believe his bad luck; his fans couldn't believe theirs had turned so good.

May 23, a month ahead of *Bon Iver, Bon Iver*'s official release date, a tiny square image of the album sleeve popped up unexpectedly on the iTunes store. Somewhere, an errant click had been made and Bon Iver's second album was uploaded for sale to the massive online store a month early.

The moment the error was spotted, Apple removed the album from sale. But it was too late. A "handful" of copies had been bought and downloaded before the gap could be plugged. The dreaded internet leak had begun.

Aware of how regularly hotly anticipated albums find their way online before their official release, Justin was prepared for the eventuality. He immediately posted the lyrics to the album on the Bon Iver official website so that no-one would have any doubt as to what he was singing, and sat back to watch the reaction to *Bon Iver, Bon Iver* spread web-wide.

The first thing that struck those who read the lyrics or managed to get hold of the music was that virtually all of the songs were named after places or buildings. "They're not just places I have been," Justin explained, "they're about places in general and what they mean to different people, like an emotional place or a time. The meaning is open ended."[29] "All of these place names have a story or are the emblem for a feeling or a notion."[30]

The titles also gave the album a worldly and nostalgic air, suggesting Bon Iver, the project, had spread its wings, widened its horizons and expanded from the closeted wood-shack hideaway of its birth. And from the very first tune, the suspicion was realised.

A geyser of electric guitar spurting from silence. A rumble of Union military drums and tapped drumstick marching rhythms. The distant choral drift of an approaching ghost army. 'Perth' – the song Justin had started way back in 2008, finding a rebirth of Bon Iver in the death of Heath Ledger – gradually emerged from the fog boasting grunge guitars, sleek shoegaze organs, trumpets and a spirited indie grandiosity worthy of Death Cab For Cutie or Band Of Horses. This was clearly a bolder, more confident and more ambitious Bon Iver than had made *For Emma . . .* , a statement of intent that this was Vernon reborn. "It starts out and it's kind of disarming in 'Perth'," he said, "and by the time you get to the end you're just kind of glad to be on the coast mode."[31]

Considering Justin's claims that 'Perth' represented a birth not just in rhyme but as a messy beginning to the record, the hallucinatory lyrics seemed to revolve around the final line "you're breaking your ground" as an indicator of new territory being explored, but were otherwise wilfully indecipherable, particularly since Vernon's uploaded lyrics included (arguably intentional) typing errors: "I'm tearing acrost your face/Move dust to the light/To fide your name/It's something fane". The image of "in a mother, out a moth", however, suggested the kind of transformation and reinvention that Justin had been striving for with *Bon Iver, Bon Iver* and the line "I'm ridding all your stories" a casting off of the mythology of the cabin. But what lingered from the song was more of an emotional rejuvenation: "still alive, who you love", not merely a reference to the memory of Heath Ledger living on in his video director's thoughts but an admission that even in Justin's once desolate heart, love was thriving once more.

The lyric could also be read as a literal birth from the baby's perspective, complete with baby-speak non-words like "fide" and "fane" in an opening verse that follows the child's first blinking emergence into the world, trying to fathom the meaning of its own name, awestruck by dust moving through shards of light and "still alive" in a whole new wide-open space that feels like "this is not a place" compared to the enclosure of the womb. And if we were looking for a linear thread to the album, as with *For Emma . . .* , this is a fitting reading, since Justin has admitted that the second song, "Minnesota, WI"* is about his childhood, although whatever memories it held were tangled tightly in obscure cut-up word collages – "doubled in the toes annex it/It minute closed in the morning/Did not lose it in the stack's stow/Imma lay that call back on ya". A string of references to the natural world – "ramble in the roots", "water's running through the valley where we grew", "laying in an open field", "fall is

---

* The title's combination of two states, it's been suggested, is a reference to the similarities between Minnesota and Wisconsin in terms of landscape and culture.

coming soon, a new year for the moon", "swallows swelling for the beams" – suggested that the tune could be Justin losing himself in incorporeal memories of his rural childhood. Certainly the saxophones that swept across the agitated Afro-funk verses – adding to the crystal-synth Eighties vibe that brought to mind the rolled white blazer sleeves of John Parr, Foreigner and Paul Simon and clashed marvellously with the serene banjo choruses – were reminiscent of his first jazz endeavours with Mount Vernon.

Justin's intended meaning for the song was secondary though: fan interpretations focused on the line "fall is coming soon, a new year for the moon and the Hmong here" and took from this the idea that the song was about the enforced relocation of 1.3 million Hmong people from their homes over the course of 17 years to make way for the building of the Three Gorges Dam in China, the world's largest hydroelectric project, and the dam's subsequent flooding – hence "water's running through in the valley where we grew". In this reading the Hmong were praised for their unbreakable nature*, but it's unlikely that this one reference to the ethnic group was intended to encompass the whole lyric. Instead, the impression was of an idyllic childhood, the grounding of which was imbued with enough love to see Justin through whatever trials he might face afterwards.

Thankfully, Justin has been more effusive on his thinking behind 'Holocene', the arpeggio slumber anthem loaning its guitar part from 'Hazelton' and named after the geological era that stretches from 11,500 years ago to the present. 'Holocene' wasn't only the era the permafrost of the last ice age† receded and humanity thrived, however, but also a Portland bar where Justin had a "dark night of the soul"[32], where perhaps he realised "I was not magnificent", setting the humbled tone of awakening to one's own failings and insignificance within the gargantuan sprawl of nature and humanity that shrouded the song. "Most of our lives feel like these epochs," Justin said. "That's kind of what that song's about. 'Once I knew I was not magnificent'. Our lives feel like these epochs, but really we are dust in the wind. But I think there's a significance in that insignificance that I was trying to look at in that song."[33] "[It's] a song about

---

* Although other interpretations suggested the song was a reference to Hmong killer Chai Vang who shot eight people in Minnesota in 2004 in a dispute over a deer stand, killing six.
† Coincidentally known as the Wisconsinan Glacial Period.

redemption and realising that you're worth something; that you're special and not special at the same time."[34]

Indeed 'Holocene' was also a reference to a shedding of frozen weight and a coming alive and, aside from the innate metaphor for springtime coming to free Wisconsin of its wintry shackles, Justin had a more personal defrosting in mind – the shift from his dour and depressed pre-Raleigh drinking days to his celebratory recent glories.

"The whole second verse is about those years in Eau Claire but the first verse is this weird amalgamation of the darkness that came with those times," he explained. "I set that verse in Milwaukee because it's a dark, beer-drunk place . . . and guess what adults do on Halloween in Milwaukee? They get blind drunk and try to forget about their childhoods. We were going through ideas for a video for 'Holocene', and we thought it should be adults trick-or-treating where children are handing out their past dreams. Pretty dark. The last verse fast-forwards to two Christmases ago, spending time with Nate during an ice storm, smoking weed."[35]

Though he set his first verse of drinking his woes away one Halloween, mourning a break-up and realising how small and pathetic he was when he got too drunk to stand* in a fictional Milwaukee, 'Holocene' was dotted with real-life images. Come the second verse wistfully mourning the loss of a golden period living with his friends and being introduced to Tennessee rock troupe Lip Parade, the line "3rd and Lake it burned away, the hallway/Was where we learned to celebrate" referred to a house on 3rd Avenue and Lake Street in Eau Claire where the Cook brothers lived, possibly with Justin, and Amateur Love recorded – a house where Justin learned how to drink and which burnt down in 2010. And his final verse Christmas scene with Nate included the wincingly honest reference to "tangled spines" as the pair watched their troubles waft away into space like the smoke from their joint.

By placing such personal recollections into the frame of someone acknowledging their essential unimportance in the universe, Justin did indeed find significance in the insignificance: that such tiny moments of such tiny creatures are intricately precious, moments to be treasured for their minuscule rarity, and illuminating them is the fine art of a pinpoint poet. The song would inspire reviewers to poetic heights themselves, the

---

* And the existential enlightenment he felt as a result: "I can see for miles, miles, miles".

Pitchfork critic penning its entry at Number Two in their Singles Of 2011 list, writing "the rising and falling chord changes create a sense of motion that develops throughout the whole song, a tide-like ebb and flow that ends with an abrupt denouement, so swift it withholds almost as much pleasure as it yields".[36]

"This is about having three quarters of a bottle of wine in college," Justin would introduce the next track on *Bon Iver, Bon Iver* live, "and well . . . you know what happens . . .". He'd also mention drugs, Ritalin and losing your virginity. And taking into account that the song was named after the notorious UW-Eau Claire college halls where Justin first had sex it's fair to assume there was a certain level of autobiography to the brisk, breezy 'Towers', with its jubilant combination of buoyant guitar, sleepy pedal steel, insouciant brass and "woah-oh-oh"s delivered with as much ecstasy as Justin's falsetto could muster.

It's uncertain whether Justin was referring to his own virginity being lost or that of his Rapunzel-esque conquest whose hair he'd tear out in his excitement to re-scale the Towers and be with her again, but the song swam with the intoxication[*] of romance, desire and sexuality. This "young darling" whose "faun" of innocence was soon to be "forever gone" now she was "up for it before you've grown" inspired in Justin the most passionate physical desires – "Break the sailor's table on your sacrum[†]" – and unquenchable ardour – "you're standing on my sternum[‡], don't you climb down darling". The "mischief" the girl brought to Justin's life – and what Trever Hagen's involvement in the whole scene was, since he got a mention: "Fuck the fiercest fables, I'm with Hagen" – can only be guessed at, but 'Towers' was testament to the powerful and confusing fervency that coursed through the teenage Vernon, and another blurred memory in *Bon Iver, Bon Iver*'s fast-forward through a life.

Many fans also read the aftermath of a lost virginity into the opening lines of 'Michicant' – "I was unafraid, I was a boy, I was a tender age/Melic[**] in the naked . . . know it wasn't wedded love/4 long minutes

---

[*] Quite literally: the line "from the liver, sweating through your tongue" suggested all manner of intoxicants were involved.

[†] The sacrum is a triangular bone at the base of the spine.

[‡] The sternum is the breastbone, guard of the human heart.

[**] A melic is a Greek poem performed in song; Vernon was certainly laying himself bare, albeit abstrusely, in these songs.

end and it was over."* But Justin's onstage pronouncements that the song was about "all the things you can't do in Michigan" suggested it was about either infidelity or seducing an unmarried girl.† Either way, the lyric hinted at coldness, distance and emotional struggles early on in the relationship – "the frost took up the eyes . . . pressed against the pane, could see the veins and there was poison out/Resting in a raze the inner claims I hadn't breath to shake/Searching for an inner clout, may not take another bout . . . Hon, it wasn't yet spring". That the dolorous guitar, hazy horns, swooning strings and dislocated sound effects of electronic ricochets combined to create a mood most reminiscent of *For Emma . . .* was a sign, perhaps, that the desperation that bubbled to the surface on 'Skinny Love' hadn't been completely purged during Bon Iver's inexorable rise.

Hinnom, in ancient Hebrew tradition, was a valley near Jerusalem where nameless strangers were buried and also the name given to the very gates of Hell, a land without laws. But in shifting this hallowed Hades to America's southernmost state in 'Hinnom, TX', Justin re-imagined it as "a place to bury the stranger in yourself, a place to bury past selves"[37]. He filled the song with desert imagery, mentions of the ancient Hebrew law system Noachide and death itself as a metaphor for self-healing and self-awakening, a leaving behind of old lives just as Lucinda Williams did in 'Fruits Of My Labor'.‡ Musically it certainly buried Bon Iver's past; guitar free, it ventured into futuristic reverb-heavy synths and treated piano and juxtaposed Justin's lower-toned natural singing voice against the falsetto, used exclusively for the choruses. So a husky Vernon looked back upon the decay of "bodies wrapped in white", representing "every pain" and "pasts . . . slain", watching with satisfaction as his old troubles sank into the sand, became imbued with dirt and ice and finally scattered to the wind, nothing but strangers. Meanwhile, a higher-register Justin looked forward to a life without such heavy cares: "solar peace/Well it swirls and sweeps/You just set it . . . armor down/On the wettest ground/Not to vet

---

* And, stretching credibility, they read drug references into the lyric too in the line "nose up in the globes".

† These are just two oddly illegal activities in Michigan; others include being drunk on a train, selling a car on a Sunday, a woman cutting her hair without her husband's permission and having sex in a vehicle unless it's parked on the property of the couple concerned.

‡ Her "I got outta La Grange" line is referenced here.

it". Here was Vernon moving on emotionally and musically, embracing all manner of possibilities in both spheres.

The chiming, gorgeous piano lilt, lush strings and backwards notes like the dripping of icicles that formed 'Wash.' were further signs of advancement, Bon Iver stretching into orchestral tones and chamber textures, draped with graceful slide guitar. The title referred to the Eau Claire tradition of holding out through the brittle chills of March until the April showers wash away the winter ice, and Vernon used the emergence of nature's life and abundance from "that iron ground" as spring takes hold as a metaphor for emerging from a period of cold emotional stasis when personal growth is impossible and coming alive again – "I'm growing the like quickening hues". He addressed it almost as a letter of apology to Eau Claire for leaving it when, unbeknownst to him, he needed it most ("Claire, I was too sore for sight"), and allowed the lyric to become a Joycean jumble of words as though he'd become lyrically effervescent at the relief and pleasure of his own personal spring.

Justin's marriage ode to Kathleen Edwards, 'Calgary', was set to be the album's first single on June 14, declaring Bon Iver's bold departure from the acoustic musical structures of *For Emma . . .* with its 'Hounds Of Love'-style amorphous pop pound, its haunting synth atmospheres and its cranky electric guitar squeals adding a mischievous edge to an otherwise silk-smooth song. "It's like 'yes! I am going to play guitar licks! Because that's how good I feel!'" Justin exclaimed. "It's saying goodbye to charcoal and hello to brighter colours."[38]

In the album's loose biography of a life, having grown up, become educated, overcome an emotional slump and emerged a fuller, brighter, complete human being, 'Calgary'* marked the point of becoming ready to settle down, albeit with someone you might not have necessarily met yet. "Eventually, you start waking up to the fact that you might be ready to spend your life with somebody," Vernon said, "and still feel good about who you are and what kind of changes you're going to go through no

---

* In concert, Justin has claimed that this song was inspired by a man from Calgary called Paul he met while living in Ireland. The song may well relate to Paul's story at that time, but the reference to Calgary was linked to the fact that Justin had never visited the city but, by gaining close friends from there, felt he knew it. Hence 'Calgary' became the title of a song about being intimate and comfortable with someone or something you've yet to encounter.

matter what."[39] But Justin wasn't lured in by any simplistic myth of marital bliss; he knew that marriages had to be worked at. "I really like the opening line: 'Don't you cherish me to sleep'. There's that whole thing that happens in relationships – you can love someone but, as soon as they stop loving you so unconditionally that they stop being themselves, it can be so dangerous."[40]

So amidst the language of infatuation – the lustful lingerings on his potential fiancee's "hair, old, long along/Your neck onto your shoulder-blades", his feeling that she "pinned me with your black sphere eyes" and his calling her his "starboard bride" – Justin imagined in this possibly future marriage hints of insecurity and neglect, that he was little more to her than a means to parenthood ("I was only for the father's crib"), a security blanket ("I was only for your very space") and an escape from life-long loneliness ("I was only for to die beside").

As the electric guitars bled into more turbulent frequencies the song's bridge traced more troubled times in this future couple's life together – having got along by knowing they "just have to keep a dialogue", a meta-phorical storm "on the lake" almost finishes their love off: "little waves, our bodies break . . . there's a fire going out/But there's really nothing to the south".* But as the storm subsides and the protagonist wakes up still dedi-cated to his "starboard bride" – "sold, I'm ever open ears and open eyes" – the closing moral is that a stout marriage can weather any rough patches: "the demons come, they can subside". As love songs go, the unflinching realism made 'Calgary' all the more touching.

'Calgary' was released accompanied by a theatrical video, directed by Andre Durand and Dan Huiting and filmed largely outside Justin's pole barn at April Base, wherein sperm-like white shapes floated towards an egg-like bed, birthing a woman who eventually emerged from a womb-like cave and met a man with similar stains on his skin; the couple then picked their way through a tangled woodland to cast burning coals out onto a lake together. The final symbolism of a bear rising out of a grave upside down was left wide open to the viewer's interpretation, but in general the promo was an artful modernist take on 'Calgary''s trepidatiously-ever-after.

* The line "there's really nothing to the south" has been suggested to mean both that geo-graphically there's little of note in Canada south of Calgary and that the relationship was suffering from a lack of bedroom activity.

After 93 seconds of modulating ambient drone, random bleeps and backwards guitar called 'Lisbon, OH', *Bon Iver, Bon Iver* ends with the death to 'Perth''s birth. 'Beth/Rest'* didn't just lay to rest Bon Iver's high-pitched acoustic roots – drenched, as it was, in Bruce Hornsby brass, Dire Straits guitar licks, the Eighties AOR Korg M1 synths of Phil Collins or Sting and sampled electronic vocals in lower register – and represent the knell of the album's life cycle, it found Vernon singing, with immense joy and emancipation, of the demise of his insecurities.

"It's about inviting love into your life and not being afraid," he said. "People run away from relationships because they're afraid of losing their independence. It doesn't have to be that way. For me it's about trying to get rid of the insecurity that caused me to think those things. There's a death in that, but it's beautiful. It's like I'm saying goodbye to the days of dread, and the reasons I had to make *For Emma* . . . . It was self-referential, it was self-loathing. It was important, I guess, but you don't have to be afraid of linking up with another person and having faith that they're not going to try to change who you are. That's the 'rest' part. I'm talking about true love, I'd given up on it."[41]

For just such reasons, Vernon admitted weeping while working on 'Beth/Rest', so pleased he'd been able to communicate something uncomplicated and innocent but full of personal meaning, albeit largely impenetrable from an outside listener's perspective. "I'm the most proud of that song," he said. "It's definitely the part where you pick up your joint and re-light it."[42] "'Perth' is this awakening or this birth . . . it's sort of that moment when you have decided to wake up and take control. And 'Beth/Rest' is the death, but it's a good death. It's good winter. But it's a rest; it's not this final thing . . . what's weird is that the record was imagined before any of this new personal relationship stuff had happened. I'm in a really good, loving relationship right now. It's really rewarding. But what's weird is that the songs kind of came as this predecessor, as an invitation, to tell myself that I was open to it and knowing that there wasn't going to be somebody coming along who's going to change me and want to change who I was. And they were going to let me be who I want to be and like me for it. Then it sort of just happened as soon as I finished writing the song."[43]

* Beth was a place invented by Justin to represent a final resting place, emotionally or physically.

"That song feels really honest to me," he'd say. "It's embracing that digital analogue pad sound I actually find really useful when listening to music, whether it's Prince or Bruce Hornsby. I wanted to go there. And I wasn't afraid to play a guitar lick. I didn't want anyone to think I was jerking around. The song's about letting go of the love of your life and letting the part of you that's selfish die. It's like a joyful sleep if you will, but it's a wakening too."[44]

He'd come in for criticism from hardcore *For Emma . . .* fans for the Eighties production values on 'Beth/Rest', but remained stoical and unrepentant. "During this whole process, I was like, whatever feels good is just right. Gayngs definitely helped with that. It doesn't have anything to do with irony. Those sounds – they just feel so good to me. It's like a song I would have written when I was 18."[45]

"People are latching onto that one because it seems like a statement," he'd say, "or it might seem like I'm trying to pull the wool over somebody's eyes, or they're just plain not into keyboard sounds like that. And I don't feel defensive about it. For me, I didn't think about it that much when I made that song. When I made it, I was like, 'I love this song. I really needed to write this song. And I need it to be last on this record' . . . it just sounds like forever. It's kind of timeless, and you can be lofted up into these very high places during that song . . . I don't blame people for having their opinions, like, 'It sounds like Steve Winwood.' But I think for me, it's kind of silly to judge something based on some production facility. It's my favourite song. It's the last thing I want you to go away with. It's innocent. And I don't want it to be some Eighties throwback song. I want it to be a current, I-get-lost-in-this song, and I love everything about it . . . It's just happy, and I want to play this song all the time. 'Beth/Rest' was more just for that certain someone, you know."[46]

Online analysts of 'Beth/Rest''s particularly obscure and unfathomable lyrics would pick out a story similar to that of 'Calgary', only more realised than imagined – a married couple whose "star" of love had lost heat and allowed rain to waterlog their relationship's "vessel". Though the struggle to repair their problems was often arduous – "it is steep, it is stone/Such recovery" – and their love "heavy-mitted"[*], ultimately their bond of marriage would see off dangers and allow them the rest of the title, a scene

---

[*] A reference to romance clumsily held or likely to scald if handled too closely.

of settling in and with 'Beth', the death of life's emotional fluctuations.

And so closed a challenging, surprising, brave and boundary-breaking follow-up to one of the alt.folk albums of the century. An album, in fact, that instantly distanced Vernon from the bearded-folkie tradition he'd seemed to epitomise on *For Emma . . .* , made the likes of Iron & Wine and Bonnie Prince Billy seem woefully traditionalist by comparison and proved Vernon an artist with far greater sonic ambitions, as adventurous in musical spirit as Fleet Foxes, Sufjan or Modest Mouse, and willing to take on board an ounce of the psychedelic futurism of Animal Collective or MGMT.

When they first heard *Bon Iver, Bon Iver*, those close to Vernon heard all of his potential realised. "When I first heard it," said Frenette, "I knew it was the album he was supposed to make and I was blown away."[47] "[It was] a lot to take in on the first listen," said Ed Horrox, who'd heard no music at all from the Vernon camp until the completed album was delivered to 4AD, "very expansive, big, deep, wide, detailed. A beautiful, beautiful thing. It was pretty mind-blowing. I didn't really have a hope [for what I wanted to hear], I just knew whatever was going to come was going to be very special. Because the music he'd made and released as Bon Iver, there were many different places, there was sonic experimentation and detail and there was great songwriting, sometimes there was simplicity, sometimes there was complexity – on *For Emma . . .* there was all of that and obviously there were the side projects. So there were so many possible roads he could've gone down, I didn't know what he was going to do."

On June 21, Jagjaguwar posted a piece on its website by Justin's author friend Michael Perry, eloquently describing the album. "*Bon Iver, Bon Iver* is the frozen beast pressing upward from a loosening earth, one ear cocked to the echo of the ghost choir still singing, the other craving the martial call of drums tumbling, of thrum and wheeze. The desolation smoke has dissipated, cut with strips of brass. Celebration will not be denied, the cabinet cannot contain the rattle, there is meat on the bones . . . There is a sturdiness – an insistence – to *Bon Iver, Bon Iver* that allows him to escape the cabin in the woods without burning it to the ground . . . In the absence of solid ground, the whirlwind becomes a whirlpool, and *Bon Iver, Bon Iver* is Justin Vernon returning to former haunts with a new spirit. The reprises are there – solitude, quietude, hope and desperation compressed –

but always a rhythm arises, a pulse vivified by gratitude and grace notes, some as bright as a bicycle bell. The winter, the legend, has faded to just that, and this is the new momentary present. The icicles have dropped, rising up again as grass."

The album's reviewers were similarly lachrymose. In *Mojo*'s four-star review James McNair described it as "a record that invites us to reconnect with the seasons and the endless cycle of life", claiming the "synthesized textures . . . exit your speakers with the slow-creeping drama of ink on blotting paper . . . As a listener, you feel as if you're up Fall Creek sans sat-nav, but the sense of disorientation is welcome, almost soothing."[48] *Q*'s Victoria Segal, meanwhile, heard "a horizon-widening record . . . this sense of space and movement matched by the expansiveness of the songs [creating] an eerie feeling of loss and yearning."[49]

The *Evening Standard*'s David Smyth called it "expansive stuff, dramatic and complex where its predecessor was barely there . . . some of the most beautiful music you'll hear . . . if his last album struck a chord, this one strikes dozens."[50] Neil McCormick at the *Telegraph*, awarding four stars, praised its "degree of inventiveness and creative confidence that suggests there was nothing accidental about his original success". The record was, he continued, "an amorphous merging of lateral strands strung together by melody and emotion" incorporating "the everything-at-once futurism of Radiohead" and "locating human spirit in digital technology, Vernon gives Auto-Tune a good name"[51]. Further five-star reviews were forthcoming from the *Sunday Times* and *Independent*, whose reviewer stated "the lyrics are even more opaque than those on his debut . . . the kind of poetic stream-of-consciousness that renders lyric sheets pointless. But more importantly, it's a beautiful, flowing series of sounds and images, like a half-remembered dream to which you long to find the key . . . one . . . simply gives oneself up to the immersive experience of the music." "It's all unfathomably beautiful," they gushed, "with meticulous attention paid to the creation of a complete, self-sufficient sound-world . . . Justin Vernon may just be the most important figure in popular music right now."[52]

Writing in *Uncut*, another five-star appreciation of *Bon Iver, Bon Iver*, Bud Scoppa found hints of Sufjan Stevens, the Seventies Californian rock styles of Carl Wilson and Mike Love and even elements of Marvin Gaye in these grooves. "The full-bodied ensemble work results in an album with pace, scale and stylistic variety, but all of this sound and rhythm feels purposeful . . . 'Beth/Rest' has the satisfying resolution of the end title theme of a classic Western score . . . a majestic payoff."[53]

Pitchfork and Paste would vote *Bon Iver, Bon Iver* their album of 2011 and, despite the initial iTunes leak, it hit number two in the *Billboard* chart and number four in the UK album chart.* Ed Horrox was pleasantly surprised by the album's reception. "I think some people expected it, but being so close to it, I didn't presume that it was going to be received so rapturously."

And, unbeknownst to Vernon's cloistered clique, that rapture was about to go mainstream.

---

* *Bon Iver, Bon Iver* would also hit number one in Denmark and Sweden and Top 10 in Switzerland, Ireland, New Zealand, Australia, Canada and Belgium.

CHAPTER THIRTEEN

Stepping Up, Winding Down

O N November 30, 2011, Twitter lit up with one bemused question. "Who," it read, retweeted across the Twittersphere for every Lady Gaga fan to fathom, "is Bonny Bear?"

It was, after all, a shock to the system of mainstream culture to hear a name they don't recognise creep into the list of nominees for the 54th Grammy Awards, especially when it's mentioned so often. Bon Iver picked up four nominations, for Record Of The Year, Best New Artist, Alternative Album Of The Year and, for 'Holocene', 'Song Of The Year.* "We were sitting there together watching," said Justine, "and then he was nominated in the first category and so we kind of 'whew' and sat back, you know? And then when he ended up with four for the night, you just can't hardly believe it. It's just so surreal."[1]

Justin's Tweets during the announcements displayed a distinct lack of interest. "Watching the badgers game with @danhuiting. super a lot better than last time we hung out. #notpenisfest" he typed shortly after the Record Of The Year nomination came in, then, on his appearance on the list of nominees for Song Of The Year, he wrote "whats the difference between song and record?! ahhH! super weird butterflies! thank's y'all. the badgers are playing UNC. don't forget!!". His last Tweet of the event, though, proved he was staying tuned right through until Jason Aldean was nominated in the Best Country Album category: "Aldean is INDIE! I love Jason Aldean. Fucking real country music! Also, Ludacris has never pissed me off. Cool! #backtobadgers".

Vernon wasn't just uncomfortable with showing an interest in the Grammys, but also with the idea of attending a major award ceremony at

* Engineer Brian Joseph also received a nomination for his work on 'Holocene'.

all. He'd made his views clear in a fuming post on his Blobtower blog on August 29, angered at watching the slick commercialism of the MTV Awards and raging disparagingly against musicians who put money before art. "Why do we NEED this shit so bad?" he wrote. "Why don't we just have MUSIC? DO music? Soul? I don't know. I don't mean to criticise. Anyone. Actually. Except for MTV. You might have had a very large opportunity to be stabilise your self as a global presence of culture and art about 15 years ago and you fucked the dog. Sorry. I'm with my girls on this one. It's becoming increasingly clear as I think about it more and more, that the dollars, if they ARE a part of why you are doing something . . . they are a part of why you are doing something. That's fucked to me. That's the absence of spirit, glue, fabric of what makes us a person. It distracts us from what we could be doing: WORK. On EARTH . . . one last thought: What would Bill Hicks say?"[2]

It was clear enough why Vernon felt he didn't particularly need or covet the dubious honour of Grammy nods. Over the course of 2011 he'd become very much the master of his own destiny. His gigs had become huge; a theatre tour of the US in July and August with support from The Rosebuds sold out instantly. "He told me, 'They took me on my first real tour, so I want to take them out,' "[3] Bon Iver's tour agent Adam Voith said of The Rosebuds being booked for the first 12 dates of the US tour, despite a huge influx of requests from bands to play with Bon Iver. The tour opened in Milwaukee where Justin was spotted punching the air along to The Rosebuds' 'The Woods' and the rammed crowd went wild to the line in 'Holocene', played early on in the set – "you're in Milwaukee, off your feet". By the time the show finished with a sumptuous 'Calgary' and the squealing solos and *Top Gun* horns of 'Beth/Rest', some of Bon Iver's now nine-strong band* even slipping on shades for the song to add to the Eighties vibe, the crowd were in paroxysms. "I wasn't shocked, because I know what Justin is as a frontman," Ivan Howard said on seeing the audience's reaction to Bon Iver that night, "and I wasn't shocked at people's reactions to it, because I know how people react at shows. But I was so proud of these sounds – the way it came together, the bigness. It was really moving. It was perfect."[4]

---

* Rob Moose, Greg Leisz, Colin Stetson and CJ Camerieri all joined along with Reginald Pace on horns.

He'd also surrounded himself with a close-knit clique of family and friends to tour with, in an effort to keep him grounded as the world opened out for him. "They just make you remain who you are and who you were," Vernon said. "By being good friends they hold you accountable, I guess, and they always have. I think it's really easy to see . . . a lot of falsities about how things actually are. Like the whole fame thing, and how there are famous people talking to famous people. There's the industry, even at an indie level, and that can just be not real sometimes, even though it pretends to be. Not in a negative way, it's just not aware of itself. I just feel like by knowing that, you kind of remain far away from some of that and know that you're not a part of something that's weird."[5]

"The way Justin views everyone he works with is very heartfelt," Darius Van Arman adds. "He's not uncomfortable with mixing or blurring the lines between friendship and business. That can spell the path to ruin for many artists, but I think Justin's also a very good judge of character. He has very good instincts with who to trust in the people around him. His batting average on that is very high, which is why it's functional."[6]

From that early July/August raft of *Bon Iver, Bon Iver* shows in large clubs, casino halls, theatres and small open-air venues – the Ryman Auditorium in Nashville, the Boston House Of Blues, New York's United Palace Theatre, The National in Richmond, the Amphitheatre in Raleigh – the gigs expanded exponentially. Occasionally sharing the bill with Kathleen Edwards, sometimes with Fleet Foxes, The Walkmen or Other Lives, by the time the September dates stretched into Canada and Europe Bon Iver had begun playing multiple shows in cities; two nights at San Diego's Spreckels Theatre, two nights with Edwards at London's 5,000-capacity Hammersmith Apollo. The capacities of the US venues he was playing on his return from Europe were approaching the size of mini-arenas – 7,000 filled the UIC Pavilion in Chicago to watch him and, just weeks after the Grammy nominations were announced Bon Iver were due to round off the first leg of the *Bon Iver, Bon Iver* tour with two sold-out shows at Eau Claire's 3,500 capacity Zorn Arena, a personal milestone for Vernon which would cement him forever as a true Eau Claire Local Hero. He'd even donate the proceeds from the shows to a local shelter for women and children fleeing domestic abuse, the Boston Refuge House.

"Professors of mine were there," Vernon said, "people who helped form who I am. It was near Christmas and it just felt very Christmas-y and thankful and a lot of gratitude involved. A very happy, shiny situation."[7]

What's more, offers had started to filter in from the bookers of the 2012 festival season; Bon Iver were offered the headline slot at both the high-brow Latitude festival in the UK and at Washington's Sasquatch! festival. Vernon had not only expanded his insular intimacy to fill large halls with tides of noise and grace, he was ascending to the upper echelons of the alternative rock vanguard without having once compromised his art and principles.

"One of the most amazing things about this band is it hasn't changed from day one," said Voith of a series of shows two years in the arranging. "Its operations, its motivations, its measures of success, its decisions – it hasn't changed. They haven't made one compromise."[8]

As with live shows, so with music. In August, announced just the day before via an enigmatic Tweet, Justin's collaboration with James Blake had hit YouTube, swiftly racking up a million views. 'Fall Creek Boys Choir'* hooked Justin's vocodered electro-soul flurries, multi-tracked and singing entirely different songs over each other, onto Blake's doomy dubstep desolation, complete with cranky woodblock beats, psycho synth interludes and noises like barking wolves. Yet there was an eerie beauty and grandeur to the track, due partly to Blake's gracious piano refrains and partly to Vernon's lyrics of utter loss – "all went in the fire, drowning in the sea . . . I'll wait for you, you know, and we both end up alone". Although no other tracks would emerge from the pair for the time being, Blake hinted that more joint projects may be in the works.

"There are a couple things, we'll see," Blake said. "I'm happy with the things we've done, but I do feel like Justin is the sort of person who . . . I think anything I do with him, it deserves more time than just sitting on a bus and doing it, or making it in a hotel room. I want to spend a bit of time and really think about something. I think it'd be nice to get on stage together at some point and do something, but . . . again, we barely have any time. Our tours are almost always on opposite sides of the country, or the world. It's not really crossing paths all that easily, but we try to stay in contact."[9]

---

* The first track from Blake's *Enough Thunder* EP and a bonus track on the deluxe edition of his eponymous debut album.

Vernon was also branching out into other media. "We've been working on a film," he told *Dazed And Confused* in the summer, "this non-narrative art-video project that will be a visual compliment to the record, so I've been doing a lot of photography and filming on my own."[10] The project hit the shelves in November, a deluxe edition of *Bon Iver, Bon Iver* including videos accompanying each song. 'Perth' came with film, directed by Isaac Gale and David Jensen, of landscapes shot from airplane windows and then manipulated, distorted or mirror-imaged along firm lines in the image and flooded with colour to resemble kaleidoscopic alien worlds as the song reached its stirring, cataclysmic reveille climax. Dan Huiting and Ryan Thompson's film for 'Minnesota, WI' was all ink unravelling in water, neon ice sculpture images of leaves dripping melt-water and dust motes refracting the spectrum as they floated in the air, nature's glory blindingly exaggerated. 'Holocene's film, also by Dan Huiting, with Andre Durand, took a more naturalistic view of the same thing, its footage cut to a rhythm reflecting the track's lull and lustre; slow motion shots of ice cliffs, broiling waves crashing in reverse, woodland frozen thick with frost like opaque cables, the breathtaking sculpture of winter. The magnificence of the glacial earth – the jagged vacance, thick with ice – highlighted the song's sentiment of humanity's lower standing on the planet. Then, for a glimpse of frivolity, sensuousness and life reflecting the lyric, 'Towers', directed by Huiting and Thompson, flipped the shutter to spring, following the withering, decay and re-bloom of bright swathes of flowers.

Dawn scenes of woodland and crop fields, dotted with incongruous floating mirrored planks or men dragging illuminated sacks, gave a hazy, hallucinogenic feel to Isaac Gale and David Jensen's short for 'Michicant' and their film for 'Hinnom, TX' tackled sunset over an icy highway, the sun an exploding, hellish furnace and the roadway shifting with spectral sands. Then, as the album enters its final phase, humans finally appeared. Motion-capture cameras followed a pair of feet walking across wet sand into the shallows in Isaac Gale's film for 'Wash.', the cameraman throwing himself into the onrushing waves and surfing back to shore.

The commercial video for 'Calgary' and a film of a corridor filled with smoke and lasers or lit by a slowly creeping light on the floor to accompany 'Lisbon, OH', shot by Isaac Gale and David Jensen, as was the final video for 'Beth/Rest', which brought the video project to its climax.

Simple, static shots of spotlit trees at night swathed in smoke were mirrored in a similar style to 'Perth''s video to create woodland images resembling dry-ice flooded stage sets, echoing the song's Eighties arena rock style.

The deluxe edition of the album wasn't the only on-screen project Justin indulged in towards the end of 2011. For the September 5 release of 'Holocene' as the album's second single, he oversaw a new video directed in Iceland by Nabil Elderkin, featuring a young boy walking the Icelandic landscape, playing with seabirds and climbing stunning rock formations. And, on a somewhat more off-the-wall level, a short video clip of Justin playing basketball, lifting weights, running up and down stairs and talking about his daily fitness routines appeared online on December 8. At first the internet thought it was a spoof video, but Huiting, the film's director, claimed it was part of a full-length Bon Iver workout video he was producing.

"It's a legit workout DVD," he said, also claiming to be working on a feature-length documentary on the band. "Straight up, for real. [It's] 45, 50 minutes. Literally, you can work out to it and have music from all the bands we like: Bon Iver, S. Carey, Megafaun, We are the Willows and a couple others that escape me. It's like a workout mixtape. You can work out to cool music instead of something stupid . . . It's in Justin's yard, where he grew up, and it's them doing these three circuit exercises. Obviously, I can see how people will think this is a big joke . . . and technically, it's different from what you expect. But the dudes are dead serious about their health. Exercise is informing all of his other stuff, including his music. I toured with them for a month this summer and it's not like a heavy party situation. Their catering is healthy food, their rider is healthy food. They put an effort into keeping in shape on the road, unlike myself."[11]

With the deluxe edition film project an artistic success, Justin even allowed himself, strictly on his own terms, to dip a toe into flagrant commercialism. That autumn Justin would accept an offer to be photographed for a campaign called Friends Since Way Back, his image and endorsement to be used on poster advertisements for Bushmills Irish whiskey. The campaign, Bushmills' press release explained, was themed around "the lives and brotherly relationships of artists and influencers across the world" and intended to "celebrate the close friendships and camaraderie shared between lifelong friends". The stars appearing in the ads – including Elijah

Wood, Theophilus London, Chromeo and Bon Iver – would, the release claimed, be creating "custom pieces of music and art" for the campaign and, indeed, 12 months later Justin, with luthier Gordy Bischoff, would model a limited run of four guitars out of white oak wood from a Bushmills whiskey barrel, add volume and tone knobs made from bottle caps, infuse the wood with whiskey, call it the 1608 and auction one of them for over $7,000 to raise funds for the Eau Claire Confluence Community Arts Center.

But, initially and most prominently, Justin, Nate, Kyle and Brian Joseph would stand on a white backdrop in a photo studio in late 2011 and be snapped clinking whiskey glasses and holding the whiskey out to each other, symbolising the product because, according to a Bushmills spokeswoman, they were as "unique and discerning" as the whiskey.

"I owe everything to the creativity of my friends and neighbours who have all influenced and supported me along the way," went Justin's quote in the release. "Bushmills approached Bon Iver about collaborating with them on 'Since Way Back', and I didn't hesitate when I knew all of us – Nate, Kyle and Brian – could be involved. The way the campaign was presented to us, as a program that rewards groups of friends who have built success around what they love, made it feel right and appropriate for us to participate. The founders of Bushmills developed a recipe that lasts. We hope to do the same with our music."[12]

Justin toed the PR line outside of the photo studio too. "To be honest with you, man, it was more about people working in the field of advertising that weren't assholes," Vernon told *Billboard*. "It's interesting, being part of Bon Iver, it's like a band that started out as nothing and became something and in the process seeing how quickly to become that something has merit . . . And for something like Bushmills, it's been around for 400 years and has traversed centuries of alcohol laws and lobbyists and global corporate whatever. The fact of the matter is they've somehow figured out a way to still manage a small get-together in New York City and have it be about what it is about. It's an advertising company, but at least it's advertising something that I tend to believe brings people together."[13]

"Our friend Jeff [Rogers] who works out with us as our trainer," he said in an interview for whiskey trade website Refinery29, "he tries to make us exercise and we try to get him to drink whiskey. We trade off – the day time is his time, the night time is our time."[14]

What Bill Hicks would say we can only presume. But what long-absent sample-based rap troupe The Avalanches would say, we know only too well.

On December 2, in the wake of Vernon's four Grammy nominations, *The New York Times* posted online a snippet from an interview its reporter had conducted with Justin early in 2011, before his nominations were announced. "I don't think the Bon Iver record is the kind of record that would get nominated for a Grammy," he said, when asked about his feelings on Arcade Fire winning an award at the 2011 ceremony. "[But] I would get up there and be like, 'This is for my parents, because they supported me', because I know they would think it would be stupid of me not to go up there. But I kinda felt like going up there and being like: 'Everyone should go home, this is ridiculous. You should not be doing this. We should not be gathering in a big room and looking at each other and pretending that this is important'. That's what I would say . . . 98 per cent of the people in that room, their art is compromised by the fact that they're thinking that, and that they're hoping to get that award."[15]

The Avalanches responded to these quotes, alongside Vernon's appearance in the Bushmills campaign, on Twitter: "a musicians 'art is compromised' if he/she desires a grammy .but endor$ing a product with proven devastating health risks is ok? a product which kills 100k p/a in the US alone..man kids look up to you. # rememberwhenitwascoolNOTtosellout". The Tweet storm escalated – Justin replied "talk about 'desire.' do u drink whiskey?" to which The Avalanches rebuked "actually vodka is more my thing, but this aint no rock n roll pissing contest. i have seen alcohol destroy many families . . . including my own.. and you are making money off this shit . dont try and justify it.". Vernon responded "I'm not. I was asking questions. Fucks sake. Glad I get to play guitar tonight" and, later, "literally not upset at you or anything. Was kinda into a talk". A conciliatory "same here . . . " from the Avalanches camp and the online spat sputtered out.

"I would've said the same shit," Justin later admitted. "That's the only fucking thing pissed me off over that whole thing is that a whole bunch of people tried to make it out to be like it was a thing. But hey, people are just trying to get shit off their breastplate you know what I mean?"[16]

So after a year of standing fast to his integrity, his creative vision and his decisions on how best to handle his business and public persona, he was in no mood to bend over backwards for such a flimsy edifice as the 55th

Grammy Awards. He told the organisers he would be happy to perform his songs at the Grammys ceremony before a televised audience of 39 million people, but when word came back that he could only play live if he collaborated with one of the other nominees, Vernon refused.

"We wanted to play our music, but were told that we couldn't play," he said. "We had to do a collaboration with someone else. And we just felt like it was such a large stage, we're getting nominated for this record that we made. Me and Brian [Joseph] and a bunch of our fucking friends and we were given accolades for it, and all of a sudden we were being asked to play music that had nothing to do with that. We kind of said 'fuck you' a little bit and they sort of acted like they wanted us to play, but I don't think they wanted us to play . . . [they suggested] awesome people. People that I would love to play a song with. But you know what? Fuckin' rock' n'roll should not be decided by people that have that job. Rock'n'roll should be the fucking people with guitars around their backs."[17]

As if scrubbing himself of the philosophical filth of Bushmills and the Grammys, the coming months saw Justin embark on some achingly cool and credible endeavours. As his headline slots at Sasquatch! and Latitude were announced at the start of February 2012, he stripped back his band to just himself and Sean Carey to prepare for a 4AD session on February 17, an intimate set of five songs* they'd play on two pianos, facing each other across Lyndhurst Hall at London's AIR Studios, a stunning converted church. And on February 4 he appeared on US late-night comedy institution *Saturday Night Live* to play 'Holocene' and 'Beth/Rest', his first of two appearances on the show in a fortnight. Sort of. His second 'appearance' was in the form of a spoof by Justin Timberlake in a skit about a variety of movie and music stars arriving at the mansion of Jay-Z and Beyoncé to pay their respects to their new baby, Blue Ivy Carter. After comedy visits by actors impersonating Prince, Taylor Swift, Nicki Minaj and Brad and Angelina, the butler announced "we have one final visitor . . . Bon Iver" and Justin Timbalake entered boasting a convincing comb-over and an acoustic guitar.

"Sorry I'm late," 'Bon' said. "I was just wandering barefoot in the woods of Wisconsin. Fashioned this guitar out of a canoe, and I wrote a song for your baby."

---

* 'Hinnom, TX', 'Wash.', 'I Can't Make You Love Me', 'Babys' and 'Beth/Rest'.

"But Bon Iver," 'Beyoncé', played by Maya Rudolph, replied, "we were just about to put our baby to sleep."

"Trust me," deadpanned 'Bon', "this'll help."

Upon which he began playing an uncanny rendition of 'Holocene' rewritten to celebrate Blue Ivy before descending into unintelligible warbling from which the words "gravy" and "muggles" emerged and finally sending himself to sleep.

If being parodied on America's coolest comedy show wasn't sign enough that Vernon had broken into the mainstream's eyeline, or the fact that YouTube was throwing up such novelty tribute acts as Bon Joviver, a comedy mash-up of Vernon and Bon Jovi, the Grammy ceremony on February 12 would thrust him firmly into the A-list firmament.

With Bon Iver theme parties raging the length of the Towers back at UW-Eau Claire, complete with huge TV screens and a red carpet, his hometown supporters went wild as Vernon stepped up to receive two of the four awards he was nominated for – Best New Act and Best Alternative Music Album.

In preparing his acceptance speech, Vernon had been acutely aware of the admiration he'd felt for Nick Cave the time he'd taken the mike at an MTV awards show to "respectfully decline" his nomination because, he stated, his music wasn't about gongs and competition. Vernon's speech, while of a similar tone, was rather more sanguine. "It's hard to accept," he said, eyes darting constantly to his notes, "because when I started to make songs, I did it for the inherent reward of making songs, so I'm a little bit uncomfortable up here. I want to say thank you to all of the nominees, to all of the non-nominees that have never been here and never will be here, all the bands I toured with, all of the bands that inspired me." He cut out these further lines, for fear of sounding too confusing or self-reverential: "It's hard to accept this award because of all the talent out there, but also because Bon Iver is an entity and something that I gave myself to. A lot of people give themselves to it, so it's hard to think of Bon Iver as an artist. Bon Iver is not an artist. Bon Iver is an idea."

In the wake of his Grammy success, Vernon's media profile went stratospheric. News stations descended on Eau Claire, April Base and his parents' home to soak up the celebratory mood, interviewing local fans and filming Frenette in his management office pointing out Bon Iver's gold discs. "What I'm hoping for is to get one of those for the US," he said, gesturing to his gold award for the UK. "That's 500,000 there. We're at 400,000 something here. It's creeping, it'll get there soon."[18]

Justin himself seemed rather head-spun by the whole thing. "I feel like I know now," he said after the ceremony, between gripes over the self-importance of the ceremony and the likes of Chris Brown miming their performances. "I know what it's like. Whatever concerns or discomforts I have about the Grammys don't matter. For the time I was there, I just enjoyed it. Now that's it over I realise that I got pretty bent out of shape about it. I was proud to win, I was happy to, but I still think the whole thing is inherently flawed. Getting an award for music?"[19]

He'd held himself back in his speech, he revealed, not unleashed his inner anti-fakery fury. "In this last week I've realised that, whether I liked it or not, I've put up some walls and defences. I just couldn't get up there and look all those people in the eye and say, 'You suck.' Because I didn't think that at the time. I don't think that now. Any of those feelings I had beforehand were probably a combination of those defences and doubt and scepticism about what all of this means. I also didn't want to be rude. A bunch of people voted for me. I got myself involved. I said it was OK for the label to submit us for the Grammys. So, ultimately, I don't think I was ready to get up there and try to take the system down. Because I realised that (a) it's not going anywhere; (b) I don't need the shitstorm to deal with afterwards; because (c) it's just not that important. And because it's not that important, I was able to enjoy it and understand its relative relevance, while also enjoying all of its irrelevance."[20]

Justin spewed on, high on the rush of the acclaim, bruised from back-slaps, somehow stumbling upon a fresh vision and intent for his band as if the penetrating plastic glare of the Grammys had illuminated his very soul. "I want to do what's best for us and be creative. This has opened my eyes to what it's going to take to do this band the way I really dream it could be. It's going to take changing bandmates, changing sounds, changing instruments, changing voices, growing into myself, making tough decisions . . . How do I garner the sort of peace and harmony in my life that I don't have now? I don't write songs right now. I'm not worried about it and I'm being patient and I know they're going to come. But I'd be much happier if they were just around all the time and I was able to breathe and feel a flow of things . . . I wonder if there will be another record, if there can be. One of the things that I feel happy about is that I have it within me to make the call, to say the show goes on or the show doesn't go on. I won't let Bon Iver fail itself. So far, it's succeeded, so if we never make another record, it's OK with me. I'm still going to do something else. But I'm a romantic, I care about what it is. I care that it came from a pure place. Maybe it's some weird, psychotic brainchild and I'm overly protective . . . If it gets to the point where that purity is so vulnerable, I wouldn't be afraid of opting out of that world. I don't want to get it too scraped-up in that scenery."[21]

He caught himself. "To rewind to five minutes ago, where I said I might not put out another record: Fuck that, I will always do this, no matter what."[22]

And, just a few months down the long, open road, a far more satisfying world of acclaim awaited.

★ ★ ★

One drizzly summer evening, out in the wild flatlands of Norfolk, England, Bon Iver became true kings of the night.

The hanging nets transformed into mountain ranges, meteorological maps and forest glades. The crimson tide sweeping the stage for 'Blood Bank'. The tremulous lanterns lighting the intimate moments of *For Emma* . . . . Headlining Latitude Festival on July 13, 2011, Justin Vernon proved a master of the grandest outdoor ceremonies. "The visual spectacle is also something to behold," wrote Virtual Festivals' reviewer, "yet in spite of this inexorable growth, this is a man (and a band) about understatement and collaboration as much as anything, all plaid shirts and humble mumblings of gratitude . . . 'Perth', the album's opener, blasts its authoritative snares out into the crowd, highlighting the contrast between this and the more well-known, sparse and introspective *Emma* tracks . . . the band surprise in the sheer noise they create, especially on slow-build tracks like the sublime 'Holocene' [and] the highlight, and finale of all Bon Iver shows, is when the audience joins in to sing the chorus of 'The Wolves (Act I and II)', building to a joyous climax. The sheer enjoyment this communal singing reveals tonight, as the rain falls softly on the Latitude crowd, that we are as important to the experience as anyone."[23]

This visual feast of a show – merging the pastoral with the technological to blazing effect – had been touring the world since its opening nights in New Zealand and Australia in February and March, scheduled around the release of 'Towers' as the album's third single and including stop-offs at the 25,000 capacity Sidney Myer Music Bowl in Melbourne and three nights at the Syndey Opera House. Then, returning to the US to play at Coachella on its way towards Sasquatch!, the tour continued into arenas holding anything up to 12,000 people per night and venturing into outdoor venues in Vancouver, Red Rocks, Alpharetta, Georgia and Salt Lake City in May and June. Then the summer festival season had kicked in in earnest, Bon Iver paying Bonnaroo, Roskilde in Denmark and Heineken Open'er in Poland before hitting Latitude, and Belgium's Dour festival and Switzerland's Paleo as part of a subsequent European tour of major theatres.

Not everyone was as overawed by the expanded Bon Iver show as the Latitude reviewer, however. "It's weird," says Stephen M Duesner. "I like that album a lot and I really rated it high when it came out, and then I saw him live in Chicago at a sports arena. He had obviously gotten out of these smaller venues and it was very weird to see him in that kind of setting, turning these songs into rock songs. I really did not like it, in fact I left early. In my review I said it was not a good look for him. There's gotta be some conflict because what else can you do with that space except fill it, and those songs don't naturally do that. I can see the predicament, but after that it kinda ruined the album for me." It wasn't an entirely blissful jaunt for Justin either – somewhere amidst his heavy touring schedule of 2012, he and Kathleen Edwards split.

A final flurry of Scandinavian festivals in September*, however, and Vernon was ready to step up his game even further. He booked four nights at the 6,000 capacity Radio City Music Hall, and announced an arena tour of Europe taking in such enormous halls as Berlin's Arena Treptow, Madrid's 15,000-seater Palacia Vistalegre, Dublin's similarly sized O2 and, on November 8, that ultimate benchmark of rock success, Wembley Arena.

While playing such huge shows, essentially distancing and depersonalising himself from vast crowds after so many years of playing up-close shows to the whites of his audiences' eyes, it was no wonder Justin wanted to reconnect with his fans on a far more intimate level while offstage. So he

---

* Bon Iver played at Oyafestivalen in Oslo, Finland's Flow and Sweden's Way Out West before returning for the Ottowa Folk Festival on September 6.

began allowing them access not just to his music but, at a safe distance, to his bodily person. Launching a competition called 99 Designs, he offered a cash prize for the fan who designed him the best tattoo based on the *Northern Exposure* TV show, the best design to be inked onto his left arm. "I named my band after an episode of *Northern Exposure*," his competition directions explained alongside example illustrations. "In the episode a women transforms a gold rush village into a cultural place with one single dance in a tavern. They name the town after her, Cicely, Alaska. The art direction in the episode is unmistakably Mucha [Czech painter Alphonse Mucha] and I want to get a very large tattoo of this on my left arm. My favourite, hopefully what your illustrations will be based on, is the image I uploaded of Cicely with arms outstretched in mid-dance. You can't see her with the flowing scarf in her hands, but it would be cool if we could involve that . . . It's a TV show but it weirdly explained my life to me. Cicely is the metaphor for that."[24] The winning design, announced on September 26, was by Italian artist Giulio Rossi and depicted an art nouveau Cicely surrounded by flowers.

On the musical front meanwhile, in collaboration with Indaba Music in August Justin launched the Stems project, offering $1,000 prizes and spots on a forthcoming remix album for the fans who best reworked tracks from *Bon Iver, Bon Iver* from the original stems of the tracks – i.e. the individual instrument audio tracks, stripped away from the completed song, that each Bon Iver band member had been given in order to learn their parts for the live shows. *Bon Iver, Bon Iver: Stems Project* was exclusively released on Spotify in September, featuring the 16 best remixes from the likes of Teen Daze, Labstract and St. South alongside mixes by band members – Sean, Matt, Reggie Pace and even Dan Huiting tried their hand at remoulding their own music. The songs suddenly spawned all kinds of bizarre and out-landish offshoots – 'Minnesota, WI' becoming a warped Eighties pop hit in the hands of Daydreamer; 'Holocene' turned into a sweet, synthetic battle-droid waltz once fed through Stop The Car's computers.

In the meantime, in his spare moments back at April Base Justin con-tinued his steady stream of collaborations. While considering a new project with Megafaun and discussing ideas with the Blind Boys Of Alabama, he worked with Ryan Olson and Ryan's old friend, intellectual Minneapolis rapper Astronautalis, aka Andy Bothwell, recording an entire album in a weekend in April, at one point firing through an eight-hour stint of jamming and freestyling. "By the time I got there, they had about eight pieces of music done, or roughed out into song form," Bothwell said. "Then I just got down there and freestyled for eight hours over everything. When I work with Ryan, it's the exact opposite of how I work on my own records. I just give him tons and tons of material. He takes it back to his house, and dangles a cigarette out of his mouth, and works for hours on end . . . What sparked this was that [Vernon] and I are obsessive and lose our minds working on albums. Stressing out over lyric choices, and getting one word right and worrying about it for weeks on end. Whereas, Ryan is this amazing personality who motivates people to enjoy the process of making music. You just do it, and if it doesn't work, it'll get cut out . . . There were several times during those three days where I couldn't believe that a sound just fell perfectly into place. Often you get one of those when you make a record, or two of those, over the course of weeks and weeks and weeks. This process was exhilarating, and it drove us further. We were originally going to be down there for a day."[25]

At pains to point out that the crew had sunk an entire bottle of Bushmills over the weekend, Bothwell described the concept. "A lot of my fans are like, 'Oh, this is going to be amazing: Astronautalis rapping and Justin singing choruses.' It's not going to be that . . . Everyone's fans respectively are going to expect certain things . . . I think everyone should abandon their expectations of what it's going to be, because it's probably going to be very far off."[26]

★   ★   ★

As the arena tour wound to its close and the last shred of *Bon Iver, Bon Iver* was released into the wind on October 16 in the form of a single release for 'Beth/Rest', Vernon faced the coming winter ballooned with accomplishment but uncertain once more where this nebulous, runaway entity called Bon Iver would carry him next. Having billowed his tiny, intricate vision to the size of arena halls in major cities, could he so effortlessly conquer the rest of the world, become a global A-list act while expanding his musical palette into brave new sonic universes? Or, with fresh heartbreak in his belly, could he deflate the monster Bon Iver had become, bring his music back to that enclosed world of falsetto and acoustic, the listener an eavesdropper on a private world of exquisite anguish?

Or, having taken the band further than he ever imagined possible back in that cold, frosted cabin in the woods, could he simply close the book on Bon Iver, take it out into the wilderness and bury it in the snow?

"[I'm] winding it down," he said in September 2012, echoing sentiments in various interviews throughout the year that Bon Iver's days may be numbered, that he saw himself merely as the 'curator' of Bon Iver and that someone else might take over his leadership role in time. "I look at it like a faucet. I have to turn it off and walk away from it because so much of how that music comes together is subconscious or discovering. There's so much attention on the band, it can be distracting at times . . . I've already got three projects of my own that I'm collaborating on, where I'm not the central songwriter or anything. That's really important for me, to clear the cobwebs out. Because Bon Iver is really special to me and it's central to who I am and what I'm trying to express with music [but] I really feel the need to walk away from it while I still care about it. And then if I come back to it – if at all – I'll feel better about it and be renewed."[27]

Was Justin serious about shutting Bon Iver down and moving on? Ed Horrox is uncertain, but knows that Vernon has plenty of other musical avenues yet to explore. "Obviously he loves making music and he loves collaborating, and there are lots of opportunities to do that. From what I can see he takes on as much as he can and probably more than he can. He's consumed by music and that's why he's so good. It's inspiring to see someone that passionate and committed about making music and playing with people and respecting other people's talent. Since I've known him, to see that grow and to see that community of artists across different types of music – experimental music, hip-hop – to see the amount of projects he throws himself into, that's the opportunity he sees. When we first met him he made it clear that he wanted that and that has happened. It's not that he's changed, it's that he's very busy and it's great to see that."

If Bon Iver, as a concept, has gotten outta La Grange though, we can be certain we haven't heard the last from Justin Vernon, the shape-shifting, cross-cultural alt-folk icon and bearer of the heartache that throbbed throughout the world.

Happy death, Bon Iver.

ACKNOWLEDGEMENTS

Many thanks to the many who've helped try to push this book in the right direction, most notably Isabel Atherton at Creative Authors, Ed Horrox, Nathan Beezer, Jack Lawrence-Brown, Stephen M Duesner, Sarah Lowe, Ruth Drake, Kaz Mercer, Tones Sampson, Jon Polk, Hannah Overton, Hanna Gorjaczkowska, Christina Rentz, Jim Johnstone, Annette Lee, my ever-patient editor David Barraclough and all at Omnibus Press. Special thanks to Jane Lancaster for allowing me my own solitary creative winter in my fourth floor 'cabin'.

Notes

CHAPTER ONE

1. *Mojo*, Gabe Soria, Oct 2008
2. *The Times*, Phoebe Greenwood, April 12, 2008
3. ibid.
4. *The Guardian*, Laura Barton, May 14, 2008
5. WEAU.com, Jenny You, February 12, 2012
6. *Wisconsin State Journal*, Barry Adams, February 28, 2012
7. WEAU.com, Jenny You, February 12, 2012
8. ibid.
9. *Indy Weekly*, A New Residency, Grayson Currin, February 22, 200
10. *Minneapolis City Pages*, Succumbing To Bon Iver, Andrea Swensson, August 31, 2011
11. *The Current*, Andrea Swensson, September 23, 2012
12. *The Current*, The Local Show, September 23, 2012
13. *Wisconsin State Journal*, February 28, 2012, Barry Adams
14. *New York Times*, Jon Caramanica, June 3, 2011
15. *The Guardian,* Laura Barton, 14 May 2008
16. Pitchfork, February 14, 2008
17. Pitchfork, Grayson Currin, June 13, 2011
18. WEAU.com, Jenny You, February 12, 2012
19. ibid.
20. Pitchfork, February 14, 2008
21. *Minneapolis City Pages*, Succumbing To Bon Iver, Andrea Swensson, August 31, 2011
22. WEAU.com, Jenny You, February 12, 2012
23. www.uwec.edu, University Of Wisconsin Eau-Claire, Nancy Wesenberg, June 21 2010
24. *Indy Weekly*, A New Residency, Grayson Currin, February 22, 2006
25. ibid.
26. NPR World Café interview, Megafaun, November 9, 2011

CHAPTER TWO

1. *The Current*, The Local Show, September 23, 2012

2. WEAU.com, Jenny You, February 12, 2012
3. ibid.
4. *Minneapolis City Pages*, Succumbing To Bon Iver, Andrea Swensson, August 31, 2011
5. *The Times*, Phoebe Greenwood, April 12, 2008

CHAPTER THREE

1. *Chicago Time Out*, Brent DiCrescenzo, December 7, 2011
2. *Dazed And Confused*, July 28, 2011
3. *The New York Times*, Jon Caramanica, June 3, 2011
4. www.uwec.edu, University Of Wisconsin Eau-Claire, Nancy Wesenburg, June 21 2010
5. ibid.
6. ibid.
7. *Wisconsin State Journal*, On Wisconsin: In Eau-Claire Justin Vernon's Roots Run Deep, Barry Adams, February 28, 2012
8. www.uwec.edu, University Of Wisconsin Eau-Claire, Nancy Wesenburg, June 21 2010
9. *The Times*, Phoebe Greenwood, 12 April, 2008
10. VolumeOne.org, Justin Vernon: Back Tracks, Ken Szymanski, December 4, 2008
11. *Mojo,* Gabe Soria interview with Justin Vernon, October 2008
12. *Sunday World*, How Heartache Helped Shape Folk Star's Rise To Fame, Eddie Rowley, December 9, 2012
13. ibid.
14. *Indy Week*, A New Residency, Grayson Currin, February 22, 2006
15. ibid.
16. VolumeOne.org – Justin Vernon: Back Tracks, Ken Szymanski, December 4, 2008
17. *Observer Music Monthly*, Albums Of The Year, Gareth Grundy, 7 December, 2008

CHAPTER FOUR

1. *Indy Week*, A New Residency, Grayson Currin, February 22, 2006
2. ibid.
3. ibid.
4. CMJ, Chris Porterfield interview, Christine Werthman, June 18, 2012
5. ibid.
6. VolumeOne.org, Justin Vernon: Back Tracks, Ken Szymanski, December 4, 2008
7. ibid.

8. ibid.
9. *New York Times*, Jon Caramanica, June 3, 2011
10. *The Guardian*, Laura Barton, May 14, 2008
11. www.thankscaptainobvious.net, Captain Obvious, November 18, 2007
12. *The Current*, The Local Show, September 23, 2012
13. NPR Radio World Café, Megafaun interview, Nov 9, 2011
14. WEAU.com, Jenny You, February 12, 2012
15. *The Current*, The Local Show, September 23, 2012
16. *Indy Week*, A New Residency, Grayson Currin, February 22, 2006
17. ibid.
18. CMJ, Chris Porterfield interview, Christine Werthman, June 18, 2012
19. *Indy Week*, A New Residency, Grayson Currin, February 22, 2006
20. VolumeOne.org, Justin Vernon: Back Tracks, Ken Szymanski, December 4, 2008
21. ibid.
22. The AV Club, Steven Hyden, February 21, 2008
23. VolumeOne.org, Justin Vernon: Back Tracks, Ken Szymanski, December 4, 2008
24. *Volume One*, June 23, 2011
25. VolumeOne.org, Justin Vernon: Back Tracks, Ken Szymanski, December 4, 2008
26. ibid.
27. ibid.
28. The AV Club, Steven Hyden, Feb 21, 2008

CHAPTER FIVE

1. *Volume One*, June 23, 2011
2. *Indy Week*, A New Residency, Grayson Currin, February 22, 2006
3. ibid.
4. Pitchfork, Nilina Mason-Campbell, May 27, 2008
5. Laundro-Matinee, October 16, 2008
6. *The Current*, The Local Show, September 23, 2012
7. *Indy Week*, A New Residency, Grayson Currin, February 22, 2006
8. ibid.
9. ibid.
10. ibid.
11. *Indy Week*, Bon Iver's Long Wager, Grayson Currin, July 27, 2011
12. *Uncut*, Alastair McKay, June 2011
13. *The Times*, Phoebe Greenwood, 12 April, 2008
14. The AV Club, Steven Hyden, February 21, 2008
15. Pitchfork, Nilina Mason-Campbell, May 27, 2008

16. WEAU.com, Jenny You, February 12, 2012
17. *The Times*, Phoebe Greenwood, April 12, 2008
18. *Stool Pigeon*, Bon Iver's Got To Do What A Man's Got To Do, Ann Lee, April 2008
19. *Daily Telegraph*, Benjamin Secher, May 17, 2008
20. *Treble*, Dustin Allen, November 2, 2008
21. NPR radio, World Café show, November 9, 2011
22. Pitchfork, Nilina Mason-Campbell, May 27, 2008
23. *Daily Telegraph*, Benjamin Secher, May 17, 2008
24. Drowned In Sound, DiScover: Bon Iver, Alex Denney, May 6, 2008
25. *Daily Telegraph*, Benjamin Secher, May 17, 2008
26. Pitchfork, Grayson Currin, June 13, 2011
27. *New York Times*, Jon Caramanica, June 3, 2011
28. ibid.
29. Pitchfork, February 14, 2008
30. *Uncut*, Alastair McKay, June 2011
31. *The Times*, Phoebe Greenwood, April 12, 2008
32. *New York Times*, Jon Caramanica, June 3, 2011
33. Pitchfork, Grayson Currin, June 13, 2011
34. ibid.
35. Source unknown
36. *StarTribune*, A Good Winter, Chris Riemenschneider, January 11, 2008
37. *Treble*, Dustin Allen, November 2, 2008
38. Creature Fear blog, November 17, 2006
39. *La Blogotheque*, Bon Iver's Choices, Sskizo, May 21, 2008
40. Pitchfork, Grayson Currin, June 13, 2011
41. *StarTribune*, A Good Winter, Chris Riemenschneider, January 11, 2008
42. My Old Kentucky Blog, December 21, 2007
43. *Indy Week*, Bon Iver's Long Wager, Grayson Currin, July 27, 2011
44. ibid.
45. *Treble*, Dustin Allen, November 2, 2008
46. Pitchfork, Grayson Currin, June 13, 2011
47. *The Guardian*, Laura Barton, June 9, 2011
48. *Uncut*, Alastair McKay, June 2011
49. *Exclaim!*, Chris Whibbs, March 2008

CHAPTER SIX
1. Pitchfork, June 13, 2011
2. *Justin Vernon*, Creature Fear blog
3. *Mojo*, Gabe Soria, October 2008
4. The AV Club, Steven Hyden, February 21, 2008

5. *Mojo*, Gabe Soria, October 2008
6. *Daily Telegraph*, Benjamin Secher, May 17, 2008
7. *Stool Pigeon*, Bon Iver's Got To Do What A Man's Got To Do, Ann Lee, April 2008
8. *Treble*, Dustin Allen, November 2, 2011
9. Laundro-Matinee, October 16, 2008
10. Captain Obvious, November 18, 2007
11. Drowned In Sound, DiScover: Bon Iver, Alex Denney, May 6, 2008
12. *Mojo*, Gabe Soria, October 2008
13. *Daily Telegraph*, Benjamin Secher, May 17, 2008
14. Ambledown.com biog
15. *Uncut*, Alastair McKay, June 2011
16. *StarTribune*, A Good Winter, Chris Riemenschneider, January 11, 2008
17. Captain Obvious, November 18, 2007
18. *Weekend America*, Songs In The Dead Of Winter, Angela Kim, January 26, 2008
19. *Uncut*, Alastair McKay, June 2011
20. *The Times*, Phoebe Greenwood, April 12, 2008
21. *Mojo*, Gabe Soria, October 2008
22. *Daily Telegraph*, Benjamin Secher, May 17, 2008
23. *Mojo*, Gabe Soria, October 2008
24. *Daily Telegraph*, Benjamin Secher, May 17, 2008
25. Creature Fear blog, Justin Vernon
26. *New York Times*, Jon Caramanica, June 3, 2011)
27. *The Guardian*, Hail, Hail Rock'N'Roll, Laura Barton, February 29, 2008
28. Creature Fear blog, Justin Vernon, January 28, 2008
29. *The Guardian*, Laura Barton, May 14, 2008
30. Creature Fear blog, Justin Vernon, January 28, 2008
31. *The Times*, Phoebe Greenwood, April 12, 2008
32. Treble, Dustin Allen, November 2, 2008
33. Laundro-Matinee, October 16, 2008
34. *The Guardian*, Laura Barton, May 14, 2008
35. *Stool Pigeon*, June 2011
36. *The Times*, Phoebe Greenwood, April 12, 2008
37. *Daily Telegraph*, Benjamin Secher, May 17, 2008
38. *StarTribune*, A Good Winter, Chris Riemenschneider, January 11, 2008
39. About.com, Andrew Carew, October 24, 2008
40. *Exclaim!*, Chris Whibbs, March 2008
41. Laundro-Matinee, October 16, 2008
42. *New York Times*, Jon Caramanica, June 3, 2011
43. *The Times*, Phoebe Greenwood, April 12, 2008

44. *Treble*, Dustin Allen, November 2, 2008
45. Captain Obvious, 18 November, 2007
46. The AV Club, Steven Hyden, February 21, 2008
47. Creature Fear blog, Justin Vernon, September 28, 2008
48. ibid.
49. *Treble*, Dustin Allen, November 2, 2008
50. Laundro-Matinee, October 16, 2008
51 *Indy Week*, Bon Iver's Long Wager, Grayson Currin, July 27, 2011
52. WEAU.com, Jenny You, February 12, 2012
53. Pitchfork, Nilina Mason-Campbell, May 27, 2008
54. ibid.
55. *The Times*, Phoebe Greenwood, April 12, 2008
56. *Weekend America*, Songs In The Dead Of Winter, Angela Kim, January 26, 2008

CHAPTER SEVEN
1. Creature Fear blog, January 28, 2008
2. *Daily Telegraph*, Benjamin Secher, May 17, 2008
3. The AV Club, Steven Hyden, February 21, 2008
4. Drowned In Sound, DiScover: Bon Iver, Alex Denney, May 6, 2008
5. ibid.
6. *Weekend America*, Songs In The Dead Of Winter, Angela Kim, January 26, 2008
7. Drowned In Sound, DiScover: Bon Iver, Alex Denney, May 6, 2008
8. *Treble*, Dustin Allen, November 2, 2008
9. Emusic, Indie Rock Moms Sound Off, July 5, 2008
10. *The Guardian*, Laura Barton, June 9, 2011
11. ibid.
12. *Stool Pigeon*, Bon Iver's Got To Do What A Man's Got To Do, Ann Lee, April 2008
13. Pitchfork, Grayson Currin, June 13, 2011
14. Pitchfork, Nilina Mason-Campbell, May 27, 2008
15. Laundro-Matinee, October 16, 2008
16. *Uncut*, Alastair McKay, June 2011
17. About.com, Andrew Carew, October 24, 2008
18. The AV Club, Steven Hyden, February 21, 2008
19. Pitchfork, Nilina Mason-Campbell, May 27, 2008
20. Pitchfork, Grayson Currin, June 13, 2011
21. *Treble*, Dustin Allen, November 2, 2008
22. Pitchfork, Nilina Mason-Campbell, May 27, 2008

CHAPTER EIGHT

1. WEAU.com, Jenny You, February 12, 2012
2. Laundro-Matinee, October 16, 2008
3. WEAU.com, Jenny You, February 12, 2012
4. WEAU.com, Jenny You, February 12, 2012
5. My Old Kentucky Blog, June 1, 2007
6. Pitchfork, Nilina Mason-Campbell, May 27, 2008
7. *Mojo*, Gabe Soria, October 2008
8. *New York Times*, Jon Caramanica, June 3, 201
9. *The Current*, Andrea Swensson, September 23, 2012
10. Brooklyn Vegan, July 27, 2007
11. Muzzle Of Bees, July 27, 2007
12. Pitchfork, Stephen M Deusner, October 4, 2007
13. *The Times*, Phoebe Greenwood, 12 April, 2008
14. WEAU.com, Jenny You, February 12, 2012
15. *Hit Quarters*, July 25, 2011
16. Pitchfork, Nilina Mason-Campbell, May 27, 2008
17. UW-Eau Claire, The View, Once Upon A Good Winter, Forever Ago, Nancy Wesenberg, June 21, 2010
18. Pitchfork, Nilina Mason-Campbell, May 27, 2008
19. ibid.
20. Captain Obvious, November 18, 2007
21. *Daily Telegraph*, Benjamin Secher, May 17, 2008
22. Pitchfork, Nilina Mason-Campbell, May 27, 2008
23. ibid.
24. Pitchfork, February 14, 2008
25. *Clash*, Gemma Hampson, 20 June, 2011
26. The AV Club, Steven Hyden, February 21, 2008
27. *StarTribune*, A Good Winter, Chris Riemenschneider, January 11, 2008
28. *Rolling Stone*, Evan Serpick, March 23, 2011
29. Dazed And Confused, July 28, 2011
30. *Rolling Stone*, Josh Eells, June 2011
31. *Esquire*, July 2011
32. *Clash*, Gemma Hampson, June 20, 2011

CHAPTER NINE

1. *Stylus*, Ryan Foley, November 9, 2007
2. *Uncut*, John Mulvey, June 2008
3. *Mojo*, Victoria Segal, June 2008
4. *Sunday Times*, 11 May, 2008
5. *Observer Music Monthly*, Gareth Grundy, December 7, 2008

6. *Uncut*, January 2009
7. *Mojo*, January 2009
8. *Uncut*, Bud Scoppa, July 2011
9. *Daily Telegraph*, Benjamin Secher, May 17, 2008
10. *Minneapolis City Pages*, Succumbing To Bon Iver, Andrea Swensson, August 31, 2011
11. Culture Bully, Chris DeLine, November 13, 2008
12. *Mojo*, Album Of The Month review, Victoria Segal, June 2008
13. Pitchfork, February 14, 2008
14. *The Times*, Phoebe Greenwood, April 12, 2008
15. *The Guardian*, Laura Barton, 14 May, 2008
16. *The Times*, Phoebe Greenwood, April 12, 2008
17. Pitchfork, Nilina Mason-Campbell, May 27, 2008
18. *Observer Music Monthly*, Albums Of The Year, Gareth Grundy, December 7, 2008
19. ibid.
20. *Treble*, Dustin Allen, November 2, 2008
21. *The Times*, Phoebe Greenwood, April 12, 2008
22. Pitchfork, Nilina Mason-Campbell, May 27, 2008
23. Pitchfork, Grayson Currin, June 13, 2011
24. *New York Times*, Jon Caramanica, June 3, 2011
25. Pitchfork, Nilina Mason-Campbell, May 27, 2008
26. *The Times*, Phoebe Greenwood, 12 April, 2008
27. *New York Times*, Jon Caramanica, June 3, 2011
28. Drowned In Sound, Alex Denney, May 6, 2008
29. About.com, Andrew Carew, October 24, 2008
30. *Treble*, Dustin Allen, November 2, 2008
31. Creature Fear blog, Justin Vernon, June 16, 2008
32. ibid.
33. Blobtower blog, Justin Vernon, May 29, 2009
34. About.com, Andrew Carew, October 24, 2008
35. *Clash*, Robin Murray, April 20, 2011
36. Drowned In Sound, Alex Denney, May 6, 2008
37. *Rolling Stone*, Evan Serpick, March 23, 2011
38. *Dazed And Confused*, July 28, 2011)
39. *Stool Pigeon*, June 2011
40. *The Guardian*, Laura Barton, June 9, 2011
41. Drowned In Sound, Alex Denney, May 6, 2008
42. NPR Music, January 3, 2009
43. *The Current*, Andrea Swensson, September 23, 2012
44. *Spin*, The Lamentalist: Bon Iver, Steve Kandell, January 8, 2009

45. NPR Music, January 3, 2009

CHAPTER TEN

1. *People*, Bon Iver Frontman Justin Vernon: Cats Are Good For Your Brain, Jessica Herndon, August 23, 2011
2. Q, Victoria Segal, June 2011
3. Bon Iver press release, Jagjaguwar, 2011
4. Creature Fear blog, Justin Vernon, September 20, 2008
5. ibid.
6. Creature Fear blog, Justin Vernon, October 20, 2008
7. *Chicago Time Out*, Brent DiCrescenzo, Deceber 7, 2011
8. *Indy Week*, Bon Iver's Long Wager, Grayson Currin, July 27 2011
9. *Uncut*, Alastair McKay, June 2011
10. ibid.
11. The AV Club, All Tiny Creatures' Thomas Wincek, Joel Shanahan, October 6, 2010
12. *Uncut*, Alastair McKay, June 2011
13. About.com, Andrew Carew, October 24, 2008
14. *Stool Pigeon*, June 2011
15. Drowned In Sound, Alex Denney, May 6, 2008
16. *Dazed And Confused*, July 28, 2011
17. *Stool Pigeon*, June 2011
18. NPR Music, Jess Gitner, June 22, 2011
19. Laundro-Matinee, October 16, 2008
20. *Clash*, Gemma Hampson, June 2, 2011
21. *Guardian*, Laura Barton, June 9, 2011
22. *Dazed And Confused*, July 28, 2011
23. NPR Music, Jess Gitner, June 22, 2011
24. *New York Times*, Jon Caramanica, June 3, 2011
25. About.com, Andrew Carew, October 24, 2008
26. *The Sun*, Simon Cosyns, June 2, 2011
27. Blobtower blog, Justin Vernon, January 28, 2009
28. Pitchfork, Grayson Currin, June 13, 2011
29. *Citypages*, Andrea Swensson, February 17, 2010
30. *Minneapolis City Pages*, Succumbing To Bon Iver, Andrea Swensson, August 31, 2011
31. Pitchfork, Grayson Currin, June 13, 2011
32. *Citypages*, Andrea Swensson, May 12, 2010
33. *Indy Week*, Grayson Currin, July 27, 2011
34. Pitchfork, Ryan Dombal, August 13, 2010
35. *Citypages*, Andrea Swensson, May 12, 2010

36. Frontier Psychiatrist, Keith Meatto, October 18, 2010
37. *NME.com*, Anthony Thornton, May 13, 2010
38. Pitchfork, Grayson Currin, June 13, 2011
39. *Dazed And Confused*, July 28, 2011
40. Q, Victoria Segal, Album review for Bon Iver, June 2011
41. Pitchfork, Grayson Currin, June 13, 2011
42. *Minneapolis City Pages*, Succumbing To Bon Iver, Andrea Swensson, August 31, 2011

CHAPTER ELEVEN

1. Pitchfork, Ryan Dombal, August 13, 2010
2. *Dazed And Confused*, July 28, 2011
3. The Dumbing Of America, April 23, 2010
4. ibid.
5. ibid.
6. *Rolling Stone*, Adam Greene, June 3, 2011
7. *The Current*, Andrea Swensson, September 23, 2012
8. *Rolling Stone*, Adam Greene, June 3, 2011
9. Pitchfork, Ryan Dombal, August 13, 2010
10. ibid.
11. *Clash*, Gemma Hampson, June 20, 2011
12. *The Sun*, Simon Cosyns, June 2, 2011
13. *Dazed And Confused*, July 28, 2011
14. *Rolling Stone*, Adam Greene, June 3, 2011
15. *The Sun*, Simon Cosyns, June 2, 2011
16. Pitchfork, Ryan Dombal, August 13, 2010
17. *Spin*, David Bevan, June 29, 2011
18. Pitchfork, Ryan Dombal, August 13, 2010
19. ibid.
20. *Spin*, David Bevan, June 29, 2011
21. Pitchfork, Ryan Dombal, August 13, 2010
22. Pitchfork, Grayson Currin, June 13, 2011
23. *The Guardian*, Laura Barton, June 9, 2011
24. *Rolling Stone*, Evan Serpick, March 23, 2011
25. Q, Victoria Segal, June 2011
26. *Dazed And Confused*, July 28, 2011
27. Bon Iver press release, Jagjaguwar, June 21, 2011
28. *Citypages*, Andrea Swensson, February 17, 2010
29. *Citypages*, Andrea Swensson, May 12, 2010
30. *Chicago Time Out*, Brent DiCrescenzo, December 7, 2011
31. *The Sun*, Robin Cosyns, June 10, 2011

32. The Thread, Peter Blackstock, September 20, 2010
33. Blobtower blog, Justin Vernon, October 11, 2010
34. The AV Club, Joel Shanahan, October 6, 2010
35. ibid.
36. *New York Times*, Jon Caramanica, June 3, 2011
37. Pitchfork, Ryan Dombal, August 13, 2010
38. *Volume One*, June 23, 2011
39. WEAU.com, Jenny You, February 12, 2012
40. *City Pages*, Youa Vang, September 27, 2012
41. *New York Times*, Jon Caramanica, June 3, 2011
42. *The Guardian*, Laura Barton, June 9, 2011

CHAPTER TWELVE
 1. *Uncut*, Alastair McKay, June 2011
 2. ibid.
 3. *The Sun*, Simon Cosyns, June 2, 2011
 4. *Esquire*, July 2011
 5. *Dazed And Confused*, July 28, 2011
 6. *Citypages*, Andrea Swensson, September 29, 2011
 7. *Volume One*, June 23, 2011
 8. Chicago *Time Out*, Brent DiCrescenzo, December 7, 2011
 9. *Minneapolis City Pages*, Succumbing To Bon Iver, Andrea Swensson, August 31, 2011
10. *The Guardian*, Laura Barton, June 9, 2011
11. *Spin*, David Bevan, June 29, 2011
12. *Uncut*, Alastair McKay, June 2011
13. *Volume One*, June 23, 2011
14. WEAU.com, Jenny You, February 12, 2012
15. *Volume One*, June 23, 2011
16. *Clash*, Gemma Hampson, June 20, 2011
17. *Uncut*, Alastair McKay, June 2011
18. Q, Victoria Segal, 2011
19. *New York Times*, Jon Caramanica, June 3, 2011
20. ibid.
21. ibid.
22. NPR Music, Jess Gitner, June 22, 2011
23. *New York Times*, Jon Caramanica, June 3, 2011
24. *Stool Pigeon*, June 2011
25. ibid.
26. *Dazed And Confused*, July 28, 2011
27. *Stool Pigeon*, June 2011

28. ibid.
29. *Clash*, Gemma Hampson, June 20, 2011
30. *The Sun*, Simon Cosyns, June 2, 2011
31. *Uncut*, Alastair McKay, June 2011
32. *Songfacts*, December 16, 2011
33. NPR Music, Jess Gitner, June 22, 2011
34. *Mojo*, June 2011
35. Pitchfork, Grayson Currin, June 13, 2011
36. Pitchfork, Philip Sherburne, December 12, 2011
37. *Mojo*, James McNair, June 2011
38. *Esquire*, July 2011
39. NPR Music, Jess Gitner, June 22, 2011
40. Pitchfork, Grayson Currin, June 13, 2011
41. *Uncut*, Alastair McKay, June 2011
42. *Rolling Stone*, Evan Serpick, March 23, 2011
43. NPR Music, Jess Gitner, June 22, 2011
44. *Stool Pigeon*, June 2011
45. *Uncut*, Alastair McKay, June 2011
46. NPR Music, Jess Gitner, June 22, 2011
47. WEAU.com, Jenny You, February 12, 2012
48. *Mojo*, Album Of The Month, James McNair, June 2011
49. Q, Victoria Segal, June 2011
50. *Evening Standard*, David Smyth, June 17, 2011
51. *Telegraph*, Neil McCormick, June 18, 2011
52. *Independent*, June 17, 2011
53. *Uncut*, Bud Scoppa, July 2011

CHAPTER THIRTEEN
1. WEAU.com, Jenny You, February 12, 2012
2. Blobtower blog, Justin Vernon, August 29, 2011
3. *Indy Week*, Bon Iver's Long Wager, Grayson Currin, July 27, 2011
4. ibid.
5. *Minneapolis City Pages*, Succumbing To Bon Iver, Andrea Swensson, August 31, 2011
6. ibid.
7. The Current, Andrea Swensson, September 23, 2012
8. *Indy Week*, Bon Iver's Long Wager, Grayson Currin, July 27, 2011
9. *Citypages*, Andrea Swensson, September 29, 2011
10. *Dazed And Confused*, July 28, 2011
11. MTV Hive, December 8, 2011
12. PR Newswire, Oct 5, 2011

13. *Billboard*, Bon Iver's Justin Vernon On (Not) Playing The Grammys, Endorsing Bushmills, Andrew Hampp, February 3, 2012
14. Refinery29, Jessica Amason, February 9, 2012
15. *New York Times*, The Bon Iver Grammy Quandary, Jon Caramanica, December 2, 2011
16. *Billboard*, Bon Iver's Justin Vernon On (Not) Playing The Grammys, Endorsing Bushmills, Andrew Hampp, February 3, 2012
17. ibid.
18. WEAU.com, Jenny You, February 12, 2012
19. *Spin*, David Bevan, February 14, 2012
20. ibid.
21. ibid.
22. ibid.
23. Virtual Festivals, Rebecca Lawrence, July 14, 2012
24. 99 Designs, Justin Vernon
25. *Citypages*, Reed Fischer, April 10, 2012
26. *Citypages*, Reed Fischer, April 10, 2012
27. The Current, Andrea Swensson, September 23, 2012

BY THE SAME AUTHOR

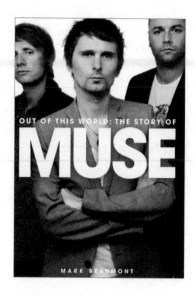

THE STORY OF MUSE
Out Of This World
by Mark Beaumont

From the first time they smashed up all the stage equipment as 16-year-old punk kids, Muse were always a stadium band in waiting, and this new in-depth biography from one of the UK's award-winning music journalists follows their every step on the road to Wembley, with detailed accounts of all four of their studio albums including the million-selling *Black Holes* And *Revelations* and all of the wild nights, theories and falsettos they experienced along the way.

This new edition of Out Of This World has been updated to include the release of Muse's album The Resistance..

Available from **www.omnibuspress.com**

ISBN: 9781849383684
Order No: OP53350

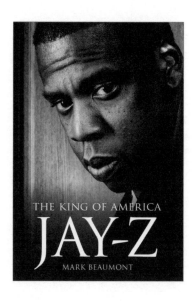

JAY-Z
The King Of America

by Mark Beaumont

A hero for our times, Jay-Z is one of the world's most successful hip hop artists, record producers and entrepreneurs, selling more than 50 million albums globally and winning 13 Grammy Awards.

Mark Beaumont has interviewed Jay-Z and many revealing insights from that encounter inform this no-holds-barred biography of a great American success story, in which musical talent and youthful criminality co-exist alongside some impressively wide-ranging entrepreneurial skills. This fascinating book tells it all, revealing how the good, the bad and the corporate are all part of the incredibly far-reaching Jay-Z legend.

Available from **www.omnibuspress.com**

ISBN: 9781780383170
Order No: OP54527